A   C L A S S   W I T H   D R U C K E R

A Class with Drucker

The Lost Lessons of the World's Greatest Management Teacher

BY WILLIAM A. COHEN, PhD

AMACOM AMERICAN MANAGEMENT ASSOCIATION

NEW YORK • ATLANTA • BRUSSELS • CHICAGO • MEXICO CITY • SAN FRANCISCO

SHANGHAI • TOKYO • TORONTO • WASHINGTON, D. C.

Special discounts on bulk quantities of AMACOM books are available to corporations, professional associations, and other organizations. For details, contact Special Sales Department, AMACOM, a division of American Management Association, 1601 Broadway, New York, NY 10019. Tel: 212-903-8316. Fax: 212-903-8083.
E-mail: specialsls@amanet.org
Website: www.amacombooks.org/go/specialsales
To view all AMACOM titles go to: www.amacombooks.org

This publication is designed to provide accurate and authoritative information in regard to the subject matter covered. It is sold with the understanding that the publisher is not engaged in rendering legal, accounting, or other professional service. If legal advice or other expert assistance is required, the services of a competent professional person should be sought.

Library of Congress Cataloging-in-Publication Data
Cohen, William A., 1937–
A class with Drucker : the lost lessons of the world's greatest management teacher by William A. Cohen.
    p. cm.
Includes index.
ISBN 978-0-8144-1418-7
1. Management. 2. Executives—Training of. 3. Drucker, Peter F. (Peter Ferdinand), 1909-2005. 4. Cohen, William A., 1937– I. Drucker, Peter F. (Peter Ferdinand), 1909-2005. II. Title.
HD31.C589 2007
658—dc22

2007020976

Printing number
10 9 8 7 6 5 4 3 2

C O N T E N T S

ACKNOWLEDGMENTS AND DEDICATION

Though the responsibility for this work and any errors in it are my alone, I want to acknowledge the following individuals, each of whom made significant contributions to *A Class with Drucker*:

Adrienne Hickey, Editor in Chief. She is an old friend with whom I have worked on a number of AMACOM books. She worked with me on this project from the beginning, and as always, did her usual outstanding work.

Barry Richardson, Developmental Editor. He had spun his magical skills over one of my previous books. He made sense in my organization where I only thought I had done so. This time he went one step further and sent me a personal anecdote which further supported my illustration of one of Drucker's concepts. I jumped on it and put it in the book.

Andy Ambraziejus. He is Managing Editor at AMACOM. He brought the whole production end together and kept me focused on responding to important editorial questions when my travel schedule kicked in to make finetuning a real challenge.

Karen Brogno, AMACOM copyeditor extraordinaire, who repeatedly challenged me to be specific and frustrated me by being right more times than not.

Most of all, Nurit Cohen, PhD, clinical psychologist. She can be my most severe critic, but is always my strongest supporter. She is also my wife and partner of forty years and without her this book would not have been written. It is dedicated to her with all my love and thanks for putting up with wars, which three times took my time and caused separation, frequent stubbornness and sometimes just downright stupidity.

What Peter Drucker Wrote About Bill Cohen

"Dr. Cohen became my student at the Graduate Management Center of the Claremont Graduate School after he had already achieved signal success in two separate careers—as a military officer and a businessman. He soon established himself as both an outstanding student and an outstanding scholar—and, after attaining the PhD degree, soon thereafter as an outstanding and inspiring teacher. He has continued to produce books of true scholarship which, at the same time, have tremendous practical applications.... In fact, Bill Cohen is a true inspiration for all of us in Academe—and, above all, for students who need a true role model, a true exemplar of the very best they could and should aspire to."

—Peter F. Drucker

FOREWORD

Bill Cohen was the first graduate of the world's first executive PhD program in management. That was in 1979 at the Peter F. Drucker and Masatoshi Ito Graduate School of Management at Claremont Graduate University. (Of course, it was just plain old Claremont Graduate School when Bill attended.) But he has never forgotten his alma mater or his professor and friend, Peter Drucker, a man who has meant so much to all of us. Bill has brought to life many of the lessons he learned from Drucker and made those insights accessible to those who weren't privileged to know Peter personally or sit in any of his classes.

Peter Drucker was many things to many people and to many organizations. He was, of course, considered the Father of Modern Management. He was a philosopher and an author and a profoundly thoughtful observer. He was a historian, and a father, and a husband, and an expert on Japanese art. Peter called himself a social ecologist, and he exercised courage in thought and prescription. Peter believed deeply that the human condition could be advanced by more effective management and more ethical leadership of every organization in every society—business, government, the nonprofit world, even the academy, where he resided most of his life. This is what he taught and wrote about, and Peter wrote some more than 30 books, many of them now classics. He inspired many others to pursue their own work. Think of Tom Peters (*In Search of Excellence*). Or Jim Collins (*Built to Last* and *Good to Great*), who says that either or both of his volumes could have been entitled simply: Peter was Right!

Peter's insights and friendship through mentoring and coaching helped to transform entire organizations. Think of GE under Jack Welch. Or the development of the megachurch in America under disciples such as Rick Warren. And, of course, Peter helped to inspire a whole generation of leaders in the nonprofit sector, whose role and importance and needs Peter was perhaps the first to identify and champion as worthy of management attention.

For all his distinctions and contributions, Peter was first and foremost a teacher. Fame never distracted him from his calling in the classroom, and his lectures were the stuff of legend: Seemingly unscripted, frequently unpredictable, and almost always provocative and original. The classroom was Peter's cathedral. And this is where he regularly practiced his craft of both instruction and learning. Classically trained, broad and deep in range and scope of intellect and knowledge, Peter held forth, almost as a secular prophet. And yet his ultimate humility and humanity was also demonstrated by his conviction that from his students he had much to learn from as well. Teaching was really a partnership for Peter, and an almost sacred trust between teacher and students, where knowledge was not only disseminated but also created. The classroom, then, was really Peter's first and last frontier of management, the ultimate knowledge-creating organization, a microcosm and laboratory for so many of his insights about human capital, purpose, objectives, innovation, and so much more.

Bill Cohen brings that laboratory of learning alive to those of us who didn't have the pleasure, privilege, or opportunity to sit at the feet of the master in Peter's classroom. One can feel the energy, the humor, the discipline, the interaction, the edge, the energy, the simplicity, and the relevance of Peter's practice of teaching.

There are many business schools named for wealthy donors. We are proud that we are named for a thinker, Peter Drucker. And we are also proud that our name includes an individual, Masatoshi Ito, who himself was a student of Peter's, and who put Peter's principles to practice by building a small apparel store in Japan into the second largest retailing organization in the world. We are working hard to preserve Peter's legacy of teaching and scholarship and fulfilling his commitment to training effective managers and ethical leaders.

Forgive me for doing a little bragging. We are training and educating our graduates not only to do well, but also to do good. We offer analytical rigor, and we also value intuition and reflection. We focus on skills and core competencies, and we also challenge students to excel and to seek a unique contribution and authentic leadership. We equip our graduates for success and we encourage them to pursue significance, as well. We remind them constantly of Peter's penetrating question: What do you want to be remembered for? There is a "Drucker Difference," and that's what we teach.

A Class with Drucker comes at a time when a reflection on Peter's legacy is an important anchor as we move forward. We are in the midst of a world-wide search for a new Peter Drucker Professor of Management as a Liberal Art, as well as our first Doris Drucker Professor in Global Management. We are attracting distinguished Drucker Scholars and Drucker Fellows, and we are transforming Peter's archives into a living memorial called The Drucker Institute. Indeed, as I write these words, we are putting the finishing touches on invitations to the first Global Symposium of Drucker Societies from around the world, whose members will be meeting here in Claremont in just two months time.

I could go on and on about these and other initiatives. However, regardless of how much we do to follow in the direction in which Peter has pointed us, none of us will be able to replicate Peter's place in the classroom. But we can all take many cues from Bill Cohen's recollections contained in this useful new book and incorporate Peter's unique philosophies, which are universal and timeless.

CGU President Bob Klitgaard reminds us that at Drucker and this unique graduate university, we have the opportunity and the obligation to conduct "conversations that matter." It was in Peter's classroom that conversations that mattered took place—about topics ranging from ignorance (a virtue) to marketing to make selling unnecessary, from common knowledge (frequently wrong) to predicting the future (by creating it).

By recreating this conversation in the classroom, Bill Cohen has performed a marvelous service and has made a valuable contribution. One reads through Bill's narrative and one hears the voice of master teacher and devoted student, engaged in dialogue and conversation about things that mattered to them both—and continue to matter to us all.

Ira Jackson
Dean, Peter F. Drucker and Masatoshi Ito
 Graduate School of Management
Claremont Graduate University

INTRODUCTION

Peter Drucker was a true genius—an amazing individual who changed modern management forever. He wrote forty books and numerous articles. There are thousands of references to him and his work, hundreds of articles about him, and several books, too. Why then this book? Although so much has been written about Drucker, his consulting work, and his philosophies, little has been written about how or what he taught in the classroom.

Peter Drucker was my professor in probably the first executive PhD program in management in academic history. I was his student from 1975 to 1979, and the first graduate of this program at Claremont Graduate School, which today is known as the Peter F. Drucker and Masatoshi Ito Graduate School of Management and is part of Claremont Graduate University. This was a program to which Peter committed his life from the first class. Our relationship continued through the years until shortly before his death.

To say that I learned much from Peter Drucker would be a gross understatement. What he taught literally changed my life. When I met him I was a young struggling ex–Air Force officer only recently involved in business management, with no academic experience at all. Beginning with my graduation from Claremont's program, and following many of Peter's lessons that are contained in this book, I was re-commissioned in the Air Force Reserve and rose to the rank of major general. I entered academia and eventually became a full professor and a university president, even teaching several times at my alma mater as an adjunct professor. In fact, at one time when Peter was not teaching at Claremont in 1985, and I was, he allowed me to use his office. I became an author and wrote books which were published in eighteen languages. Peter was generous enough to call my books "scholarly." For all this, though he would deny it, I credit Peter Drucker.

A Class with Drucker contains my recollections of what it was like to be in a Drucker class as a Drucker student during this early period. I have used my notes, old papers, and other information to reconstruct some of his lectures and our conversations to give the reader the best picture possible of how things actually were. I have tried to come close to capturing his actual words, but in any case, I believe I achieved the spirit of what he said and how he said it. My aim is to put the reader in the classroom as if he were there with me at the time hearing Drucker and participating in every interaction I had with him.

I debated whether to re-read Peter's books before writing this book. I decided not to do so in order not to corrupt my perception of what he taught at the time. I occasionally referred to my well-worn copy of *Management: Tasks, Responsibilities, Practices* to jog my memory about a particular lesson, as this was our only textbook when I was his student, and even this volume was not always helpful, since much of what Drucker taught in the classroom was not in his books, or had a somewhat different emphasis.

I didn't want to stop with just what Peter taught, but what I did with his knowledge. Peter did not tell us how to do things. He frequently taught as he consulted, by asking questions. That showed us what to do and got us thinking how to do it ourselves. So, after explaining Peter's lesson, I have tried to bridge this final gap by giving the reader my interpretation of what Peter meant and how I used and applied his teaching, and perhaps how the reader can as well.

The first chapter of the book tells much of my background at the time and how I came to be the first executive doctorial graduate of the "Father of Modern Management." The second chapter sets the background of the Drucker classroom and explains how Peter taught. Chapters 3 through 19 cover a variety of Peter's lessons, from "What Everyone Knows is Frequently Wrong" (Chapter 3) to "Drucker's Principles of Development" (Chapter 19), and how to apply them.

Peter Drucker was a man not only of great ability and insight, but of great integrity. I have tried to be true to his story and my own as his student. At this point, Peter would have said, "Enough. If your book is worth anything, let's get on with it." I hope you agree that it is.

Bill Cohen—June, 2007

CHAPTER ONE

How I Became the Student of the Father of Modern Management

This book consists of wisdom that I learned in the classroom and in personal dialogue with Peter F. Drucker, arguably the greatest management thinker of our time. It also describes how I applied these insights which he so generously imparted. However, this first chapter is mostly about me and how I came to my relationship with Peter Drucker. The lessons themselves were received over a thirty-year period, from when I first met Peter Drucker in 1975 until his death in 2005. His management approach continues to be taught at the Peter F. Drucker and Masatoshi Ito Graduate School of Management at Claremont Graduate University. I know that it gave him a great deal of satisfaction and pleasure that his university would continue the legacy of his work both in spirit and practice.

My lessons from Peter ended on November 11th, 2005. It was then that I received a most unwelcome e-mail announcement from Claremont Graduate University regarding this man from whom I learned so much, and who in so many ways changed my life. Peter F. Drucker, The "Father of Modern Management," had died peacefully several hours earlier at age of 95, a couple of weeks before his 96th birthday.

While death at an advanced age does not come as a complete surprise, such an announcement cannot come without a profound sense of loss. This is because Peter was who he was and did the things he did, and because he made such major contributions to the lives and thinking of many generations of management practitioners, researchers, thinkers, and students. In my case, I felt this loss especially keenly because it was personal. Until not long prior to his death, I spoke with Peter by telephone often and saw him at least once a year. I was not a campus colleague, except twice when I taught at Claremont Graduate University as a part time adjunct professor. During one such period in the mid-1980's, Peter allowed me to use his office as my own.

Peter Drucker was both my friend and mentor. He was more than a former professor with whom I had studied for my doctorate some thirty years earlier. But I hasten to add that many, perhaps thousands of students and non-students alike felt the same about him. Peter had a gift of making everyone he came into contact with feel as if he or she were an especially close friend. And he seemed to remember and have special affection for his former students. Many maintained contact with him.

The lessons I learned from Peter were extraordinary and significant to my thinking and practice, not just of management, but of life. One of the highest honors I have ever received came as a result of my teaching a challenging course in strategy, planning, and decision-making to a group of doctoral students at CETYS University in Ensenada, Mexico in 2005. One student representing the group was generous enough to say, "As you have quoted and furthered the ideas of Peter Drucker, in the future, as we progress in our careers, we will quote you and further your ideas."

How I First Heard About Peter Drucker

In 1973, I had returned from Israel after living and working there for three years. Previous to that, my background was totally in the military, I was even born into a military family. I knew little outside of the military, and less about business and how it was practiced. I did know something about management and how to direct research and development activities since I had done this work in the Air Force and in Israel. Moreover, on my return to the U.S., I had become director of research and development for a company developing and manufacturing life support equipment, primarily for aviators and airplane passengers. This company was located in California, near Los Angeles. As a practicing manager, I decided that I had better learn something about business, so I committed to reading at least one business book every week.

I soon discovered Drucker. I read his classic works such as *Concept of the Corporation* and *The Effective Executive*. His book, *Management: Tasks, Responsibilities, Practices,* was published the same year as I began as an executive in industry, and I eagerly devoured the thick volume that I would later study as his student.

My First Drucker Lesson was Not from the Classroom

I received my first Drucker lesson before I even met Peter Drucker. As the senior manager heading up research and development, I attended the company's annual off-site sales conference. One of the items on the agenda was a discussion of a Drucker concept developed in *Management: Tasks, Responsibilities, Practices.* In this book Peter had written that "the first task of any business management was to decide what business it was in." I soon realized that it was not only a profound statement about business: it was true about every endeavor anyone might undertake in life.

Let me explain what I mean. I had at that point recently completed my first-ever job search. A few years later I became a headhunter. Both as a job seeker myself and as a facilitator in this field, I discovered that many job candidates fail to get hired by companies because they don't know what they want to do. They want "to keep their options open." Even some managers who have extensive experience in many industries make this mistake. They put together a very general resume which says that they have done many different things in many different areas and for different companies. They promote themselves as a "jack of all trades," able to do anything. Unfortunately, their resumes do not emphasize what "business" they are really in. This comes across as the second part of that old saying ". . . and master of none."

As a consequence, not infrequently, a job candidate with a lot less experience who makes it clear by the way his or her experience is presented that this is the one "business" that the person is really in, is the one who lands the job. This happens even though the candidate's experience in the discipline is frequently far less than the one who tries to be everything to everybody.

The same is true when it comes to managing our time in order to achieve our goals, and Peter was a master time manager. Each of us has the same amount of time, 24 hours a day. But some fritter away and waste their time on work which has no bearing on what they would like to accomplish or where they would like to be one, five, or ten years in the future.

Once you decide on "your business," the non-essential work that you do becomes obvious. Maybe you are in the wrong job for where you want to be in ten years or for what you want to become. If that job is supporting you as you struggle to gain knowledge or in other ways work toward your "real" professional goal, you probably have to stick with it for the time being. But you are much less likely to reach your goal than someone who knows what "business" he or she is in and focuses on that to the exclusion of other activity non-essential to this goal.

This doesn't mean that you must avoid washing dishes or digging ditches to earn necessary money while you are preparing yourself in other ways to do what you really want. But it does mean that you need to decide what you want, and then stick to activities which support "your business" goals. From this first preliminary lesson I realized that this individual, Peter Drucker, had something to say which was very valuable indeed, and I applied it at once.

I Become Peter Drucker's Student

I was heading up research and development for a company, but I felt I had much to learn. On the technical side, I was well-supported by some first-rate engineers. However, some of the business concepts I was dealing with were unfamiliar. I had only a BS degree from West Point and an MBA, so I decided the best solution was to further my academic education in business.

At first I just wanted to take some additional courses. However, I soon decided that what I really needed was a higher level of business education. That meant a doctorate in business. I called two well-known universities in my geographical area. Representatives at both institutions said that if I wanted a doctorate, I had to quit my job and work on the doctorate full-time. They told me that there was no such thing as studying for a doctorate without becoming a full-time student. This didn't sound right to me then, and I am even more convinced today that it is not right.

What happens in most cases is that full-time students are forced to teach or assist the full-time professors in order to support themselves. This amounts to a full-time job. They are paid a small fraction of what they earned previously or could earn outside of the academic environment. Arguably, they are exploited, to one extent or another, by the universities that accept them as doctoral students. I suppose those who do this rationalize that this is how would-be doctorate candidates "learn their trade." Fortunately for me, this situation turned out not to be true at Drucker's university.

Seeing an advertisement in *The Wall Street Journal* by a university that claimed to offer doctoral degrees part-time for employed executives, I responded and was invited to meet the dean for an interview. Much to my surprise and disappointment, the "university" turned out to be a suite in a hotel. The "dean" told me that I could get a doctorate in any field I wanted, not just business but in engineering, psychology, or anything else. There were no courses. All I had to do was to write a "dissertation." And of course pay several thousand dollars in tuition upfront.

"It has to be a real good dissertation," the "dean" told me, "and it should take you about six months to complete." The "dean" misread the look on my face and quickly added, "Of course, under special circumstances and if you work real hard, you can finish your dissertation and get your doctorate in a week." I was aghast and terminated the interview.

On my return to my office, I immediately called the California State Board of Education. I was amazed to discover that this university was actually empowered by the State of California to grant these degrees. This was a type of school known as a "diploma mill." It wasn't a real university at all. In those days, California educational laws were very loose, and these so-called "universities," all non-accredited, flourished. Fortunately, California law was tightened considerably in the late 1980's and these phony universities have all but disappeared. Today, nonaccredited universities in California must be approved by the State, and in order to gain this approval they have to meet stringent standards, including site visitations. Soon after this incident, I received a printed advertisement at work promoting an MBA. In smaller letters at the bottom of the flyer were the words: "New PhD program for executives—call the dean's office." It gave a telephone number. The university was called Claremont Graduate School.

Not being from the Los Angeles area, nor having much dealing with academia, I had never heard of this university, and I even suspected that it might just be another diploma mill. I called the telephone number and was soon connected with Dean Paul Albrecht. I didn't know Paul Albrecht when I called, but he was one of the leaders in higher education—an innovator who in many ways changed education as we know it.

Dean Albrecht told me that this new PhD for executives had just been approved by Claremont's president and its academic council, and that a limited number of students would be admitted to the first class in the fall of 1975. He told me that this was not a program for specialists or those who wanted to become professors to teach and do research. It was designed for executives who wanted to reach the top levels as practicing managers. Potential students wanting to get into the program had to be practicing managers with a certain minimum number of people reporting to them as evidence of their management background and potential for further promotion.

Albrecht questioned me extensively about my background and about the research and development organization which I headed. Finally, he said: "If you are interested, you seem to meet the basic requirements. Why don't you send me your curriculum vitae?" He had to explain to me that "a vita" was the academic way of saying "resume." I sent it. Several weeks later his secretary, Lois, called to set up an interview for me at Claremont.

After a week or so I was heading toward the small town of Claremont, California, about thirty miles due east from my home in Pasadena. I wondered whether I was to be disappointed again with another diploma mill. I was much relieved when I arrived at the university and I found it to be one of a consortium of educational institutions called "The Claremont Colleges." It looked real, but after my earlier experience, I was still somewhat suspicious of California schools.

I met Dean Albrecht and he explained what in academia we call "the theory construct" of his new doctoral program, the first class of which was just forming. It was based on an equally demanding MBA executive program begun several years earlier.

"Management is becoming more and more complex," he said. "Even an MBA is no longer sufficient. Our new program differs substantially from our regular PhD program. Our regular program requires a high degree of specialization. For example, if you wanted a PhD in finance, you must take mostly finance courses and pursue this one discipline in some depth. Then, of course, you must do research and write a dissertation in that discipline.

"In this new executive PhD program, you will still be required to do research and write a dissertation on a specific business topic. You must also meet the requirements for traditional research tools, such as taking a qualifying examination and a proficiency examination in two foreign languages. The difference is that your doctoral courses will not be in one area, but will cover all of the various disciplines of business and economics."

The requirement for two foreign languages was later changed to either one foreign language and one research tool, or two research tools. I understand that some years later the traditional requirement of mastery of a foreign language was finally dropped altogether.

"Also," the dean continued, "You will be required to take several courses from Peter Drucker, as his management concepts are the basis of the program."

The magical name, "Peter Drucker," grabbed my immediate attention. I could not believe that the number-one managerial thinker and writer in the country, and probably the world, was teaching at the very university at which I was interviewing, one I had even suspected might be a diploma mill. I didn't want to insult Dean Albrecht about my disbelief that this world famous professor could be at this university with which I had previously been totally unfamiliar. So, I asked, "Which 'Peter Drucker' is this?" I guess it was a rather inane question, but it was all I could think of to ask at the time to confirm that we were talking about the same individual.

"I believe there is only one Peter Drucker," Albrecht responded. I don't recall now if he was smiling or not when he said this to me. As Paul described himself, he was a "taciturn German." However, he was taciturn with a sense of humor. I recall thinking at the time that he seemed somewhat amused at my question. "Our new program has much to do with Drucker's ideas and way of thinking, and if you join us, you will be required to take several courses from him as a minimum," he repeated.

I decided right then that this was exactly what I wanted. I applied for Claremont's new program and was eventually accepted. A couple of months later I was in a class with nine other executive PhD students with perhaps the greatest management thinker of our time, teaming up with the man behind the program, Dean Paul Albrecht. It was the first class of the new program, limited to ten new executive doctoral students, and conducted in a lounge room at the university faculty club. The class was completely informal, with both Paul Albrecht and Peter Drucker leading the class in discussing a number of important managerial issues of the day. I was off and running, learning Drucker lessons and wisdom first-hand.

The Oral Lessons and Lost Wisdom

Despite Peter Drucker's extensive writing in books and articles and edited collections of his works, some of his wisdom has probably never been published, and much has been published incompletely. The reasons are not difficult to understand. An author focuses on the subject matter of the topic at hand. Thus Drucker wrote on "The Concept of Management;" *Management: Tasks, Responsibilities, Practices; Innovation and Entrepreneurship;* and more. But many important concepts are left out of the specific topics on which he writes. Moreover, much is probably imparted through voice intonations and gestures and in providing feedback, and his interaction with his students. What Drucker really wanted to emphasize is sometimes missing from any published material, even though Drucker was a master of the printed word.

Fortunately, while Drucker may have not have covered everything he wanted to get across through the single mode of communication of his writing, or even in the many oral interviews he did with journalists and business writers, he frequently elaborated more in his lectures and discussions with his students. The new doctoral program and its courses were developed by him and Paul Albrecht. Four years later in 1979, I was proud to be the very first graduate from that program.

Although Dean Albrecht applauded my advancement to become a senior military officer, at the time I wasn't even in the military, having resigned my commission when I accompanied my Israeli wife to Israel. However, though I eventually became a major general in the Air Force Reserve, I'm not certain that Paul was ever comfortable with the fact that, contrary to his intentions when founding this program, his very first graduate, the new manager with doctoral training, jumped ship and became an academic. (Even as I write this, I cannot help but remember how Drucker, in editing my writing, would have underlined the words "jumped ship" and boldly written: "Too glib!" It's a sad testimony to the fact that he was not a hundred percent successful in altering all of my bad habits.)

In any case, I think Peter was actually pleased that I became an academic, although some years later when, having some challenges in my academic career, I asked his advice, and complained to him, "You got me into this." He instantly retorted, "Don't blame it on me!"

During the period that I was his formal student from 1975 to 1979, Drucker and I developed a friendship that continued after my graduation and the award of my doctorate and lasted until his death. While I did not see him with the frequency of Mitch Albom in *Tuesdays with Morrie,* we did maintain contact, mostly by telephone, but also through my occasional visits and lunches in Claremont, California.

I do not mean to imply that I was the only former student that he mentored. Without a doubt there were many, and I am personal friends or am acquainted with a number of them. At a memorial for Peter several months after his death (it was actually a celebration of his life), the master of ceremonies said, referring to the TV show, *The Apprentice*: "We are all Peter's apprentices." She was absolutely accurate in her assessment.

However, Peter was not accessible to all. He was careful not to allow himself to be exploited. Not that he had an inflated sense of self-importance. Rather, he knew his time was valuable and limited. He was willing to give his time generously as an investment, but only if he thought that investment would have some value for the future, not to him personally, but to some higher cause. I'm told that he had a scrap of paper that he routinely returned to those making requests. On it were printed words to the effect that he did not honor requests for interviews, testimonials, or speeches, etc. Although, of course he did, if he was convinced that it would positively contribute in some way to society. I also heard from others, some high up in management, who wanted to see him, but were denied this opportunity.

I do not know what he saw in me, or for that matter, how I even got accepted into this new and experimental program. When I first met Peter I was a struggling young husband and practicing manager trying to support two small children. I had an extraordinarily poor business background for becoming a top business executive, the stated objective of the program. I stood far below most of my nine doctoral classmates in business accomplishments. Several of them were already presidents or vice presidents of large organizations (the term "CEO," being not yet fully in vogue).

I had graduated from West Point, but with an academic average that put me toward the bottom of my class. I was once told that I had the lowest passing math average since George Armstrong Custer graduated in the class of June 1861. I had done well in the Air Force, and I had been accepted at the University of Chicago and earned an MBA. However, I suspect that the latter achievement was based more on my perceived potential than demonstrated academic brilliance.

Now thirty-five years of age, I had just returned to the U.S. after three years in Israel. And I was trying to establish myself as a serious business manager. Partially due to my aviation and research-and-development background, I managed to land a job as head of research and development in a company developing life support equipment for aircrew. That's when I entered Claremont's first experimental doctoral class for practicing executives.

I was not a top student in Claremont's program either—except in Drucker's classes. Yet, Peter saw something in me that maybe I didn't see in myself, and he gave me access and his attention when I asked for it, and even sometimes when I didn't. Later, he was kind enough to recommend one of my first books, despite being besieged for testimonials by others. He also recommended me for several important academic positions and later supported me for a major teaching and research award at my university.

Moreover, several years later, as I advanced in the Air Force Reserve and became a distinguished graduate from the Industrial College of the Armed Forces in Washington, D.C., Peter accepted an invitation to fly across the country to speak to these military students at my invitation, a request he was unable to honor only due to last-minute illness. This was truly unique because toward the end of his career, Peter would rarely go anywhere to speak requiring an overnight stay. Without a doubt, I was a very fortunate student of Drucker's. I miss him and greatly honor his wisdom and the lessons he taught me. I have tried in the past, and will continue to do everything I can in the future, to make good on his investment in me.

Much of Peter's oral wisdom from the classroom is both unique and important and is not really lost, for all of his many students from his classes have received it. Yet, even having lived an academic life as full as Peter did, only a tiny percentage of us would have the good fortune to have sat in his classrooms. This is unfortunate, for what he taught, much of which was far from intuitive, has saved me time and again in business and in life and has had a significant impact in whatever success I have achieved. For this it is well that Claremont Graduate University carries on his work.

In the next chapter, I'll have more to say about Peter and how he ran his classes. The remaining chapters cover the various lessons that I took from his instructions and how I used them.

Drucker in the Classroom

At the time I was Peter's student, Albrecht Auditorium and the newer modern teaching facilities at Claremont did not exist. Drucker's classes were all in Harper Hall. Even then it was old, and used not only for business and management studies, but also for other subjects, such as for classes in religion and ancient languages.

Peter's classes were always conducted in the largest room available because most classes were taught to both masters and doctoral students simultaneously. The classroom usually held 50–60 table-student chairs, the kind used by students in classrooms all over the world. Drucker would arrive early and engage whichever students were interested in conversation before the formal class began. There were few women in any of these classes in those days, perhaps three or four in each class. Nevertheless, they have made their presence felt, and today these women are at the head of universities and companies or are successful entrepreneurs.

In all of the classes I took from Peter, he always used a single textbook. This was *Management: Tasks, Responsibilities, Practices,* an 839-page tome which he had written several years earlier, the one in which he had written the material about deciding what "business" you were in. I heard that in some classes he required no textbooks, only recommended a couple of books that he had written. That's right, recommended. He did not require them, or any textbooks, in these classes.

Anyway, in the courses I took his *Management: Tasks, Responsibilities, Practices* was required. It is still in print and selling well today. It's an outstanding book. Moreover, this is a regular book, not a textbook in the usual sense of the word, a fact that was much appreciated by Drucker's students. I think the book sold for about $20 in those days. This was expensive for a book, but regular textbooks thirty years ago were priced at more than twice that. So my one-time cost of $20 or so meant a savings of more and more money in every course I took with him.

Saving money on books, however, was definitely not the reason he had such a large following. You took the first couple of courses from him because of his reputation and maybe because it was required. Thereafter, you signed up for Drucker because there was great value in what he had to say.

But, back to his "textbook." Most professors tend to try to cram an entire textbook into whatever time period over which the course is conducted. Drucker's syllabus always covered reasonable amounts of the book, to digest. He felt that books needed to be "mastered," not simply skimmed with a host of facts and a few techniques committed to memory. So, he did not try to assign the entire eight-hundred-plus pages over one seven-week "module." The idea was to focus on one section and to master that.

Frankly, my own experience is that few actual textbooks are ever completely read by students, and certainly not "mastered." I don't exclude the several textbooks of which I am the author. There is simply too much material for the ten-to-sixteen weeks over which a course is usually taught at most universities. Moreover, the classes in the executive program at Claremont were taught in seven-week modules because we had to take more courses than the regular doctoral students.

If an author attempted to write a textbook which could be read and understood in the time available, it probably would fail in the marketplace. This is because it is the professors who make the decision as to which textbook is adopted. Students might like it, but most professors would view a 200- or even a 300-page textbook as lacking substance.

Most professors would definitely turn their noses up at a professional book like Drucker's, even if it met their length requirements, because it was not academic. And his idea of concentrating on one section per course would be equally frowned upon. However, to me, the value of Peter's classic book is immeasurable.

Drucker the Rebel

Drucker was a man of great courage in his thinking, writing, and in his teaching, and not only in his unorthodox use of the same book for many courses. As a result, though he made unequaled contributions to management thinking in the 20th and 21st centuries, he was frequently ignored, and shockingly, even ridiculed by some fellow academics. Much of this was pure jealousy, but it has a basis in the type of research an academic is expected to do and how he is supposed to disseminate the results of his research.

Peter frequently said, "The corporation is my laboratory." He meant that he observed what was going on in a company or companies, analyzed what happened, and drew relevant conclusions which he published in a way that could be understood and put to use by management practitioners. Most academics didn't buy that. To them, there is only one kind of research: scientific research based on mostly quantitative methods. This research is disseminated by publishing in "the scientific journals" of business, not by books or practitioner-read journals like *The Harvard Business Review* or *The Wall Street Journal*. Moreover, these "scientific" articles are not written for practitioners, but for fellow academics. Drucker was an academic, but he wrote for practitioners, and he wrote to be understood. Many academics didn't like it and resented his success.

I didn't realize the prejudice in the academic community against Drucker until I began to interview for an academic position. When some professors with whom I interviewed learned that I had studied under Drucker, they let loose with a variety of snide comments. I remember one senior professor at a mid-level university telling me, "If Drucker were interviewing for a job here, we *might* be willing to offer him a junior level position." This comment originated from a professor who had contributed little, if anything, to management thinking and development. I could barely control my anger, and it must have been noticeable. I did not receive an offer from that particular university. Well-known business author Tom Peters once wrote: "Drucker effectively by-passed the intellectual establishment. So it's not surprising that they hated his guts."[1]

In November 1984, when Peter turned 75, *The Los Angeles Times* did a special report devoted entirely to him and his accomplishments. They asked a few well-known academic writers, including Rosabeth Moss Kanter from the Harvard Business School and Warren Bennis from the University of Southern California, what they had learned from Peter Drucker and what they thought that he had contributed to the management discipline. As I recall, this list included Tom Peters, who while not an academic, had co-authored the mega-best seller, *In Search of Excellence*. All wrote short pieces extolling Peter's accomplishments and wishing him a Happy Birthday.

However, one writer used this public forum for praising Drucker to show his disdain instead. This was a professor who had authored a best-selling book a few years earlier which set off what became a well-known management fad, but he was basically an academic researcher in the traditional sense. His contribution to this special *Los Angeles Times* tribute was something to the effect that he really couldn't comment as he had never read Drucker, since Drucker, he said, didn't publish in scientific journals.

Peter really didn't care. Those kinds of criticisms never bothered him. He went on his own way as an academic rebel and made major contributions which frequently challenged conventional wisdom, were not based on quantitative studies, and significantly changed management and how it was practiced.

Drucker invariably did what he thought was right. For example, each of his courses required several short papers. Though he might have sixty students, he graded every single paper himself. He never once used a teaching assistant to grade for him. I might have "Too glib," or "Now I am more confused than ever," scribbled across a paper, which I had thought was pretty good. However, if this happened, it was written by Drucker himself, and not some graduate assistant who was assigned to help him grade papers. Except in 2003–2005, when I taught at an online university whose official policy it was to have graduate assistants and subordinate professors grade all except doctoral papers, I did my own grading. And since my students have also complained about being unable to decipher my comments, I may have acquired this habit from Peter. First of all, I always thought it was right, but also I thought, "If Peter Drucker can do it, so can I."

Class Begins

Everyone knew when Drucker was ready to begin. He always wore a jacket and tie. The jacket would come off. He would roll his sleeves up. Then, the tie would come off or be loosened and he would begin.

The first day of class, he would offer to autograph his book for anyone who wanted. "You'll probably get more money for it autographed when you sell it," he often quipped. This was a joke. I suppose it happened, but I never knew of a student to sell Drucker's book.

I wasn't comfortable taking the time to have him autograph the book until the second class I had with him. I was still a bit uncomfortable. "What do you want me to write, Bill?" he asked. My discomfort in interacting with famous people, coupled with an abominable sense of humor, frequently appears out of nowhere in such situations and leads me astray. And so, middle-aged smartass that I was, I answered, "Just write: 'To Bill Cohen, to whom I owe everything.'" He didn't pause but wrote something. For a moment, I wondered whether he had actually followed my irreverent request. Alas, he wrote only "To Bill Cohen, with best regards, Peter F. Drucker."

Peter's modus operandi in teaching was straight out of his birthplace, Vienna, Austria, from where he had fled the Nazis: He lectured. As to the subject, we rarely knew what to expect, even for a first class of the term. Peter did not waste a lot of explaining what the class would be about and doing class introductions. Syllabi were typically distributed when we signed up for the course, but not by him.

Peter did not rely on notes for his lectures, either. He would begin speaking on a topic he considered important that applied to the class subject matter. He would continue unless interrupted by a question or he decided to ask a question of his own. As his thoughts unfurled, depending on the events or the weather, his lectures might go anywhere. They frequently went off in unexpected directions, and yielded valuable lessons like unearthed diamonds. These gems might surprise and delight, or could even bore his students on the rare occasions that the topic he selected was perceived as less interesting.

In answering a question he might go off in an unexpected direction which seemingly had nothing to do with the question asked. Before you knew it, he was giving a lecture within a lecture. You might think that this was due to some sort of professorial absentmindedness. However, if you stayed with him, and sometimes it took as long as an hour, he would suddenly conclude and you would realize that everything tied together. He felt that you needed all this additional information to understand his answer.

Peter was not a captivating speaker by his style or manner of speech. In fact, his Viennese accent sometimes detracted from his style, but his content was always right on the money. If you stayed engaged you would learn a lot and you would receive invaluable wisdom you could gain nowhere else.

Sometimes he would get stuck. He couldn't remember an individual's name, a company, or perhaps where he was going to go with his lecture. Most speakers or instructors in this predicament just go somewhere else with their presentation. Not Peter, his eyes would roll up as if trying to find the information in a file—in many ways I guess he was—then invariably he would find it and say exactly what he had intended. He never failed to find what he was looking for in his "mind file." It must have been a great filing system. I'm kind of sorry I never asked about it, since it was so clearly effective.

Another sign of his independence was that he did not always go by the clock. He completed his lectures when he was done, not when the clock said it was time. However, when it came to the break for dinner, he was always on time. So, I knew that he knew what he was doing, and controlling his time. However, classes were supposed to end at 10:00 PM. (Note I said PM not AM—these were all evening classes). This didn't always happen. Early on, I was in a class that went to 11:00 PM and I stayed until the end. But after this, I walked out of his classes that went this late. I'll have more to say on my walking out on Peter and its consequences in a later chapter.

Drucker the Man

I think it important for you, the reader, to understand Peter Drucker, the man, and what people thought about him. He was a complex human being. Ethnically Jewish, he was raised a Protestant.[2] From Doris Drucker I learned that Peter's father received an award from the Austrian emperor for his services while an official in the Austrian government.

Peter was an academic, but he never did what many, if not most, academics considered acceptable academic research. Professor James O'Toole at the University of Southern California noted that he would never have attained tenure in most top-tiered universities.[3] And, as I mentioned, I encountered anti-Drucker bias when I sought my first job in academia. Yet no one had a greater influence on management and how it was practiced. About 1999, I was present for the acceptance speech of a senior professor for a major research award at a national academic conference. Peter was not present. I'm not certain that he even had ever attended an academic conference. In the speech, this top-ranked academic researcher mentioned the one individual who most influenced his research. That individual was Peter F. Drucker.

Finally, I want to quote a particular laudatory, but insightful paragraph about Peter. He would not have wanted me to do so. He was always impatient and dismissive with accolades, no matter their source. Were he reviewing this chapter, or listening to me as I read it out loud, he would have interrupted me at this point and said: "That's enough—get on with the lessons if you think you have something worthwhile sharing." Sorry, Peter. This one's mine. The following is quoted verbatim from his memorial celebration. I do not know who wrote it, but it is inaccurate only in its understatement of his stature.

> "Peter Drucker was a man of great intellect, vision, humor, and curiosity. Outside of his expertise in journalism and management, he was an avid collector and scholar of Japanese art. In his younger days he would ski, fish, and ice skate with his son. He loved classical music, hiking with his family, and reading—history, Charles Dickens, and Jane Austen.
>
> "Peter Drucker was a renaissance man. He has left his mark on those who knew him personally, studied with him, benefited from his counsel, or simply admired him from afar.[4]"

Learning from Drucker

I took copious notes of everything Drucker said. I know that many others did the same. These were not important for my grade as he gave no exams. His grades were based solely on the papers that you were required to write for his classes. I thought that I would use these notes for my qualifying exams at the end of my coursework. This turned out not to be the case.

Qualifying exams, sometimes called "comprehensive exams," are given at the end of a doctoral student's coursework, and usually prior to his beginning the research for his dissertation. The idea is for the student to demonstrate his knowledge from everything previously studied. The exams are graded by the professors who taught the courses. And it is most definitely not a "rubber stamp." It is a screener for those seeking the title of "doctor." In the executive program, we took a wide variety of courses. This made it a little tougher, because we had to study more than a single discipline. In my case, I had five or six different professors grading my exams. We were advised to call each professor and ask what textbooks we should review.

Every professor I called recommended textbooks in addition to those we had used in class. That is, every professor except Peter. When I asked him what textbooks I should review, he answered, "None. Don't review anything. You already know everything you need to know to pass my exam. Don't study or review anything." Inasmuch as I knew my preparation for the other professors was going to cost me more than a hundred dollars in books and several weeks of cramming, I was happy to follow his instructions. Of course, when he evaluated my paper answering the questions he posed, he kept his word and gave me a high pass.

Nevertheless, my notes were important because they were extremely valuable for their content. It is from these notes and my memories of his classroom teaching, as well as our conversations out of class as a student and as "a Drucker apprentice" later on, that many of the lessons in this book come. I not only applied them, but I taught them as well. They are in every book I have written and in every lecture I have given, and in most actions I have taken as a manager.

Like many others, I owe much of whatever success I have achieved in my life and career to Peter Drucker and his wisdom. They were invaluable to me in my careers as an Air Force officer, an academic, an academic administrator, a writer, and an entrepreneur. I believe Drucker's lessons will continue to prove invaluable to tens of thousands of others in the future, whether from his books, the writings and teaching of his "apprentices" like me, or his work still being taught at Claremont and elsewhere.

I have presented these lessons pretty much as I received them, and I tried to describe the situations in which they occurred as accurately as my memory recalls the circumstances. I have tried to give you the flavor of the time, not only to help you to understand Peter's lessons and my thinking about them, but also to put you, so far as is possible, in his classroom.

Peter never began teaching any point without ensuring that you had the necessary facts to understand what followed. You now have the background and facts you need, so let's begin.

What Everybody Knows Is Frequently Wrong

y first class with Peter Drucker met in the fall of 1975. I didn't know what to expect. Drucker was a world-famous celebrity. I was a young man with limited business experience. Needless to say, I was more than a little intimidated with the thought of dealing with this prominent professor face-to-face.

I was actually taking two courses with Peter that first term. The other class had yet to meet. It was to meet Wednesday night in the faculty club, and Peter and the dean, Paul Albrecht, were teamed as instructors. It was open only to the ten students in the new doctoral program for practicing executives.

However, this was Monday night, and the class was entitled "Module 300: The Management Process." This particular course, and even the course numbering system then used, no longer exists. Peter taught it by himself. There were no other professors, and no graduate students assisting him. The class was open to both master's students and the ten doctoral students and was taught over a seven-week period. In the Claremont system, there were three semesters a year with two seven-week modules in every semester. This allowed students to take a variety of courses.

In later years, Drucker classes met in Albrecht Auditorium, and other ultramodern complexes built long after my own graduation. However, since the larger and more modern facilities didn't exist then, Module 300 met in probably the largest room available on campus in Harper Hall. It held fifty or sixty of the old-style seats for students with a table top that folded over your lap to allow notetaking.

I arrived early. About half of the class was already there. I didn't know anyone. We were all working professionals, and there were no orientation programs for new graduate students in those days. However, I discovered that many of these students weren't new to Claremont, and had taken classes with Drucker previously.

"What's he like?" I asked. "Oh, Peter's fine, you'll like him" seemed to be the most common reply. I noticed that just about everyone called him "Peter" not "Drucker" or "Professor Drucker." I discovered that this was his preferred form of address. He seemed to dislike any form of honorific or deferential treatment. I don't want to describe him as modest, but rather I would say that he considered himself beyond any special behavior and thought that this sort of thing was a waste of time. This does not mean to imply that he was timid in any way or encouraged disrespect. I never saw anyone ever treat Peter with disrespect, and he absolutely was not bashful about correcting any student.

After several minutes Peter strode confidently into the classroom. He was in good humor and engaged several students in conversation who apparently had been his students previously. He was of medium height, wore glasses, and was balding. He was energetic and appeared to be in excellent health. He had a copy of a thick book under one arm. As the time for the class to begin approached, he removed his jacket and held a copy of *Management: Tasks, Responsibilities, and Practices* aloft with one hand. "This is your textbook," he said with a heavy Viennese accent. "Anyone wanting me to autograph it, please line up over here to the right side of the classroom near the window."

There was a scrambling as maybe fifteen or sixteen students formed a line to get the coveted autograph. I did not. I didn't know what to make of this action at the time. Somehow it rubbed me the wrong way. I guess I thought it egotistical. The rest of the students continued their conversations while the autographing took place for another ten minutes or so. Then Peter went to the front of the classroom and began to lecture without reference to notes or his book.

The Story of the Two Vice Presidents

GE

Peter began with a story about a company he had observed. As the president of the company grew older, he knew that he should begin thinking about succession. Fortunately, he had two vice presidents, both equally outstanding, and of the right age, and each with a record of outstanding prior accomplishments with this firm. He increased the responsibility of both subordinate executives and gave them each the new title of executive vice president. He called them in together and announced that he intended to retire in five years and that one of them would be named to succeed him as president.

Both men thanked the president for the opportunity. The president had confidence that he had picked the right candidates. Although both were ambitious, he knew that both would put the company before themselves in whatever they undertook. He knew that either would make an excellent replacement.

Over the five years of their apprenticeship a differing pattern began to emerge from each of the prospective presidents-to-be. Although both men did well in every task given them and were equally successful in accomplishing their assignments, the process each followed was quite different. One would be given a task by the president. He would request the information needed and would ask when the job was to be accomplished. He would go off, gather his subordinates together, and would invariably present the president with a completed job well done days, weeks, or months later. Unless he needed some specific information or permission to do something a little out of the usual process, he would do this without ever bothering the old president.

The other executive vice president took an entirely different approach. Given a project by the president, he too would organize his subordinates to complete it successfully. However, there was a big difference. The first candidate worked independently and didn't bother the president with the details of what he was doing unless specific help was needed. However, the second candidate met periodically with the president to discuss the project and frequently requested additional meetings, continually seeking the president's advice.

"Now," asked Drucker, "When the president retired, which candidate did he pick to succeed him, the executive who was always successful without bothering him or taking his time, or the one who continually seemed to seek his help and approval?"

Many hands shot up, including my own. Drucker called on several students. Each stated his opinion that the president picked the executive who was able to succeed on his own without having to report back until the job was done unless there was a specific problem. This was my opinion too. Our thinking was that the new president would need to operate on his own and would not have the old president's counsel to fall back on.

Peter asked for a show of hands as to how many agreed that the president selected the executive who demonstrated that he was able to operate independently and without the president's ongoing approval. A large majority agreed with the students Peter had previously called on. Only a few thought that the second executive who constantly bothered the former president had been the one selected.

Peter stated the results: "Most of you are wrong. The former president selected the candidate who continually consulted with him." The class was in an uproar. This went against everything we knew about management and leadership. Everyone knew that the candidate who demonstrated that he could make decisions on his own should and would be selected.

Drucker's Lesson: Question Your Assumptions

"What everybody 'knows' is frequently wrong," Peter continued. "We are dealing with human beings. Most top managers want to feel that their policies and legacies will be continued. The constant contact and interaction with the second manager gave the president that confidence.

"Both executives were outstanding, but while the president felt that he knew and understood the executive who maintained contact, he was less certain about the other executive and he was less invested in his success. After picking candidates based on accomplishment, he went with his gut instinct, a perfectly correct way in which to make such an important decision after considering all the facts. Unless the president's preferred style was to let those who reported to him operate independently, the first executive should have tried to adapt his preferred method to what his boss preferred, even though 'everyone knows' that continual consultation with a higher manager is less desirable."

Drucker was right, and I should have known better. I was in the process of losing the confidence of my then boss by behaving exactly like the executive who operated independently. That in itself is an important lesson, but the idea that what everyone knows is frequently wrong proved even more important to me, and I think many other of Drucker's students. Over the next few years, I heard Peter say this quite a few times.

Maybe through repetition I finally began to think more deeply about what the words really meant. This seemingly simple and self-contradicting statement is amazingly true and immensely valuable, and not only in business. What Drucker wanted to emphasize was that we must always question our assumptions no matter from where they originate. This is especially true regarding anything that a majority of people "know" or assume without questioning. This "knowledge" should always be suspect and needs to be examined much more closely. In a surprisingly high percentage of cases, the information "known to be true" will turn out to be false or inaccurate, if not generally, then in a specific instance. This can lead to extremely poor, even disastrous management decisions.

Things Once "Known to Be True" Are Now Known to Be False

Of course there are many old "truisms" once thought by everyone to be true which we laugh at today. "The world is flat." "The earth is the center of the universe." The ancient Greeks knew that everything was made up of only four elements: earth, air, fire, and water. Of course, in modern times we learned that they were mistaken. When I took chemistry in high school, I learned that a Periodic Table of Elements had been formulated by a fellow named Mendeleev and that it had been established that there were exactly 93 elements, no more, no less. We got an "A" if we could name them all. Today, there are 102 elements— or so "everybody knows."

Questions Raised by 100 Percent Agreement

Interestingly, Drucker's lesson goes back over the millennia. In ancient Israel, the highest court was called the Sanhedrin. It corresponded roughly to the U.S. Supreme Court today, although it had a lot more power. The Sanhedrin tried the most important cases, and it had the power to exact capital punishment. In this high court, there were no prosecuting or defense attorneys and no appeals. The Sanhedrin court consisted only of judges. Some historians say 71 judges, others 23. The actual number is unimportant to some factual points.

The judges could examine the defendant, the accusers, and any witnesses either side brought before it. To exonerate a defendant required a majority of one, while to find him guilty required a majority of two. But perhaps the most interesting aspect of this ancient Jewish legal body was that if all judges found the accused guilty of a capital crime, he or she was allowed to go free! This was because the ancient Hebrews were convinced that there is a defense to be argued for every individual accused, regardless of the gravity of the crime and the persuasiveness of the evidence. If not a single judge thought that the defendant's case had merit, then it was clear that no matter how heinous the crime, something was wrong in the situation and it was likely that the accused was innocent. In other words, when every judge "knew" something to be "true," it probably wasn't.

In modern times, the impact of mass agreement on an issue has been addressed and confirmed in psychological research. In one experiment, subjects were asked to rate the attractiveness of individuals depicted in selections of photographs. However, there was only one real subject and the results were rigged. Unknown to the subject, the other participants were part of the scientist's team of experimenters. These participants were to agree about the most attractive individual depicted in any particular set of photographs at random. It was found that the subject could usually be influenced to agree with any photograph that the group selected, regardless of merit. This experiment demonstrates the influence of social proof, while it confirms one reason why Drucker's theory that what everyone knows is frequently wrong is correct. Accepting what everybody knows without any examination will often result in faulty decisions.

The Tylenol Case

Is Drucker's wisdom valid or important in business? Back in 1982 someone laced a popular over-the-counter drug with cyanide. A few who bought the poisoned product died. This led to an almost instantaneous nationwide panic. One hospital received 700 queries from people suspecting they had been poisoned with the tainted product. People in cities across the country were admitted to hospitals on suspicion of cyanide poisoning. The Food and Drug Administration (FDA) investigated 270 incidents of suspected product tampering. While some of the product had been tampered with as some sort of a sick joke, in most cases this was pure hysteria with no basis at all in fact. This panic in itself demonstrates part of Peter's thesis, but there is more that is critical to business decision-makers.

At that time, the product, Tylenol, was almost thirty years old. Over the years, it had built up a well-deserved trust with consumers. Nevertheless, sales of the product plummeted overnight and Johnson & Johnson, the product's maker, launched a recall and stopped all sales. The company advised consumers not to buy or use the product until further notice.

Virtually everyone predicted the demise of the product. One well-known advertising guru was quoted in *The New York Times*: "I don't think they can ever sell another product under that name. . . . There may be an advertising person who thinks he can solve this [crisis] and if they find him, I want to hire him, because then I want him to turn our water cooler into a wine cooler."[1]

Tylenol once dominated the market. Everyone knew that those days were gone for good. An article in *The Wall Street Journal* commented sadly that the product was dead and could not be resurrected; any other notion was an executive's pipedream. A survey of "the-man-in-the-street" found almost no one that would buy the product regardless of what the company did to guarantee its safety or promote its sale.

Despite what everyone knew, Johnson & Johnson retained the product Tylenol and its now famous brand name, which had become infamous through no fault of the product or its maker. Johnson & Johnson launched one of the most effective public relations campaigns for a product in commercial history. As a result, sales began a steady climb only a few months after the poisonings, returning Tylenol to its previous position as the number one analgesic controlling 35 percent of a two-billion-dollar market.

Where would Johnson & Johnson have been today had this established brand, built through thirty years of advertising, performance, and reliability, been allowed to disappear? How much would it have cost Johnson & Johnson to attempt to introduce and build an entirely new brand to replace Tylenol? Could this have even been accomplished? We'll never know. Nor do we know whether Peter Drucker was called in to consult with Johnson & Johnson.

What we do know is that Johnson & Johnson did the right thing when this tragedy struck and then took the right actions to reintroduce the

Tylenol product successfully. These actions today are studied in business schools as an almost perfect example of a successful public relations strategy and execution in the face of a crisis. However the basis of this was that Johnson & Johnson executives, knowingly or not, decided, "What everyone knows is frequently wrong." They went against what all the experts and even the consumers "knew" and went on to resurrect Tylenol to be even more successful than it was previously.

Analyzing Assumptions

How can this Drucker wisdom be applied in business? There is no question that applying this lesson requires critical analysis, because while "what everyone knows is frequently wrong" may be true, sometimes "what everyone knows" is actually true. So the problem is in how to know when common knowledge is true and when it is not. The first thing we need to understand is that what everyone knows, or so-called common knowledge, is simply an assumption.

An assumption is any belief, idea, hunch, or thought that you, a group of people, or any internal or external experts have about a subject. These assumptions are crucial because we use our assumptions to guide our actions and decision-making. This is sometimes complicated by the fact that frequently these assumptions are implicit and unstated. Decision making can be disastrous if we accept assumptions as fact without analysis. In the previous example, Tylenol would have been dropped as a product and Johnson & Johnson would have lost millions of dollars in revenue, plus it would have had to spend further millions of dollars to develop and market a replacement product.

So how can you analyze an assumption? The following steps will help:

Look at the Source's Reliability. The first step in analyzing an assumption is to look at the source's reliability. Reliability refers to consistency in measurement over time. Many years ago, I was involved in the selection of one of two designs for a new aircraft from two different companies. The companies were The Boeing Aircraft Company and McDonnell Douglas Aircraft Company. (Those who know this industry also know that the former company eventually acquired the latter, but this has nothing to do with our story.) Both companies proposed modifying one of their standard airline designs which was already in production and in use. Periodically we would meet with each aircraft company's design team individually to assess progress on each company's proposals, acceptance of which would be worth hundreds of millions of dollars to the winning contractor.

On one occasion we discussed ways in which we might lower the cost of each aircraft. The McDonnell Douglas manager stated, "You can save $10 million for each aircraft produced if you will allow us to deviate on the size of the escape hatch by two inches. That would be the standard size of the hatch on our DC-9 airliners. They successfully passed all FAA tests with no problems." I promised to look into his request, since it could save a lot of money.

Find the Ultimate Source. In this case, the initial source was the engineer who had put this requirement into the package listing design specifications that we had sent to the two aircraft manufacturers. However, frequently, you need to conduct a process I call "peeling the onion," because the initial source isn't the end of the story. What we are looking for usually lies inside one, maybe more layers that we need to peel away to get to the center—the ultimate source.

As soon as I could, I contacted the engineer responsible for the aircraft specification that McDonnell-Douglas wanted waived. "We can't do it," he told me. "This requirement comes directly from our aircraft design handbook with specifications that we must use for all new transport type aircraft." This means that the source had a sub-source. The sub-source was the design handbook. Not only did it produce a predictable and repeatable result, but "everybody knew" that these dimensions were the correct ones for the escape hatch and that we were required to use them.

Suppose Johnson & Johnson had investigated the sources for those who said that the demise of Tylenol was irreversible. These sources were the advertising and business experts who wrote for the business journals. They were usually right on the money in their judgments regarding advertising and how poor publicity could ruin a product's reputation. They were reliable sources based on past history.

Is the Source Valid? Both reliability and validity are concepts that come from testing. The validity of a test tells us how well the test measures what it is supposed to measure. It is a judgment based on evidence about the appropriateness of inferences drawn from test scores. But we're not looking at test scores here, we're looking at assumptions. So where did this particular specification in the aircraft design handbook come from? Knowing that source could help me decide whether this particular specification was valid for the aircraft we now wanted to build.

So, I peeled the onion again. I knew that every specification in the aircraft design handbook was referenced as to where it came from and what it was based on. I asked the engineer to do the necessary research to find out what tests this particular design specification was based on. Surprise, surprise, this specification was based on an aircraft test done with propeller-driven aircraft almost thirty years earlier. That aircraft traveled at about 120 miles per hour. The aircraft we were working on traveled at about 500 miles per hour.

Obviously, in this instance, the design specification was not valid. We turned it over to one of our aeronautical designers. He advised us to forget what everyone knew (the design handbook) and that the two inches would make no difference at the air speeds we were anticipating for an emergency bailout. We took his advice.

In the same way, the Johnson & Johnson decision makers probably evaluated the sources advising them to drop Tylenol and find something else. They probably asked what the success rate was for a product that was reintroduced in this way and under similar circumstance. That would have been peeling the onion. They probably discovered that there wasn't much of a data base to go on because no one had even attempted something like this before. They had taken the high road all the way, and felt that despite what everybody knew, it was worthwhile trying. The results, as they say, are history.

Drucker's wisdom reminds me of Roger Bannister's stunning achievement. Bannister, an Englishman and a medical doctor, broke a record in running once thought to be impossible. This was the famous "four-minute mile." No one had ever run a mile in four minutes. The world record of 4:01.4, had been set in 1945 by Sweden's Gunder Haegg. The experts knew that it could not be done, and some said it was dangerous for an athlete to even attempt. Today, the fastest mile record is 3 minutes, 43.13 seconds. Some high school runners even break the 4-minute mile. However, the fact is that when Bannister achieved this on May 6th of 1954, many, if not most, knew that it was an impossible dream. He was knighted for his achievement.

I was in high school at the time and I remember a radio interview with an doctor of kinesiology shortly before Bannister broke the record.

He stated that the human body just wasn't built to run this fast and that it couldn't be done. He predicted that Bannister would never succeed. Bannister knew better. What most "knew" was wrong, and Bannister understood this.

Drucker Lesson Summary

What everyone knows is frequently wrong. It is wrong because people make one or more erroneous assumptions and then everybody else buys in. To use this wisdom effectively, a decision maker needs to look at the source and determine its reliability and validity. Usually this involves "peeling the onion" to get to the very core source.

Self-Confidence Must Be Built Step-by-Step

One warm day in the Drucker classroom he passed on a lesson which was not explicit. This was unlike Peter, who was usually very explicit in both his writing and his speaking. I was a little out of sorts at the time that he gave us this wisdom; and consequently, I missed some of the preamble to his lesson, which might have made the lesson he taught more obvious to me.

At the time I was working at McDonnell Douglas Astronautics Company in Huntington Beach, California, in charge of advanced technology marketing. That was about fifty miles down the road, southwest of Claremont, and it usually took me about an hour to drive to class. My main car in those days was a lime-green Plymouth Arrow. Because it was small, it reminded me of the sports cars that I craved but could not afford with a wife and two young boys to support. I tried to convince people that it looked something like a Porsche. It didn't.

The Arrow didn't have a tape system, and so I would take a portable tape player with me, put it on the passenger seat, and run it from there. It was not stereo, but that didn't matter because I listened mostly to tapes on business or self improvement. I thought I could use a little of both, especially the latter. Unfortunately, the tape in my recorder kept sticking. I would take it out and pound it against my right leg, reinsert it, and turn the player on again. It would play for a short time, and then stick again. I was getting more and more frustrated and my leg was getting sore.

If that weren't enough, I ran into a traffic jam on the freeway and I arrived at Claremont late for class. Then I couldn't find a parking place close to Harper Hall. I finally found something, but it was several blocks away. I tentatively stuck my head in the classroom to see if I could sneak in unobserved. Not a chance. Drucker was already sans jacket, sleeves rolled up, tie loosened, and lecturing. I usually sat right up front, but being late, all the front row seats were taken. I nodded to Peter and found something at the back of the room. At that precise moment, I heard one of my classmates ask, "So, Dr. Drucker, how did you happen to become a management consultant?"

By then, I had learned that Peter didn't care for titles. He liked to be called "Peter." My impression was that he especially didn't like the title "doctor." I don't know why that was. In addition to his many honorary doctorates, he had a doctorate in International Law from the University of Frankfurt. He told us that he had selected law because it was the easiest doctorate to obtain. Whether this was true or not, I don't know. It was equally unclear what Peter thought of management consultants, although, of course, he was reputed to be the world's preeminent consultant in the management field.

There are a lot of books published on management consulting today. In fact, I wrote one (*How To Make It Big as a Consultant*, AMACOM, 1985, 1991, 2001). However, this was not always so. In the 1970's, management consulting was just becoming popular in the business community and there was a great deal of interest in the subject. There was a considerable mystique about what management consultants did and how they operated. Peter had consulted for some of the largest corporations in the world, including General Motors. His project with General Motors, actually a study, was the basis of his book, *Concept of the Corporation*, which helped to establish him as the foremost thinker in the field of management. So whatever Peter was lecturing on that led to this question, the question was probably honestly, if somewhat brashly, asked by my classmate. In any case,

I eased into the empty classroom seat I had located and listened closely to hear what kind of response such an impudent question would elicit.

How Peter Became a Management Consultant

Surprisingly, there was no rebuke, and Peter answered right to the point and with no side commentary regarding my classmate's brazenness in asking the question. He said that his experience with management consulting started just prior to the U.S. entry into World War II. With a doctoral degree, he was mobilized for the war effort in a civilian capacity and ordered to report to a certain army colonel. Peter was told that he was to serve as a "management consultant." Drucker said that he had no idea what a management consultant was. He checked a dictionary, but couldn't find the term. He said he went to the library and the bookstore. "Today," he told us, "you will find shelves of titles on management. In those days, there was almost nothing. The few books didn't include the term, much less explain it." He asked several colleagues and had no better luck. They didn't know, either.

On the appointed time and date, Drucker proceeded to the colonel's office, wondering exactly what he was getting in to. A receptionist asked him to wait, and then an unsmiling sergeant came to escort him to the colonel. This must have been a little intimidating for a young immigrant who not too many years earlier had fled from the military dictatorship of Nazi Germany, where almost all party members wore one sort of uniform or another.

Peter was led into the office by yet another stern-faced assistant. The colonel glanced at Peter's orders and invited him to be seated. He asked Peter to tell him about himself and questioned him at some length about his background and education. But though they seemed to talk on and on, Drucker did not learn what the colonel's office was responsible for, nor was he given any understanding as to what he would be doing for the colonel as a "management consultant." It seemed as if they were talking round and round, to no purpose.

Drucker was more than a little uncomfortable in dealing with the colonel. He hoped that he would soon get to the point and explain exactly what kind of work he would be involved in. He was growing increasingly frustrated. Finally, Peter could take it no longer. "Please, sir, can you tell me what a management consultant does?" he asked respectfully.

Drucker told the class that the colonel glared at him for what seemed like a long time and then responded: "Young man, don't be impertinent." "By which," Drucker told us, "I knew that he didn't know what a management consultant did, either."

Peter knew that someone who did know what was expected of a management consultant had made this assignment. Having lived in England and read Arthur Conan Doyle's Sherlock Holmes stories, Drucker knew what a "consulting detective" did. With that knowledge, and the insight that the colonel did not know anything about management consulting, Drucker asked direct questions about the colonel's responsibilities and problems. Peter then laid out some options about what should be done and the work, he, Drucker should do. The colonel was interested and clearly relieved. He accepted Peter's proposals in their entirety. This proved to be Drucker's first successful consulting engagement. So, Peter Drucker was not only the Father of Modern Management; he may have been the father of modern management consulting as well.

Moreover, if you consider the fact that Drucker's writing career was built on his consulting practice, and that during sixty-five active years of consulting, Drucker consulted for some of the world's largest corporations and nonprofit organizations—including the governments of the U.S., Canada, and Japan, this meeting with the colonel was clearly a pivotal point in his career. Therefore, though the lesson was not explicit as to what we were supposed to learn, and Drucker said no more on this subject, this story and its hidden lesson is of some value and significance.

Where Did Drucker Get His Self-Confidence?

I pondered Drucker's story for quite some time afterwards. Usually Peter was quite unambiguous in disseminating his knowledge. He would state his proposition clearly, and then give examples to support his thesis. On occasion, the order was reversed—the story came first, followed by his thesis. But the lesson or lessons were always explicit. This time his lesson was not immediately apparent and the inherent wisdom was hidden.

I could imagine the young Peter Drucker, a new immigrant to the United States in time of approaching war, and not only born in what had become part of the potential enemy's country, but actually in Austria.

Therefore he was born in the same country as Adolf Hitler, the Nazi dictator himself. How did he find the courage to question a senior officer of the army of his new country, and his new boss? Even more surprising was that when he realized that even his boss-to-be didn't know the duties of a management consultant, he had the confidence to make recommendations to a much older and more experienced man based on his flimsy knowledge about a fictional 19th century detective.

Most new immigrants at that time and under similar circumstances would have said nothing and taken pains not to challenge or question the colonel in any way. Drucker hadn't been in the U.S. long enough to become a U.S. citizen. Non-citizen Jews were denied U.S. asylum just prior to World War II, and some of whom who probably had equivalent credentials to Drucker at that time were sent back to Germany, where they wound up in concentration camps. Years earlier, Drucker had written an anti-Nazi tract which had been banned by the Nazis. Although he had lived in England for several years, to have been returned to Germany or his native Austria would have been a sure death sentence. Under these circumstances, and from Drucker's lack of full knowledge of either the power of an army colonel or his personality, to challenge him seems almost foolhardy. Where did such self-confidence come from?

Of course, Drucker's character and personality had no small bearing on this. Drucker possessed unusual strength of character and great integrity when I came to know him, and probably had possessed this trait at the time of the incident. Character and personality are basically fixed in childhood. However, I never knew Peter to talk about himself or brag about his achievements, and certainly never to make claim to unusual traits not possessed by others.

I never heard Drucker tell a story that did not have an important lesson for his listeners, even in answer to a question which might have been asked merely to satisfy idle curiosity. Drucker never told stories to no purpose. He taught and gave lessons. He never wasted anyone's time, especially his own or that of his students. A lesson implies that there is something to learn. If Peter intended a lesson in the story about meeting the colonel, it was more subtle. In searching for a lesson in this case, I decided to research Drucker's background and experience before the incident he described had occurred.

Searching for the Source of Drucker's Self-Confidence

What struck me regarding Drucker's background was the wide variety of different experiences he had had and the range of tasks he had successfully accomplished by the age of 30. His family were government employees. Even today, Doris Drucker has a document signed by Kaiser Franz Joseph awarding Peter an order for his services. Visitors to his home in Austria included famous economists with whom he was encouraged to engage in dialogue even while still in his teens. The family vacationed with others similarly accomplished in their academic or professional pursuits. Drucker himself stated, "That was actually my education."[1]

Drucker's father wanted him to immediately enroll in a university. Instead, after completing the equivalent of what we call high school (but in the Europe of that day, this was in many ways equivalent to what was taught in the U.S. in the first years of college), he left for Hamburg, Germany. At the age of 18, and on his own initiative, he started and completed a one-year merchant apprenticeship with an established trading company. This was his grounding in business.

My thought was that he must have identified with the theoretical economics he had discussed with his family's visitors and done this with a definite purpose in mind. Shortly after completing his apprenticeship, he left for Frankfurt. Clearly, he did not intend to continue the work for which he had apprenticed. The fact that he completed this year-long apprenticeship, yet immediately moved on, speaks volumes about what must have been his principles of self development, of which I will have more to say in the last chapter.

In Frankfurt, Drucker began to write a number of articles on economics as a freelancer. As a result, he was hired by a well-known Frankfurt newspaper as a journalist. Gaining an interest in politics, he attended meetings of a conservative political party in Germany. At the same time he started and completed his doctorate in law at the University of Frankfurt.[2]

Leaving Germany immediately after the Nazi takeover in 1933, Drucker found refuge in England. Here, he obtained work first for an insurance company as a security analyst, and later as an economist with a private bank. He also wrote his first book, *The End of Economic Man*, which analyzed the rise of Nazism in Germany and was reviewed favorably by none other than future British Prime Minister, Winston Churchill. In 1937, he immigrated to the United States, and again he became a freelance journalist, and found a job teaching part-time at Sarah Lawrence College in New York. From this timeline, he was still a freelance journalist at the time of his meeting with the colonel. He then accepted an appointment at Bennington College in Vermont as a professor of political science.[3]

In summary, by the time of his meeting with the colonel, although he was only about thirty, Drucker had already interacted with well-known intellectuals, completed a successful apprenticeship for a business, written articles which were good enough to be published, worked as a freelance journalist in three different countries, worked as a securities analyst for an insurance company, as a journalist for a newspaper, and as an economist for a bank, was a youth leader for a major political party, wrote a book acclaimed by a major political figure in England, and completed a doctorate degree. No wonder Drucker had the self-confidence to speak forcefully and successfully to the colonel. The colonel might have been the one who was intimidated had he known everything about Drucker.

One could write the whole thing off to Drucker's good fortune in parents or his native genius. But there are thousands of men and women who had these same advantages of parent, genius, and more. Yet few of them became "Druckers," and a good many of them squandered their advantages. Others without these advantages, but with the self-confidence of a Drucker, go on to great and near-great accomplishments.

Self-Confidence Is Based on Past Success   Discuss

One manual on leadership says, "No man can have self-confidence if not convinced in his own mind that he is qualified to perform the job he is assigned."[4] In other words, if you know that you can succeed at something, then you will automatically have self-confidence that you can do it. That's a big advantage in any situation. That's why Peter was so self-confident in dealing with the colonel, even though he only guessed at what a management consultant really did.

There is an old saying that "nothing succeeds like success." This means that success breeds success, or that if you have been successful in the past, you have a better chance of being successful, or at least will tend to be successful in the future. That's at least partly because you gain confidence with every success. That's how Drucker did it. But how can you become successful until you are successful the first time? It's like the chicken and the egg. You can't have a chicken until you have an egg, but you can't have an egg until you have a chicken. It sounds like an impossible contradiction.

Fortunately, there is a way of resolving this issue not available to the chicken: you can have a smaller success before a larger one. And a little success counts just as much as a big success as far as building self-confidence and knowing that you will succeed in the future.

Successful bodybuilder, movie star, and more recently, Governor of California, Arnold Schwarzenegger described how his confidence began to develop while in high school after he started bodybuilding. "Before long people began looking at me as a special person. Partly this was the result of my own changing attitude about myself. I was growing, getting bigger, gaining confidence. I was given consideration I had never received before. . . ."[5] Bodybuilding is a good analogy to increasing self-confidence through increasingly greater successes. No matter how weak he is at the start, a bodybuilder begins to exercise with a weight he can handle easily. Then as he grows stronger and his self-confidence increases at the same time, more and more weight is added.

This is not a new concept. Milo of Croton was the most famous athlete of the ancient world. It was said that he was able to lift and carry a full-grown bull on his back. How did he become capable of performing such a feat? He started with a newborn calf and lifted and carried it every day until it was fully grown.

So that's the first lesson in developing your self-confidence: accept responsibility and start to do small things. It's a long way from simply being willing to engage accomplished adults in conversation to confronting a senior boss who seems to hold all the power. But by starting small and performing more and more challenging tasks of different types, you can build up your confidence step-by-step, as Drucker did. Then you can do most anything else you choose, like another immigrant from Austria, who arrived in the U.S. penniless and uneducated, became a wealthy, famous movie star, and eventually was elected Governor of California.

Four More Ways to Develop Self-Confidence

Here are four additional ways I've found of implementing Drucker's "hidden lesson" of approaching situations armed with self-confidence based on past success:

- Become an uncrowned performer.

- Develop your expertise.

- Use positive mental imagery.

- Act confident to become confident.

ANYONE CAN BE AN UNCROWNED PERFORMER

One easy way to develop your self-confidence is to become what I call an "uncrowned performer." This is someone who does not hold a permanent appointment for the responsibilities he has taken on, but may take them on at any time and in an ad hoc manner.

You don't need to be a supervisor, manager, or director in order to assume such added responsibilities. Even without a title or position at work, there are hundreds of opportunities to become an uncrowned performer. If you stop to look within your work environment, you will find at least one opportunity, and probably even more, every day. The truth is, people around you are positively crying out for you to help them. This means that you must accept new responsibility opportunities outside of your normal duties, for which you may or may not be compensated directly. But the self-confidence you will get from doing uncrowned performance and the skills you will acquire, will more than make up for lack of immediate and direct benefit.

The first rule for becoming a successful uncrowned performer is to accept responsibility cheerfully on the job or in any club, association, or at home, every chance that you get. In fact, look for opportunities to accept new responsibilities at any time and at any place.

Maybe there is a special report that needs to be done. Perhaps your boss is looking for someone to organize or coach your company's softball team. Does your office want to buy a new computer? Who's going to handle the job of selecting and buying it? Do you have office parties or weekend social events? Entertainment committee chairmen are performance positions also. Every organizing opportunity is another chance to be an uncrowned performer. The more you do this, the easier it gets. The more others will look to you as the one who gets things done, the more self-confident you will become in the future in taking on new and challenging tasks that you have never done before.

Since there are far more uncrowned performance opportunities than there are individuals willing to do them, you will find opportunities like this everywhere. For example, you will find many opportunities where you live. There probably are organizations such as the "neighborhood watch" to help your local police guard against crime. There are committees to beautify the neighborhood, to get out the vote, or to organize youth sports programs. There are numerous boards that require leadership or performance positions if you live in an apartment building, condominium, or co-op.

You also will find opportunities in your place of worship, professional organizations, trade associations, political organizations, boy and girl scouts, and many others. Look especially for unpopular jobs that no one wants to do. Volunteer to do them and have fun doing them. Your self-confidence will soar as you complete these tasks and become more and more successful. In most cases, you won't need to compete for them. All you need to do is raise your hand and volunteer.

SEEK TO DEVELOP YOUR EXPERTISE

Research has demonstrated conclusively that there is an important source of power that will automatically give you increased self-confidence. That source of power is your expertise.

Expertise is in-depth knowledge or skill about any subject. Let's look at the expertise Peter had acquired by the time of his pivotal meeting with the colonel. He knew how to speak with important people; he had acquired the basic skills of business operations; he had developed proven abilities as a writer and journalist; he had expert knowledge regarding international law from his doctorate; and he had developed his analytical skills in political economics.

You can develop your expertise in anything: economics, marketing, flying, leadership, stock analysis, record keeping, investments, buying a car, getting a loan, bowling, or baseball. Expertise can also be on what to eat, how to jog, or even the best way to mow your lawn. Expertise can be about anything that human beings do.

Numerous, perhaps most, successful corporate leaders got to the top by developing their expertise. People like Steven Spielberg, Bill Gates, Steve Jobs, and Mary Kay Ash shared a common attribute. They had expertise in a topic that was of some importance to others. Interestingly, all four of them were either college dropouts, or had never even attended college before attaining success. This demonstrates that there are many paths to the development of expertise and that they don't depend solely on a formal education.

Steven Spielberg, CEO of DreamWorks, is the most financially successful motion picture director of all time and has won three

Academy Awards. He has been making movies since he was fourteen years old. He took any unpaid job he could find to develop his expertise and made his first film for theatrical release before the age of 21. He started college at California State University, Long Beach, but dropped out at the age of 22 to take a television director contract with Universal Studios.

Bill Gates is founder and chairman of the Microsoft Corporation, with almost $40 billion in annual sales. Gates discovered his interest in software and began programming computers at the age of 13. He entered Harvard University, but left during his junior year to devote himself full time to Microsoft, which he had started while still a student.

Steve Jobs attended one semester of Reed College, but dropped out of college to co-found Apple Computers with his friend Steve Wozniak. His actions changed the personal computer industry at the time and also had a major impact on building it into what it is today. But the decision to drop out of college and found a computer company was not done without self-confidence. Jobs had been working on computers as his main interest even in high school. Moreover, Apple did not immediately start designing and manufacturing computers. The company Jobs and Wozniak founded built circuit boards first.

Mary Kay Ash built her self-confidence and success step-by-step over the years. She didn't have the money to attend college during the Great Depression. Having to support a family as a single mother, she started by selling books on child psychology door-to-door. Her success at that built her self-confidence. She progressed to selling for the Stanley Home Products Company, and over a thirteen-year period, she again was a highly successful salesperson. Denied entry into top management, Mary Kay left to become National Training Director for the World Gift Company and gained more expertise and self-confidence.

In 1963, she started Mary Kay Cosmetics with $5,000 and nine saleswomen. By then remarried, she planned to keep the company going on her husband's income until she could get a positive cash flow started. Two weeks before she was to open her doors, her husband died of a heart attack. However, she had developed the self-confidence to keep going, so she didn't quit until she was earning a profit. Before she died in 2001 at the age of 83, Mary Kay Ash saw her company, Mary Kay Cosmetics, reach a billion dollars in sales.[6]

DEVELOP SELF-CONFIDENCE THROUGH POSITIVE MENTAL IMAGERY

One of the most important exercises you can do to develop your self-confidence is to practice positive mental imagery. Just as negative images can hurt your self-confidence, positive images can help your self-confidence significantly. I never knew just how much until I read about Dr. Charles Garfield's work years ago in the pages of *The Wall Street Journal*. The article told of Dr. Garfield's research regarding what he called a kind of "mental rehearsal." Garfield found that the more effective executive speakers frequently practiced mental rehearsal for speeches, whereas less effective executive speakers did not. I began to formally practice some of his techniques myself, and to teach them to my students.

Garfield was also an amateur weightlifter. He later wrote a book, *Peak Performers* (Avon Books, 1986), in which he described how Soviet scientists got him to bench press 365 pounds, more weight than he ever imagined he could handle. They did this by putting him in a state of extreme relaxation and then having him see himself making this difficult lift. He not only lifted the 365-pound weight, but was also astounded to discover it easier to lift than a much lighter weight he had lifted earlier, which he thought was the maximum weight he could ever lift.[7]

Today, the technique that the Soviets used with Garfield is well known to psychologists in a variety of fields, not just sports. It is possible because part of the mind believes what you tell it, whether it is true or not. So, in a state of extreme relaxation, meditation, or self-hypnosis, your mind will believe the images you put there. When no longer in this state, you will often be able to do what you imagined. This is because you have the self-confidence to do those things which you previously thought were impossible. However, this comes with one major caveat: you will not be able to do things which are contrary to physical laws of nature. For example, you can see yourself flying like Superman, but if you jump off a building in an attempt to imitate him, you are going to have an unpleasant surprise.

Still, there is much that you can do with mental imagery, and this kind of imaging tends to become reality in a number of cases. This is why many physicians teach patients with cancer and other terminal diseases imagery techniques. By using them, the patient sees the cancer cells being destroyed in his or her mind.

I once heard Norman Vincent Peale, the author of *The Power of Positive Thinking*, relate how he had helped a girl who wanted to find a suitable husband. He had her write a description of the man she wanted to meet on a slip of paper and put the statement of attaining her goal in the present, not the future, tense. Three times a day she was to take out this paper and read it aloud to herself. When he heard from the woman later, she had found a husband and she attested that the technique had worked. Peale claimed that this technique was infallible. I believe it is closely associated with mental imaging, because you cannot read the words without seeing the images of success.

ACT CONFIDENT TO BECOME CONFIDENT

Mary Kay Ash instructed her salespeople, "Fake it 'til you make it." She meant if you act as if you have already achieved something, eventually you will achieve it. So if you act as if you are confident, eventually you will become confident.

This has been confirmed many times and by many people. Walter Anderson, who wrote the book *The Confidence Course,* says: "If you act as if you're confident, even though you may not feel sure of yourself, your confidence *will* grow. If you firmly *fix the image in your mind* of the person you'd like to be, you *will* begin to become that person."[8] Heavyweight boxing champion Muhammad Ali confirmed this. He said: "To be a great champion you must believe you are the best. If you're not, pretend you are."

George S. Patton, the famed World War II general, employed the same techniques. In World War I, Patton was a young, 29-year-old colonel leading the first American tanks ever built against the Germans in France. Patton wrote his wife that every day he practiced in front of a mirror looking absolutely determined and confident. He called this his "war face." He maintained that this look helped his troops and gave them the confidence they needed to face the Germans. Until I read that, I had always assumed that Patton was just naturally confident in everything he did. However, there is little doubt that acting as if you have already achieved perfect confidence, even if you are a little uncertain, will eventually make it so.

Mayor Rudolph Giuliani was asked how he managed to lead New York City out of the tragedy of 9/11 after so much destruction and death. He responded, "I used Churchill to teach me how to reinvigorate the spirit of a dying nation. . . . During the worst days of the Battle of Britain, Churchill never stepped out of Downing Street and said, 'I don't know what to do,' or 'I'm lost.' He walked out with a direction and purpose, even if he had to fake it."[9]

Drucker Lesson Summary

Confronted by a new boss, an army colonel for whom he was to serve as a "management consultant," a job he couldn't even define, Drucker showed remarkable self-confidence. The reason was that he had built his confidence step-by-step over the years, as he achieved success in a wide range of areas.

Your self-confidence will increase as you accomplish various tasks successfully. So do smaller and easier tasks first. Take on all that you can. Then, progress to more difficult tasks. You will find them to be much easier than you thought.

In addition, here are four action steps I recommend to build your self-confidence:

1. Become an uncrowned performer by seeking out and volunteering for a variety of tasks, especially those that you have never done before, whenever you can.

2. Develop your expertise. Expertise is a major source of confidence and power.

3. Use positive mental imagery. Simulations in the mind are rehearsals for success. They are interpreted by the mind as real experiences. They will boost your self-confidence as if you had the actual experience.

4. Act confident and become confident. Behave as if you are already confident of success in any situation, even if you are uncertain.

CHAPTER FIVE

If You Keep Doing What Worked in the Past You're Going to Fail

e had all had a tough session in class, Peter most of all. He had lectured for almost two hours without stopping, and after a tough day at work I was pretty tired from just sitting and trying to follow his thinking. This was not a day in which I easily engaged, so as Peter lectured, I was ill-prepared for what was to come. As I recall, Peter's lecture had to do with reorganization.

A number of companies were reorganizing, and the business journals were excited with the concept, many companies reporting great success from their reorganization schemes. Still, there were cautionary tales and Peter's main message was rather negative. He said that reorganization just for the sake of reorganizing was never the thing to do. He said some recently appointed top executives were doing this, and it was just plain wrong and caused more problems than any possible benefit. It was time-consuming, expensive, and confusing to workers and managers alike. He told us if reorganization were really needed, to go ahead and do it, but we must keep in mind that reorganization was major surgery.

I thought this was a "no-brainer," and maybe this was why I felt that there wasn't much new to learn from what he said. I was employed at McDonnell Douglas Astronautics Company at the time. Over a one-year period, we had gone through three major reorganizations. Perhaps fortunately, I don't even remember what happened on two of them now, except that they didn't work. One was so ill-conceived that I'll never forget it.

Several of the company's major research and development programs were running behind schedule and with cost overruns. Top management had come up with a "brilliant" solution which involved reorganization. Every functional vice president, in addition to his other duties, would be assigned to a program to "help." The idea was to get top management's attention for these critical areas. I couldn't believe it when this reorganization was announced. The assigned functional VP would be responsible to top management for cost overruns and scheduling delays on that program. Never mind that each of these multimillion dollar programs already had a senior manager in charge. Never mind that this would split the functional VP's time, responsibilities, and set up some real conflicts of interest both within each program's organization and when the functional manager made decisions about which programs got priority on various resources.

The new organization was announced with much fanfare. What a mess! Fortunately, this crazy idea only lasted a couple of months. No one even announced its demise; it just faded away. This wasn't only major surgery, it was management malpractice.

Anyway, with this in my personal background, Drucker was preaching to the choir on this subject as far as I was concerned. I was already tired and impatient for the dinner break at about the midpoint of the class. The standard procedure in those days was to take a break at the halfway mark. We started class at 4:30 PM. The hour-long breaks for social activities and dinner were staggered for different classes, beginning about 5:50 PM. At break time, we would all adjourn to the Claremont Faculty Club, several blocks south of Harper Hall where classes were held. The staggered times for different classes were necessary because there were probably several hundred executive graduate students in both the MBA and doctoral programs in the evenings. This was too large a group for the faculty club to accommodate at the same time.

For a half-hour after arriving at the faculty club, we would socialize and enjoy an open bar with faculty and classmates. This was a good time to unwind and to talk with executives and managers from many different companies and industries, as well as with the Claremont faculty who were teaching that night. The open bar mixer was a very popular device for getting to know one another and for getting away from classroom pressures for a while. When the half-hour was up, we would be called to meals and would join a cafeteria-style line. Like the drinks, everything was "on the house." It was a nice fringe benefit of being an executive student at Claremont in those days. "All part of the service," Dean Paul Albrecht would comment.

To digress briefly, Paul's great success as a dean and in building the executive program transformed the graduate business college at Claremont from a sleepy boutique school that few had heard about into a major force in education in the country. When he hired Peter Drucker, it really put the school on the map. Moreover Peter's teaching was the perfect instrument for what Paul wanted to accomplish. Today there is an Albrecht Auditorium named in his honor.

I understand that the practice of the funded socializing over drinks, as well as the community dinner, has long since been discontinued. Whether for financial or other reasons, I cannot say. Someone may have pointed out that should one of these executive students have an automobile accident on the way home, the university could have been held responsible. Or perhaps the evening programs got so large that there was no way that the faculty club could continue to accommodate all executive students, no matter how staggered the times. In any case, while the socializing and meals with faculty were in place, they were very popular, and I believe of significant benefit to the students intellectually as well as socially. But that's just one former student's opinion.

On this night, I am ashamed to say that I wanted to avoid Peter during both the open bar and the meal afterward. As I said, I was tired and wanted to neither talk nor think very hard. Peter would force me to do both. Moreover, though Peter went out of his way to put all of us at ease when he spoke to any of us in or out of class, he could still be a little intimidating. After all, this was *the* Peter Drucker. No matter how personable and engaging, and Peter was both, his intellect and his fame could be a little overwhelming. I held him in such awe and high regard that despite my sometimes irreverent comments in class and bravado in other academic situations, I was a little uncomfortable in interacting with him, especially when feeling tired and out-of-sorts.

Because of this discomfort, rather than seeking him out and trying to join him in conversation over either drinks or food, I took the opposite tack and tried to steer clear of him completely. After having acquired the evening's repast on a tray, I planned on finding some table to sit where there were no professors, much less someone of the stature of a Peter Drucker. Alas, a more buoyant classmate saw me, called my name, and beckoned me to his table. I found myself seated with Peter and three of his other students.

Wisdom at the Dinner Table

One of the students, a senior executive in an aerospace company, was holding forth. "Once we learn how to do something," he proclaimed, "we don't let it slip away. In my company, we institutionalize it and we make it permanent. We call it 'modeling success.'"

I perked up. I was interested. I was always happy to pick up a new technique which worked.

"Do you do this in all instances?" Peter asked.

"Absolutely," the student responded. "I think it is the main secret of our success in this industry."

"What if the success you are modeling is a product? Do you continue to optimize that product without planning for eventual withdrawal?"

"That is exactly what we do," the student said. "When we get a successful product, we just continue to improve it. We keep doing that no matter what. In this way we continually stay ahead of our competition. Of course, at some point the next generation of the product is introduced. We plan for withdrawal of the product in that sense. But as far as the general type of product goes, when we find a winning horse we continue to ride it. We have a major product that we sell to NASA which has gone through more than a dozen generations and improvements. It's still going strong," he said proudly, "But we don't just do that with successful products; we institutionalize our successful policies and procedures, too. In that sense we're like 'Big Blue' (IBM). Those guys know what works so they keep doing it, and so do we. As I said, we model success." In those days IBM was considered the master corporation of the business world. Its own success formula seemed to include a uniform of white shirts, dark ties, and blue suits, a dress code which hadn't been changed in years, although since that time, it has.

[handwritten note: W, W, the Way, And is there a Better Way!]

"That's very interesting," said Drucker. "But what do you do when your environment changes?"

"I'm not sure what you are getting at," said my classmate, a little testily. "If the environment changes, we make the changes necessary in the product or procedures to accommodate changes in the environment. We just keep making it better. Once we find a success, we concentrate on making it better and staying ahead of our competition," he repeated. "That way our competition never catches up."

Peter put down his knife and fork and thought for a moment. Then he spoke. "I congratulate you on your and your company's success. However, I must tell you that your modeling strategy will work in the short term only. In the longer term, unless you have thought ahead to create your own future, any organization which continues to do what brought it success in the past will eventually fail. Moreover, when a significant change occurs, unless management is willing to quickly readjust to the new situation in which it finds itself and does not try to optimize the old model, it will fail even faster."

Drucker Explains His Lesson

The student blanched slightly, but said nothing. The rest of us waited to hear a fuller explanation.

"Look," Peter continued, "every environment changes. Eventually that change is sufficiently severe that you cannot adapt either a product or a procedure, no matter what you do. Sometimes this change is technological. Someone invents a mass-produced automobile. Think what this invention did to the buggy whip or the carriage industries—it destroyed them completely, and in a very short period of time.

"However, the change in the environment can be cultural, political, or something else. You mentioned NASA, so my guess is that this may be your only customer in this market for this particular product. What if NASA as a customer disappears or its funding is severely curtailed? Such changes do not cause incremental results. They are revolutionary.

"So long as your environment is fairly stable," he explained, "your company's actions are correct, and I am not suggesting that they should be discarded. However, you must be prepared for major change in the future, and you must start now. If someone else's revolutionary innovation catches you unawares, you must abandon what made you successful and take an entirely different course immediately. If you are not prepared to do this and do not drop the product or the procedure, you will certainly fail as an organization."

Drucker paused. Then he added, "Of course, the best procedure is to obsolete your past successes yourself to stay ahead of your competition. And not just by incremental improvement, either. That way, you will maintain control and create your own future."

Peter gave us several other examples of companies, even whole industries, which disappeared even though they optimized past successes, sometimes to an extraordinary degree. I do not recall them now, but I immediately understood what he meant. In the military we were constantly warned that we should avoid fighting the next war based on the methods, weapons, and tactics of the most recent successful one. Peter's lesson was clearly one that applied in many aspects of human behavior.

All of us were mesmerized to such an extent that time ran out before we completed our meals, and the discussion continued around the points Drucker had made. Before we knew it, it was time to return to the classroom, where Peter took up an entirely different subject. But before he started to lecture on the new subject, I scribbled some quick notes to myself on what he had said during the dinner break. I have emphasized them many times in my own writing and teaching.

Here are what I consider the important implications of Drucker's lesson:

- Continuing what led to past success will invariably lead to eventual future failure.

- If caught unawares, organizations must be willing to instantly abandon what was formerly successful.

- Better yet, an organization should assume an eventual revolutionary change is inevitable. Therefore, an organization should take actions to create its own future by making the revolutionary change itself, even though it means obsolescing the products or methods of its current and past success.

Examples Are Everywhere

Classic business cautionary tales of those ignoring this concept include the demise of the buggy whip industry and everything having to do with equestrian transportation (which Peter mentioned in his comments), but changes within the automobile industry itself.

After the automobile industry was well established, a very successful Ford Motor Company dominated the market due to its development of mass production and its implementation of the production line. However, it lost its market leadership to General Motors for fifty years when founder Henry Ford failed to acknowledge that customers wanted variety. They were prepared to ignore the mighty Model T in black with a single set of features and pay more for a variety of colors and options. General Motors successfully challenged Ford by offering customers a choice. Ford, who had built the Model T on the premise of no options and the lowest price possible, did not respond to GM until it was too late.

There are numerous examples in every industry. The railroad, that great invention of the 19th century which helped win the American west and, in the process, created "railroad barons," "robber barons," and some of the wealthiest men in America, was relegated to a greatly diminished role in the late 20th century by the introduction of superior technology by the airline transportation companies. The legendary and mighty railroad companies shrank to mere shadows of their former eminence.

In the mid-1980's, the entire billion-dollar vinyl record industry vanished almost overnight and vinyl record manufacturers lost millions when they failed to prepare for the growing threat from compact disc technology.

Slide rules, once carried by every engineer worldwide, are no more except for very specialized roles and in museums. Handheld slide rules were manually manipulated, non-electronic, analog computers. The basic models had two stationary rules with a central sliding rule. A clear sliding piece with a crosshair, called a cursor, completed the basic model. With this device, engineers could accomplish a variety of complex mathematical and algebraic computations. Every single engineer in the world owned at least one. Major companies like Pickett and K + E dominated the industry. They introduced improvements in their product every year. They optimized the slide rule. Yet, their markets disappeared within two years of the introduction of the handheld electronic calculator. Because these companies failed to anticipate such an innovation and could not respond fast enough, these companies disappeared, too.

I could go on, but you get the idea. Like a light bulb which burns its brightest just prior to complete failure, many of these companies and industries were at their best just a few years or, in some cases, just a few months prior to their demise. They optimized their success and it led directly to failure, exactly as Drucker stated. Although now recovered, IBM suffered the largest single-year corporate loss (almost $5 billion) in U.S. history in the late 1980's and early 1990's by continuing to do precisely what had won its reputation and made it so successful previously in marketing policy. As a result, the rise of PCs and changes in how customers viewed, used, and bought technology took the purchasing decision out of the hands of IBM's traditional customers. Moreover, IBM missed out on both the rise of the personal computer and the market power of Microsoft's operating system. According to one source, IBM had just 100 days left before cash ran out. Fortunately for IBM, Lou Gerstner took over the company and turned things around.[1]

Why does this occur? Why can't a company or an organization continue to do what has made it successful in the past? What happens is, as Drucker explained, the environment changes in some critical way that invalidates all the old rules. In IBM's case, it was the personal computer.

Environmental Changes

Environmental changes may include:

▪ *Technology:* something new like the automobile comes along and downgrades the horse as the basic means of personal transportation.

▪ *Economics:* the economy falls into a recession or becomes inflationary. One condition might cause potential customers to hold on to their money; the latter to spend more freely and in a much shorter period of time.

▪ *Culture or Social Change:* bathing suits covering the entire body go out of fashion. Ten years ago, a simple change in a uniform jacket put several firms making silver braid out of business when that item was removed from two million uniforms in the Air Force.

▪ *Politics, Laws, and Regulations:* what was once legal becomes illegal, and vice versa. The sale of alcoholic beverages becomes illegal, or becomes legal (both happened in the 1920's in the U.S.). Or, the law places restrictions on the ownership of firearms or how they may be sold. The gun industry suffered major losses when mail order and other purchases of firearms were severely curtailed by law after President John F. Kennedy was assassinated with a weapon easily purchased for a few dollars through the mail.

▪ *Actions of Competitors:* if a competitor is successful in an action that you have not anticipated and allowed for, you can be in serious trouble. Apple Computer opened the market for personal computers and dominated the market. IBM was very much a latecomer because it had been caught unawares by the success of the personal computer market. But "Big Blue" responded fast and with an excellent counter strategy. Whereas Apple did not allow anyone to create software for their operating system, IBM not only allowed, but encouraged anyone and everyone to do so. As a result, the amount of software available including games, business programs and more for IBM's operating system soon far exceeded Apple's. Through this strategy, IBM was able to take over and dominate this market for many years with even a late start and entering the fray with a product that was technically inferior to its competitor.

▪ *Unexpected Major Events:* the terrorist attack on 9/11 led to reduced air travel and created a demand for much greater security. A major earthquake or a war can affect the environment similarly. So can an unexpected national outbreak of an e-coli bacteria in food items.

Executives Have Trouble Changing

You might think that senior executives can easily anticipate and readily prepare for change, but this is rarely the case for several reasons. These executives are in power because they "made it" under the old paradigm. Their prior actions made them and their organizations successful. They are comfortable with the old way, not some new, usually unproven idea. Many leaders are afraid to deviate from what they know, afraid to make a mistake. They invested heavily in the old modus operandi and avoid anything that says that they must invest again and start over. It takes an exceptional individual to do this, or even to utter the words that imply that anything will change. However, the truth is that the new model may hardly be rocket science once you accept the fact that there will be change, like it or not.

One of the most remarkable cases of an organizational leader who was able to recognize that future change was inevitable was not a business executive but a military leader. His name was Henry H. "Hap" Arnold. He was the commander of the U.S. Army Air Forces during World War II.

After the U.S. Air Force was given the status of an independent military service after the war, he became the first and only five-star general that the

Air Force ever had. But getting there hadn't been easy. General Arnold had fought his entire career for an air force independent of the U.S. Army, with full career opportunities for the pilots who flew the airplanes which made up any air force. Previously, when the Air Force had been under the control of non-flying senior officers of the Army, pilots were allowed to command only flying organizations. They were rarely permitted to head up the non-flying divisions, corps, and armies, without which they could not reach the top posts in the U.S. Army.

Soon after the United States Air Force was created, and despite a lifetime of fighting for this flying air force and equal career opportunities for pilots, General Arnold wrote words then considered heresy by those who flew. He said that Air Force officers must be flexible and forward looking in their vision of the future of this new military service. "There will come a day," he stated, "when the airplane will be outmoded as a weapon system and the Air Force must be ready to adopt other means of fulfilling its mission." General Arnold said this at a time when airplanes were the essential vehicles in the Air Force's arsenal. Space weaponry and other unmanned systems didn't exist except as experimental prototypes in our military. Today, missiles and even unmanned flying machines take an increasingly larger share of the Air Force mission.

Asking Questions the Drucker Way

As a management technique, Drucker was famous for asking questions of his consultant clients. Jack Welch, former CEO of General Electric, has been called the pre-eminent CEO of the 20th century. He was also the youngest CEO in GE's history. When he became CEO in 1981, the company's market value was about $12 billion. When he left, it was worth more than 25 times that figure. According to Welch, Drucker's two simple questions helped propel him to this amazing feat. The first question was, "If you weren't already in the business, would you enter it today?" This Drucker followed with a second, more difficult question, "What are you going to do about it?" According to Welch, Drucker's questions led him to shed unprofitable businesses and streamline GE into its extraordinary success.

I have heard that some forward thinkers in the airline industry are anticipating the day when business travelers, a major source of revenue, are no more. How are they approaching this? Let's imagine we are these forward-looking airline executives looking at business travel. What questions should we ask ourselves?

The first question might be: What drives business travel? Obviously, the answer is the need to do business face-to-face. Are there alternatives to doing face-to-face travel other than alternative means of transportation? Sure. One can not only talk on the telephone, but can fax material, e-mail material, communicate over a computer, or even have a video conference. These methods are a lot quicker and less expensive than air travel. If this is so why is business travel preferred for business? Business travel is necessary when face-to-face meetings are essential because other means of communication are less effective.

The next question is whether there could be any other way enabling face-to-face meetings aside from travel? We already noted video conferences, but there are limitations. There are time delays, blurred images, and other issues. Still, technology is advancing. Without too much imagination, one can visualize a holographic video conference incorporating stereophonic sound. Maybe two companies are in the final stages of negotiations, but on opposite sides of the world. After several days of serious negotiations, no executive from either company has left his or her home city. However, from all physical clues, it's as if these executives have been involved face-to-face, and only separated by inches rather than thousands of miles. Through holography, each side has seen the other in three dimensions. With high quality sound systems, the images of all parties look and sound real.

An executive from one company puts a document in a fax machine on a table. Instantly the document arrives in the fax machine on the table of the other company thousands of miles away. It takes not much longer than if the document were passed across the table, hand-to-hand. Would such a negotiation save money over having one set of executives fly halfway around the world? You bet!

I'm told some airline-industry thinkers are redefining their business, at least for the business travel market. They are considering re-inventing their future by investing in communication technology instead of faster or more economical jet aircraft. They want to do what the mighty railroad companies that dominated transportation in the 19th and early part of the 20th century failed to do. That is, invest in the potential of a newer future technology instead of focusing exclusively on optimizing the instrument of their past success.

How to Recognize the Future

Despite the need for forward thinking, it would be foolish, even dangerous, to abandon successful products, organizations, strategies, or businesses while they are still very profitable and useful. When is the airline
example about forward thinking, and when is it a costly waste of time and
"not sticking to one's knitting?"

Drucker himself agreed that tactical modeling of success works. How
then can we recognize the possible onset of environmental conditions of
significant magnitude that we must prepare for revolutionary change?

To do this, consider implementing the following practices:

■ *Make an effort to know what's going on, not only in your industry, but in
the world.* Familiarize yourself not only with new products, but with trends
in the environment that could remotely affect your operations in future
years. This means a regimen of continually reading of trade journals, newspapers, the Internet, and other relevant media and thinking about what this
means or will mean in the future. You should never stop this as a process.

■ *Ask yourself not what will happen, but what can happen, based on current
and anticipated developments.* Play a "what if" game with your present business. What would you do if . . .?

■ *Watch developments closely.* If sales drop over several quarters, find
out why. Do not assume that everything will "return to normal." There is
no normal. If sales increase in certain areas, also ask why. When the
American automobile first tried to emulate the small foreign cars, mostly
Volkswagen in those days, they failed miserably. The Ford Falcon, Plymouth Valiant, and Chevrolet Chevette all lasted but a few years as sales
dropped every year. However, only Ford noted and capitalized on the fact
that as sales were falling, certain options, such as a padded dash, bucket
seats, and "four-on-the-floor" gear shift options, were all increasingly
requested. Ford connected the dots and developed the Mustang—a spectacular success.

■ *Recognize that nothing lasts forever.* Prepare yourself mentally for
change and take immediate action when necessary, regardless of your previous investment in time, money, or resources. Never forget the accountants' credo that sunk costs are sunk costs, and that nothing lasts forever.

■ *While you should not change just for the sake of change, establish a pro-*

gram of continual review of every product, strategy, tactic, and policy. Aggressively seek opportunities to change and use change to stay ahead of the competition, to make what you are currently doing obsolete.

▪ *Adopt new ideas; and change from previously successful methods to ones that are even more successful for the future.* In this way, you'll not only succeed, you'll succeed in a big way.

Drucker Lesson Summary

Companies that cling to their past successes will eventually fail, sometimes in a spectacular way. Change is inevitable if you are going to stay successful. Be ready to turn on a dime and abandon everything that has made you what you are. Better yet, be a forward thinker and create your own changes and your own future.

Approach Problems with Your Ignorance—Not Your Experience

*W*hen Peter first began instruction on this lesson, we thought he was making an outlandish statement to make a point. Drucker was certainly not the sort of professor to brag about any of his accomplishments. This was in contrast to some professors I have met as a student or later when I became a professor myself. Drucker was never arrogant or "full of himself." But he was not above relating anecdotes that later proved to be less than accurate to illustrate a point, although the point itself was always absolutely true and immensely powerful.

A Chilly Afternoon in Drucker's Class

In any case, this Drucker lesson began unexpectedly on a chilly afternoon in January of 1976, a little after 4:00 in the afternoon. I can't place the date any closer, but I recall the weather. It was not chilly in the sense of a northern or eastern winter. In fact, it was not cold inside the building.

Still, I remember that it had been what we considered chilly outside. This was Claremont, California, forty miles east of Los Angeles. The temperature rarely dipped lower than 60 degrees Fahrenheit during the day in the winter season. Sometimes it really warmed up. Visitors from other parts of the country proclaimed our winter climate to be "balmy." Still, we termed it "chilly" and, for whatever reason, I remember this fact when remembering Peter's giving us this lesson.

This class met in one of the larger classrooms in Harper Hall. Harper Hall was an old building on the Claremont Graduate School part of the campus which The Clarement Colleges had allocated to it. The Colleges are a consortium of five undergraduate colleges and two graduate institutions and a central organization that provides general services to all seven institutions.

Large portraits of past professors and academic administrators from the Claremont Colleges, most in full academic regalia, hung on the walls of Harper Hall. This particular classroom was the first room one encountered on the ground floor immediately upon entering the building. The classroom was large because it had to be. This was a Drucker class.

A Drucker Gem

This evening's lecture was far from boring. Moreover, the important lesson that came right away was a gem. Drucker began to reminisce about his work with various corporations both here and in Japan. He told us that it was often very simple things that an outsider could do which would have a major impact in the company he assisted. This was because inside people were generally much too close to the issues, and also because they assumed things from their past experience that they incorrectly thought were identical in the present situation. An outsider would wonder and question these things that a practicing manager in the organization frequently missed, although all managers needed to train themselves to ask questions.

Asked the secret of his success in these endeavors by a student, Drucker responded, "There is no secret. You just need to ask the right questions."

Unexpectedly, one of my classmates raised his arm and exploded with three questions in rapid succession. "How do you know the right questions to ask? Aren't your questions based on your knowledge in the industries in which you consult? How did you have the knowledge and expertise to do this when you were first starting out with no experience?"

"I never ask these questions or approach these assignments based on my knowledge and experience in these industries," answered Drucker. "It is exactly the opposite. I do not use my knowledge and experience at all. I bring my ignorance to the situation. Ignorance is the most important component for helping others to solve any problem in any industry."

Hands shot up around the room, but Peter waved them off. "Ignorance is not such a bad thing if one knows how to use it," he continued, "and all managers must learn how to do this. You must frequently approach problems with your ignorance; not what you think you know from past experience, because not infrequently, what you think you know is wrong."

Liberty Ships Prove the Value of Ignorance

Drucker immediately launched into a story to prove his point. His stories generally covered the wide range of Drucker's reading and thinking—from the Catholic Church to Japanese culture, politics, history, Jewish mysticism, warfare, and of course, business. The stories were usually fairly short, but sometimes they were much longer. Many times I heard Peter launch into an answer to a question and his "answer" wasn't an answer at all. It was a story that led to a story within a story that led to another story within that story.

I am ashamed to say, and sorry too, that sometimes I got lost and allowed my mind to become disengaged from his line of reasoning. This was truly unfortunate, because although Drucker might lecture for an hour or more in this fashion, all of the stories and information were linked. In the end, he would tie it all together, and if you stayed with him you could see that to understand his answer completely, it required that you understand everything else he had talked about, including the Pandora's box of stories.

However, on this particular chilly day, his tale was neither long, nor linked to other sets of information. Moreover, it had to do with a subject with which I was familiar. When I was a cadet at West Point, the Hudson River, for several miles was packed with hundreds of immobilized, no-longer-used ships. Each looked the same, about 400–500 feet long and clearly inactivated. I was told that these sleeping giants were called Liberty Ships and had been built on an emergency basis during World War II. Drucker now proceeded with the story to illustrate his point.

"After World War II broke out in 1939," he began, "the British were losing thousands of tons of shipping to German submarines. This was not unimportant, as the British needed the supplies and munitions these ships brought to feed their population and to continue to fight the war.

"In response to the demand and their high losses due to German submarines, the British had come up with a design for an inexpensive cargo ship. These ships were so cheaply built and basic in design that the ships weren't even expected to remain in use more than five years. They were slow, bulky, and inefficient. However, they had a major advantage and that was the reason that they were built. They could be constructed much faster than any other cargo ship. This was the critical factor. It only took about eight months for each ship to be built from start to finish. This was a significant improvement over the time it took to build a merchant cargo ship previously.

"Unfortunately, there was still a problem," Drucker went on. "Though England was the first great seafaring nation with centuries of experience in shipbuilding, it still took experts and skilled workers to build a ship, even a vastly simplified design like this one. Britain was fully engaged in all aspects of fighting the Germans. The manpower, shipyards, and production facilities to build the fleets needed simply didn't exist.

"So, the British looked to the United States, which at that time was not yet in the war. Now the United States did not have a terrific record for merchant shipbuilding on the eve of World War II. In fact, in the previous decade only two ocean-going cargo ships had been built in the United States. However, England was so desperate that it was willing to turn to a country that had little experience and no expertise in building the types of ships needed. The hope was that with the British design and with British help, it might take about a year to build each ship. Since the United States was not yet in the war, it was just possible that the Americans could put enough manpower on the project to produce the ships in numbers which would make the project viable. Anyway, there was no alternative, as German submarines were sinking merchant ships every day."

Drucker continued his story: "Since few Americans knew anything about building merchant cargo ships, the British cast a wide net and didn't limit themselves to shipbuilders or those with a lot of experience in the industry. One of the individuals that the British contacted was industrialist Henry Kaiser. Kaiser knew little about shipbuilding and was completely ignorant about cargo ships. However, he looked at the British design and proceeded not with British help and expertise, but out of his own ignorance.

"The British used expert workers who had not only general, but in-depth shipbuilding knowledge. Since he didn't have such workers, Kaiser asked himself how he could proceed without such expert workers. He came up with a unique solution based on his ignorance of shipbuilding. Kaiser redesigned the assembly process using pre-fabricated parts so that no worker had to know more than a small part of the job and was much easier to train. Moreover, he introduced American assembly-line techniques.

"The British knew that for close tolerances in high quality ships, heavy machinery was necessary to cut metal accurately. Kaiser didn't know this, and, anyway, he didn't have heavy machinery. Again, he asked himself a question: 'How do I cut the metal?' Again he came up with a solution, but not the one the British had been using. In his ignorance he told his workers to cut the metal using oxyacetylene torches. This turned out to be cheaper and faster than the traditional British methods. In his ignorance, Kaiser replaced riveting with welding, also cheaper and faster.

"Kaiser called his ships 'Liberty Ships.' He started building them and it didn't take him a year for each ship. It didn't even take him eight months. He started building them from start to finish in about a month. Then they got production time down to a couple weeks and, for publicity purposes, they constructed one Liberty Ship in just four and a half days."

Drucker paused for a moment to let this idea sink in. "Approaching this problem out of his ignorance, Kaiser built almost 1,500 ships at two-thirds of the time and at a quarter of the cost of other shipyards previously. Other American shipbuilders immediately adopted his methods in building these ships. Interestingly, despite the fact that they were not built to last, a couple are still around and in use."

Henry Kaiser knew nothing about building merchant ships and approached the problem out of his ignorance, not his knowledge in this area, and the results were astounding. Concluding his story, Drucker went on to say that he looked at situations, about which he knew nothing, and asked questions stemming from his ignorance, much as Kaiser was forced to ask himself and his staff questions out of his ignorance. Those who Peter helped were frequently surprised that these "ignorant" questions led to effective solutions that helped them with their problems.

Drucker then went on to his original topic and continued lecturing, his lesson on the importance of approaching a problem from a position of ignorance complete.

What to Do; Not How to Do It

This was typical of the way in which Drucker disseminated his lessons. Drucker taught what to do. He was very specific about this. However, he did not teach how to do it. That was left up to the student or to his consulting clients. Shortly after his death, a tribute in *The Los Angeles Times* quoted former GE Chairman Jack Welch. Welch credited Drucker with helping him to understand what to do in order to restructure his giant company, a company that was in many disparate businesses conducted in many different geographical locations around the world.

I've mentioned this previously, but it is worthwhile repeating here because it reinforces the value of ignorance. Most consultants would not have done what Drucker did. They probably would have begun an expensive and lengthy study of the organization and structure of GE and the location, nature, and profitability of these varied businesses. Drucker cut right to the heart of the issue. He didn't know much about GE or its businesses, but he did know that it was a mess and required a simplifying process. According to Welch, Drucker asked only: "If you weren't already in a business, would you enter it today? And if not, what are you going to do about it?" Welch's comment to his interviewer for the article was: "Simple, right? But incredibly powerful."[1]

Coming from a position of his ignorance about GE, Drucker had asked two questions that caused Welch to analyze GE businesses using Drucker's questions as a starting point. Welch had to answer the primary question and then come up with a decision to act, or a conscious decision not to act.

Welch decided that if GE couldn't be number one or two in the marketplace for any business, he would never have chosen to enter the business in the first place. He gathered the information he needed to determine whether GE could become first or second in the market in each business. Using these criteria, he ruthlessly dropped businesses that he would not have chosen to enter. As a result of this pruning, GE became much more efficient and concentrated its resources on those businesses which it could really exploit. GE became more efficient and effective, and its stock began to skyrocket. This helped to make Welch's reputation as one of America's most effective and celebrated executives. Not bad for starting with a little ignorance.

Analyzing Drucker's Lesson

At the time of Drucker's lesson, I knew I was on to something profound, and so I jotted down a few quick notes about approaching a problem primarily with ignorance for later consideration. Then I transferred my attention to the new topic Drucker had already embarked upon.

Later, back home, I began to think about how to apply what Drucker had said regarding what managers should do in applying their ignorance to problem situations. I knew that Drucker didn't mean to exclude one's prior experience, knowledge, or expertise completely. If that were true, how would Drucker have known even where to begin? Moreover, his injunction to begin with ignorance had to be based on a model developed through knowledge, experience, and expertise. I suspected it was his background as a journalist that may have given him the inspiration for this concept.

In addition, I realized that as a manager got involved in following Drucker's advice based on a question, whatever it was, he would be unable to accurately understand the issue if he didn't already have considerable knowledge. Drucker was not talking about tactical decisions that needed to be made immediately and on the spot. Such decisions had to be based on prior knowledge and experience. Peter was talking about more strategic decisions for which one had the time to reflect. Moreover, since Peter had said on many occasions that managers needed to trust their gut feelings, it didn't mean ignoring intuition, either.

I concluded that what Drucker meant was that a manager should not jump in with an immediate solution. And while a manager's experience and intuition were not to be excluded, he or she had to approach these problems first with an open mind. Thus the manager needed to recognize, even emphasize, his own ignorance in organizing resources to solve the problem. To rely primarily on expertise was in fact, dangerous to the problem's optimal solution. That this was in fact what Drucker meant was confirmed some years later in a personal discussion.

Using Ignorance for Problem Solving

Starting with Drucker's concept, I began an investigation of problem-solving methodologies. I categorized two major approaches to managerial problem solving, both of which involved beginning from a point of "ignorance." Essentially, these involved the left-brain and right-brain methods emphasizing, or if you wish, relying on logic and analysis versus relying on creativity and emotion. Of course, the two approaches can be combined. Again, the important element is to enter with ignorance—even though both methods may involve amassing and analyzing additional information available.

The Left-Brain Solution

I had already been exposed to an effective left-brain methodology previously. It was used in staff studies and was extremely effective not only in organizing complex problems and reaching logical solutions, but in presenting this information to others to convince them of the validity of the problem solver's solution. I had understood that this was developed by the military in the 19th century. However, during my investigation, I discovered that this method was also used and taught at Harvard University. Later yet, I learned that other professions, such as the law, have used a very similar approach to analyzing and reaching logical conclusions when confronted with difficult and complex problems.

The left-brain approach involves:

- defining the problem;

- deciding on the relevant information bearing on the problem;

- developing potential alternative solutions to the problem;

- analyzing these alternatives;

- developing solutions from this analysis;

- and finally in making the decision.

Problem Definition

You can't get "there" until you know where "there" is. That's not one of Peter Drucker's injunctions; it's one of mine. That's my way of emphasizing that in order to solve any problem, you've got first to understand exactly what the problem is. That's the "there" in a problem situation. The shipbuilding problem was not to be able to build the ships the British way, it was to build ships. Drucker saw Welch's restructuring problem as having to do with trying to manage a number of businesses that didn't fit the strengths of the overall corporation.

You can see here where Drucker's instruction to begin with ignorance is so important. With the shipbuilding problem, the problem previously had been defined incorrectly. It had been defined as: "How can we build the ships the British way without the same human and physical resources?" The fact was, you couldn't. If Kaiser's ignorance hadn't been brought to the problem so that this problem statement was redefined, Kaiser and other potential American emergency shipbuilders might still be working on the problem, or long since decided that it couldn't be done. Using 1940's technology available at the time, the problem just couldn't have been solved.

Similarly, had a large consulting concern accepted GE's problem and defined it as simply the restructuring of GE, they probably would have embarked on a massive program of analysis of each individual business owned by the corporation. While eventually a common theme of which businesses GE should or should not have shed may have emerged, it would have taken far longer and used up many more resources to arrive at this solution. Further, it might have ignored Welch's eventual strategic criteria since Welch himself would never have been forced to struggle with the issue of which businesses he would have GE enter if it were not already in the business.

Relevant Factors

Both Kaiser's and Welch's problems had a number of factors that were directly relevant to each problem situation. Therefore, both needed to gather additional data. Kaiser knew what he didn't have. He needed to know what resources he did have available. Kaiser looked into this, did his analysis, and decided that he could build these particular ships cheaper and faster. Similarly, Welch had to decide which businesses he would or would not cut or retain, measured against a common standard. He decided to get rid of those businesses in which GE could not be number one or two in the market.

Alternative Courses of Action

In this part of the left-brain decision process, Kaiser had to decide on alternatives to solve the problem. One option might have been to develop new tactics. Maybe he could have started a worldwide search for expert shipbuilders in neutral countries and offered them high wages. Maybe he could have designed new metal-cutting machinery and produced it quickly using his methods. It is possible he did consider these or other options. Likewise, Welch might have used different criteria, say, eliminating those businesses that don't have the potential to reach a certain level of profits.

All alternatives have both advantages and disadvantages. Welch probably sold off some valuable companies using his criteria. He knew that this could, and probably would, happen in certain instances. That was a disadvantage to this alternative.

Kaiser took an enormous risk with his solution. He had millions of dollars invested in it before he built his first ship. Many of the methods he used had never been employed previously and many were extremely innovative, to say the least. It was reported that because it took years and extensive training to enable novice fitters to tightrope across the high structures of the ship as it was completed, Kaiser hired ballet dancers as fitters.[2]

Analysis, Conclusions, and Decision

During the analysis, the manager essentially compares the relative importance of each alternative's advantages and disadvantages. Some alternatives have few disadvantages, but no great advantage, either. In any case, the manager needs to think it through and document his thinking. This helps the left-brain method to be really effective in explaining the decision to others after the decision is made.

In the cases discussed here, the conclusions are from the analysis and the eventual decision should be obvious. I'm sure Henry Kaiser went through this process in detail in explaining what he wanted to do to his managers, workers, and his board of directors. He would have left nothing out, concluding that despite the risks, the best way to achieve the desired results was to implement the building of the British design in the way he outlined it. Similarly, Welch would have explained the situation to his board, and eventually to GE stockholders, as to why certain businesses, even if profitable, had to be sold in order to secure the future growth and higher profitability of the overall corporation.

The Right-Brain Solution

The right-brained approach to problem solving still works by starting out with an assumption of ignorance. However, unlike the very structured procedure that is part of the left-brain approach, the right-brain method uses no fixed sequence of logical steps to arrive at a solution.

One of the best examples of its use in American business was by the famous inventor Thomas Edison. While Edison had no formal education past high school, he was the inventor of numerous "high tech" devices, from the light bulb to practical motion pictures. His right-brained approach, according to his assistants, was to go into a dark room and sit there—sometimes for hours—until a solution to his problem presented itself.

Another example of the use of this right-brain method was Einstein's description as to how he formulated the Theory of Relativity. One would think that anything as quantitatively complex or as mathematical as the development of this theory would require thousands of white-coated scientists working for months at blackboards covered with hundreds of chalk-smeared formulas and equations, plus advanced work in laboratories. Even were today's technology available to Einstein, these scientists would have used up an awful lot of computer time. Yet Einstein stated that he thought the whole thing up by himself by simply closing his eyes and imagining himself riding on a beam of light and as what would transpire to time on earth during his speed-of-light trip.

Inventing the Sewing Machine

In the 1840's, Elias Howe knew nothing about sewing or the struggles of predecessors over a hundred years in trying to invent a machine that could sew as effectively, but much faster, than a human seamstress or tailor. In fact, he was a young man still in his twenties. However, Howe was fascinated with the use of a machine to increase the speed in repetitious patterns of sewing.

He had an idea that such a machine would work if he used thread from two different sources. The problem was that a standard needle threaded through a hole at the back of the needle would not work. One night he went to sleep and had a strange dream that he recalled in the morning. He was on a desert island and attacked by natives. The natives were armed with strange spears. Each spear was attached to a rope, not from its shaft as one might expect in a whaling harpoon, but from a hole threaded through the spearhead. When he awoke and remembered his dream, Howe instantly grasped this as a solution for his sewing machine needle. It was now possible in his machine for the needle to be pushed through the cloth. This created a loop on the other side; a shuttle on a track then slipped the second thread through the loop, creating what is now called a lockstitch.

The Right Brain Leads to Silly Putty

During World War II, most rubber came from rubber trees grown in the Southwest Pacific, which were under Japanese control. In 1943, General Electric engineer James Wright was attempting to create a synthetic rubber by mixing boric acid and silicone oil. He came up with a product which had extremely unusual properties. When dropped, the material bounced to an unusual height. It was impervious to rot. It was also soft and malleable. It could even be stretched many times its length without tearing. Finally, if pressure was applied, it could copy the image of any printed material with which it came in contact and to which pressure was applied. The only trouble was, with all of these properties it was not a good substitute for rubber.

Wright went on to better things, but General Electric was intrigued with this strange material and its unusual properties. General Electric had a product, but without a practical use. Fortunately, no one junked it. GE sent the product all over the world to scientists, asking them to develop or discover a use for it. None could.

A few years later, a very unlikely innovator stumbled on the product. By varying accounts he was an unemployed marketing consultant, an unemployed advertising executive, or an itinerant salesman. In any case, his name was Peter Hodgson. Hodgson went to a party at which this material was the entertainment of the evening. He used his right brain to discover what many scientists were unable to do. As he watched adults playing with and enjoying the product for its properties, he visualized a much larger market for a children's toy. General Electric sold Hodgson the rights and it was Hodgson that named it: Silly Putty®

At one point, millions of sales and many years later, I was in China teaching some MBA students about marketing as conducted in the United States. None spoke English. I took some Silly Putty with me to impress my students with American marketing acumen. I took the sample from my briefcase. Before I could speak and my interpreter could translate, there was a universal shout in unison the words: "Silly Putty."

There could be no finer testimonial to James Wright at General Electric, who knew he had something when he developed the material, but didn't know exactly what to do with it. He maintained his faith in the product until Peter Hodgson came along, unemployed or not, to use the right-brain problem solving to finish the job.[3]

Many who use this method of right-brain problem solving state that they struggle with a problem, go to sleep, and awake with a solution. Had either Kaiser or Welch cared to use this method in solving their respective problems, they needed do little more than to "sleep on it." Peter Drucker would have been proud in any case, that all of these problem-plagued individuals approached—and solved—their problems with their ignorance.

Drucker Lesson Summary

Approach problems with your ignorance, not your experience. My final conclusions regarding this Drucker lesson is that no one need be afraid of being incapable of solving any problem, managerial or otherwise. While a manager may lack specific knowledge, experience, or expertise at the beginning of a quest, this is not necessarily a bad thing. On the contrary, beginning with ignorance, and recognizing it, is possibly the best way to approach any problem to obtain an optimal solution.

Develop Expertise Outside Your Field to Be an Effective Manager

*W*hen I traveled to Claremont from home, it was a straight shot east on Freeway 210. As I approached Claremont, the freeway ended, and I continued through Foothill Boulevard, one of the main streets in Claremont, for a couple miles. Then I turned right on College Street to arrive at Harper Hall, where Claremont Graduate School was and Peter Drucker taught.

Time permitting, I would stop at a particular drug store in one of the shopping centers along the way. My purpose was to buy candy, one of my favorite vices. On this particular day, I had a full five minutes to luxuriate over my decision and still make Peter's class without being late.

Suddenly I heard loud shouting from one of the entrances at the front end of the store. I caught the words, "Put that gun away!" and "I've called the cops." That got my attention and, without thinking, I rushed toward the front end of the store. Such is the impetuousness of youth. However, by my arrival on the scene, the confrontation appeared to be just about over. Two young women, one brandishing a rifle, were still arguing loudly, but both were in the process of leaving the store. I followed. Outside, I saw a police vehicle screech to a stop and an officer approach the women. The one with the rifle put the weapon down in the driveway. I watched only long enough to see another police vehicle arrive and the women were hustled off. It was all over.

However, my distraction meant that now my time was short. I ran back in, grabbed a candy bar, paid for it, and left the store. I arrived in the classroom a little out of breath, without a minute to spare, still munching on the candy. I was just enough on time to claim my preferred front row seat, next to a classmate, Giff Miller. Giff, then in his mid-fifties, was the oldest student in the executive doctoral program. In "real life," Giff was the much respected City Manager of the City of Orange, California, a town of approximately 100,000 about thirty miles southeast of Los Angeles.

I told Giff about the incident with the two women. "I thought Claremont was supposed to be a quiet, laid-back college town," I said.

"Well, Orange has a low crime rate like Claremont, but still these things happen. You really don't want to get involved in confrontations like that," he added. "You need to stay out of it and let the professionals do their job."

"Well, I might have been needed," I said, unwilling to admit I had perhaps acted rashly, even stupidly, by rushing into something about which I knew nothing.

Enter Peter Drucker

At that point, Peter entered the room. Contrary to his usual procedure, he was carrying a large stack of papers. It wasn't a test. Peter never gave tests. It was some kind of handout. Giff and I rushed over to help him. I guess he heard the tail end of our conversation. Because he said, "Bill, unless you have previously prepared yourself to handle situations which have the potential for danger, you should leave their resolution to the experts, except if there is absolutely no alternative."

I didn't respond, but I wanted to say, "Hey, I'm a military guy, I've been in combat." However, I knew that saying anything would demonstrate a further lack of judgment, so I wisely, and perhaps uncharacteristically, kept quiet.

Peter, with help from Giff, myself, and a couple of other students, distributed his handouts. They were in packets of six. Each was titled "Case 1,"

"Case 2," "Case 3," etc. This, too, was out of the ordinary. I had not known Peter previously to use written cases. In the classes that I took from him, I never saw him do this again, although it is possible it was done later on or in other classes. I did notice as I helped to distribute them that these were not standard cases from a "case book" or those developed and sold for use in class by other universities. Each case carried a copyright with Peter's name. He was clearly the author. No case was longer than a couple of pages.

"We'll be using these as a point of discussion for the next few classes," Peter told us. He paused and considered and then said, "Please take a few minutes and read Case 4 now."

Case Number 4

Case 4 concerned a corporation in which the president had been replaced. I don't recall whether this was due to his health, death, resignation, or whether he was fired by the Board of Directors. The point of the case was that the Board of Directors had replaced the former president with the corporate attorney. The attorney was not an "acting president," but was the permanent replacement.

Traditionally, the company president had come up from one of the main business functional areas of the company: marketing, finance, manufacturing, or engineering. A corporate specialist, such as a corporate attorney, had never before been selected. The attorney was very bright and competent. He had a demonstrated track record of success in his area of expertise. He was obviously well thought of by the board and respected by senior managers in the company. However, the new president had neither functional area business experience nor an academic degree in business. I was not sure from the case whether he had even taken any business courses or seminars. This raised a number of questions which Drucker wanted us to analyze and discuss:

- Should a specialist ever be selected as a president in a traditional manufacturing company?

- Could a specialist, such as a corporate attorney, be a competent corporate president?

- Do other leaders promoted into top management face similar problems?

- If you were the corporate attorney, what actions should you take, given your lack of functional business knowledge and experience?

- How can senior corporate managers of any background best prepare themselves for general management responsibilities?

After giving us time to read the case and jot down our ideas, Peter led us into a discussion regarding the generalist versus the specialist as a successful top executive. Some of the class supported the view that the traditional functional areas were the only way to reach the top. However, Peter clearly felt that the traditional functional tracks to the top should be secondary to two other important elements in an executive's background: past proven success and personal readiness for the job. Peter emphasized that any manager's preparation for a top job was the responsibility of the individual executive. Looking at me meaningfully, he added, "Without this preparation, one should not venture into unfamiliar areas unless there is no alternative." Without pause, he then launched into what I believe was an allegorical story regarding a type of preparation he envisioned as effective.

The Secret Life of a Top Executive

I was often amazed that Drucker could so easily transition from a lecture on one topic to suddenly come forth with an absolute gem on an entirely different topic which sometimes appeared only tenuously connected to his original subject. In some cases, he might lecture for an hour on various topics which appeared not at all to be connected to what he was lecturing about when he began. He might do this in answer to a question, but at times it appeared that no special stimulus at all was required. However, if you paid close attention to these different mini-lectures, and even the lectures within a lecture, everything would become clear. He would tie it all together, and you understood that he felt that you needed to understand all of this extra material to get the basic point or understand his answer to a question that a student asked.

Everything Drucker said had value. I have frequently tried to go over Peter's lectures in my mind to find some unimportant trivia or something that I could immediately dismiss or disregard. I was never able to do it. Yet his lectures ranged widely. I learned to eagerly await these sudden appearances of unexpected lessons, and I suspect others did as well.

On this particular night, Drucker's sudden diversionary lecture was easier to connect with his main topic. Peter told us the story of the career of a highly successful corporate head. After graduating with a bachelor's degree, he had worked for five years at an entry-level position in a company. Then he had returned for two additional years' study at a well-known business school and received his MBA. On graduation, he was hired by a large corporation, and over a twenty-year period he had advanced to successively higher positions in this company, first in finance, and then several years at senior levels in marketing. He had always done extremely well, and after being named president had set out to further grow his company. After six years at the top, he had retired in his early sixties, leaving the firm at four times the annual sales and profitability from the time when he became president. Unfortunately, only two years into retirement, and still working as a respected consultant with his former company, he died.

At the funeral, hundreds of mourners attended the services from the man's former company. Not only were the company's senior executives present, but also many of the industry's leaders, even competitors. However, these mourners were amazed to find another group in attendance which had nothing to do with the deceased's former company or business. This group was not quite as large, but still consisted of equally prominent leaders. All were Egyptologists. They came from academia, museums, and several even from foreign countries. Neither group of mourners knew about the other. What were the Egyptologists doing there? Apparently the Egyptologists wondered the same thing about the business people.

This top executive had a secret life. From his undergraduate days, he had studied and become fascinated with ancient Egypt. He had developed and maintained this interest. Vacations were spent in Egypt, and he was the author of numerous articles in this discipline which had nothing at all to do with business. None of the business leaders knew that their colleague was so respected in this totally different field of endeavor. None of the Egyptologists knew that their colleague was also a successful and highly respected business executive.

I rather suspect that Peter's story was allegorical. As Peter sometimes said, "I am not a historian; I am trying to make a point." I think it is telling that Peter himself was not only a world-renowned professor of management, but also held an appointment at Claremont as a professor of Japanese art. I do not know if he was considered a world expert in this other field. I do know that he was the author of *The Zen Expressionists: Paintings of the Japanese Counterculture 1600–1800* (Ruth Chandler Williamson Gallery, Scripps College, 1982).

Master More than One Discipline

After his story, Drucker went on to tell us that it was essential that business executives master at least two disciplines, and that one of them must be outside of the field of business. He said this was important in the preparation of an executive for higher responsibilities because, like the corporate attorney suddenly elevated to general management, one never knew what future responsibilities might be thrust upon one unexpectedly. Expertise in more than one field was good training for sudden responsibilities in yet another field, and was the only evidence that the manager was capable of mastering more than one discipline.

Peter said that mastering at least two disciplines would have a number of beneficial effects. First, the executive would have the self-confidence of knowing that he was not limited to a single field. That he could, if called upon, do something entirely different, and do it well. Moreover, Drucker continued, "Great advances in any field rarely come from a single discipline. Rather, they come from advances in one discipline being transplanted to another sphere, which is totally unfamiliar with these procedures, ideas, or methods which have never been applied to problems in this other domain."

It was clear to me that mastering a second discipline was intended to help prepare the future high-level leader handle new and higher responsibilities. This would be part of the preparation needed for the high-level leaders to competently deal with situations with which he was previously unfamiliar.

I tried to follow Drucker's suggestion in my own career and I discovered his recommendation to be valuable advice. Moreover, I found another major advantage he did not mention. When frustrations, setbacks, and increased challenges in my profession sometimes seemed overwhelming, I was able to lose myself in my alternate arena of expertise and responsibilities. This somehow refreshed me so that I was able to go back and do battle in the other area with renewed vigor and determination. An even deeper understanding of the value of this lesson for success as a senior executive was to come.

Flash Ahead Twenty-Five Years

Like much of Peter's wisdom, it was not enough to just hear it. You had to think about it more deeply and see where his ideas led to get their full benefit. For me, Peter's lesson on mastering more than one discipline didn't fully come together until many years later.

Dr. Owen Jacobs at the Industrial College of the Armed Forces in Washington, D.C., and others at various civilian institutions around the country, had conceptualized the notion of "strategic leadership." They had discovered a thorny problem when previously successful lower level managers were promoted into the higher rungs of management. An inordinate number failed, despite their previous record of success. The numbers were too high to be written off as simply "some make it and some do not." This had cost the nation dearly in terms of national treasure and increased waste and losses for the companies and organizations.

In the past, those that could not make the transition to become what was now termed by some "a strategic leader" were discarded, and those that could make it were rewarded. The company bit the bullet for the cost of the failed executive, and the individual generally lost his career, or got shunted aside where it was perceived he would do no damage. However, someone finally realized that this cost was in the millions of dollars to a single organization, and probably in the billions for the nation as a whole.

According to Dr. Jacobs and his colleagues, the problem was that these failed leaders had been successful as lower-level tactical leaders, but could not make the transition to higher level strategic leaders. I was asked to analyze this concept and develop a presentation which would help successful tactical leaders to understand the problem and determine what they needed to do to become successful top managers—before they were promoted into these positions.

I agreed to undertake this task with some hesitation. The very words "strategic leadership" sounded a little over simplistic, a mere coupling of the buzzword "strategic" with the old standby, "leadership." While I was convinced that good leadership could be developed, I was less certain as to whether good tactical leaders could be turned into good strategic ones by a program.

Then, I remembered Drucker's lesson of the corporate attorney promoted to president, which he had discussed so many years earlier in the classroom and the need for preparation to prepare for what was now being called "strategic leadership." Clearly, the concept of the strategic leader is new only in its title. This was exactly the kind of thing Drucker was talking about. Expertise outside of one's profession gave one more of a strategic view of any situation.

Dr Jacob's basic concept was that as a leader is promoted, he or she must lead more and more in an indirect fashion. There are several reasons for this. At higher levels, the strategic leader must interact with numerous other specialties, in and outside of the organization, and many of these specialties are totally unfamiliar. The tactical leader had direct supervisory authority over all subordinates. However, at higher levels, the strategic leader must interact with others of similar rank, often without any authority over them.

For example, a top leader might need to deal with government officials, with the media, other complementary and competitive organizations, and even with officials and executives in other countries. Moreover, many of the leader's subordinates at higher levels in an organization would have technical knowledge and experience about which the leader would know little and in which he had little experience.

At the tactical level, the leader advanced based on increasing competency in a limited discipline. As the leader moved higher up in the organization, he or she managed more and more outside of his comfort and competency zone. His job was even more challenging because at higher levels, the leader more and more led integrated groups of multi-disciplined teams. Even basic communication could become a major problem because of different terms, jargon, and meanings.

Communicating with Other Disciplines

You may remember the children's game of "telephone," where we got in a circle and whispered a secret into the ear of a schoolmate to our right, who passed the "secret" on to another schoolmate in the same way until the "secret" got back to its originator from the last schoolmate on his left. The secret that came back was never the one that we started out with.

I've done a similar exercise with many senior management groups, from the Cheesecake Factory general managers to chiefs of police from around the country going through a special course at the FBI Academy at Quantico, Virginia. I asked each group to pick five of its most articulate members and then asked all five to leave the room. Then I had the group pick the one person they considered the most articulate to return. I read him or her a brief story from a printed sheet. This individual was then asked to identify one of the remaining four class members still outside to re-enter the room. He told the same story to the next individual entering the room, without reference to notes. This was repeated, until the last person entered the room and heard the story and retold it to the group.

The story is usually so different from what I read to the first person that it bears little resemblance to it. Males become females, jobs are different, times and actions are not done by the same person, even the basic point of the story sometimes changes in retelling. The police chiefs, especially trained to remember critical incidents, were just as bad as the others. At the end of the exercise, everyone clearly understands the difficulty of communicating a simple message through five levels of management. When backgrounds and specialties differ, communication is even more difficult.

Today's strategic leader has additional challenges. Technology enables change to take place at near light-year velocity, and with much greater penalty for failure than ever before. The penalty for the organization extends deeper than simply the loss of a leader of great promise because a leader's actions have a much longer timeline. A tactical leader may affect what happens over a period of weeks, months, or maybe a year. But, the strategic leader's decisions, both good and bad, reach farther and farther into the future.

Applying Drucker's Wisdom

Peter defined the problem early for us, and pointed the way to its solution. First, one must master at least one distinctly separate discipline, and it should be outside of business. But this is only part of what the would-be strategic leader must do. You may be the greatest leader of _____ (you fill in the blank). But if you try to lead in the same way at a much higher level, with no preparation for the higher level job, your success is far from assured. Your personal environment has changed, but you may continue to act as if you were in the same, more limited, old environment.

A very successful tactical leader I knew who didn't make it was an army officer. Let's call him "Mike." Mike was one of the finest tactical leaders that I ever came across, either in the military or civilian worlds. I met Mike while attending the Industrial College of the Armed Forces (or ICAF) in Washington, D.C. ICAF is one of the higher level schools in the military called "war colleges." Those officers who are selected to attend in residence are considered to have a better chance than others of someday becoming a general or an admiral. I think something like 20 percent actually make it.

ICAF is unique among the war colleges for two reasons. First, rather than attendees being primarily from one particular military service, as in all but one of the other war colleges, officers attend from all the military services. There are officers from the Army, Navy, Air Force, Marines, and Coast Guard, plus senior government officials, and, in current classes, even a few senior executives from civilian industry. Secondly, it is the only war college which specializes in aspects of national defense, such as mobilization and weapons acquisition, not directly involved in fighting a war.

Mike was what anyone would call a natural leader, if there ever was one. He was loved and respected by all. There was no question that in leading a unit of combat forces in his specialty, which was armor, his tank troops would follow him anywhere and he would do a superb job. In fact, several years later, as a full colonel, he led one of the leading brigades of tanks making the attack against Saddam Hussein in the first Gulf War. He performed in an outstanding manner.

Unfortunately, Mike had a weakness. He simply could not expand his thinking out of the tactical level in which he was an acknowledged expert and maybe the best. I rather suspect that one of the reasons he was selected to attend ICAF rather than one of the other war colleges which was more focused on fighting was to try and expose him to other things and other people. Unfortunately, it didn't work. One of the last things Mike said to me on our graduation from ICAF was, "I can't wait to get back to where everyone thinks exactly like I do." What a telling comment!

Some years later, I talked with a retired four-star general who had once been Mike's boss. In retirement, this senior general had been hired to run a short course for those newly promoted to general officer. He told me, "Mike was one of the finest soldiers I ever met. I kept waiting for the day that he would be promoted to brigadier general and be sent to take my course, but it never happened."

I once gave a talk on developing senior strategic leaders. I told the story of Mike and I said, "Mike, this one's for you." So is what follows, and I am sure that Peter would have echoed my sentiments.

Drucker's Approach to Becoming a Strategic Leader

The program I came up with for developing strategic leaders is not complicated, but like many simple but important tasks, it is not necessarily easy, either. However, the good news is that you can implement this program on your own. There are only one main and two supporting elements. The main component I have already introduced to you. It is to follow Drucker's exhortation to take the time to become an expert outside of your main profession. For my more cynical readers, I would suggest that the game of golf does not qualify. The two supporting elements will help you in many ways, not only in developing this second field of expertise, but also in broadening and sharpening your thinking.

To become a strategic leader, you need to become proactive and take action starting now. The object is to start to think and act strategically, and to handle the increased complexity resulting from the necessity to integrate numerous elements that are, in some cases, far removed from your basic expertise and experience. This process, as Drucker taught, requires you to develop expertise outside of your current thinking. This is the main element.

This is a good opportunity to pick up on some interest that you may have ignored in order to focus on the main aspects of your career. It doesn't matter too much what this field of expertise is. You need to become an expert in something far removed from whatever it is you do for a living. At first, this may feel a little unnatural. You may have spent so much time and energy in becoming the best at what you do in your profession that you are going to feel guilty about taking time away from this focus. Also, as you got better and better at one thing, knowing more and more about less and less, you may have come to the point that, within your profession, nothing really challenges you for very long. You could lead, in most instances, almost in your sleep.

You are so competent at what you currently do that anything new that you learn in your present field can be related to dozens of other elements in the same general arena about which you are familiar. This is not going to be the same when you decide to become a real expert in a totally different discipline. For the first time in years, you are probably going to feel inept, and less confident. Stay with it.

The fact that you learned so much in one field means that you can repeat it in another. Your confidence in what you do now is beneficial to that extent. You are supposed to feel uncomfortable as you learn something totally new. Just remember why you are doing this. Don't expect to start at the same level of expertise you hold in the area of your profession.

READ DAILY

The first supporting element for becoming a strategic thinker is based on extensive reading outside the general area of your primary expertise. I would recommend that you develop the habit of daily reading. I'll have more to say about what Peter did along these lines in a later chapter on self-development.

Of course, the big problem for most of us is to find the time to read each day. It doesn't have to be a very long time period. Thirty minutes is sufficient. If you set aside only thirty minutes for this special type of reading and do it every day, say, first thing when you first wake up in the morning, or the last thing right before you go to sleep in the evening, that's 182.5 hours a year. Or bump it up to an hour and take the hour away from watching television. Either 182.5 or 365 hours a year is impressive. That's a lot of reading.

If you do this already, keep it up. However, this should not only be reading general management and professional books in business outside of your specialty. Also read general-interest books in history, politics, economics, social issues, etc., and even fiction. Don't just read words, but engage with the author actively. If you disagree with the author's "facts" or reasoning, that is so much the better. Think it through and refute the author as if he or she were right there with you.

There was a time when professionals completed their basic education, and then bragged about not having read a book since. That time has long passed. Today, you not only must read extensively in your own field to reach the top and to be successful, but you also need to read extensively in other fields as well.

START WRITING

For the final element, become a writer. Writing may be challenging to some at first. But short of face-to-face interaction with others on these issues, it is the only way I know to really engage in the complex problems with which the strategic leaders will be faced.

What are you going to write about? Anything you want. Take as a subject material from one of the books you have read. You already thought about the issue when you read the material and engaged with the author mentally. All you need to do now is to organize these thoughts and write them down.

Years ago I was taught a very simple way of doing this. State the premise, question, or assertion in your introductory paragraph. Now, write three to five elements which support what you say in the introduction. Each one of these supporting arguments becomes a paragraph. In each paragraph, write three to five proofs of each supporting point. Now, write a concluding paragraph which restates your premise, questions, or assertion, and sums up your supporting arguments. That's it, you are done.

You can also find items from your daily newspaper. As problems and crises arise, think them through, integrating the many different aspects of the issue with which the article may or may not deal with. Take the time to do a mini-analysis and write out your conclusions and recommendations. You may even get them published if you send a letter to the editor in charge of such responses.

If you have never thought of yourself as much of a writer, this may be challenging at first. However, the more you write the better you'll get at it. If you carry this a step further to actually publish what you write, that's even better. This can net a number of additional benefits, including boosting your credibility in whatever discipline you write. It will certainly develop your ability as strategic thinker and help prepare you for the strategic tasks and actions required of a top manager.

And one final thought. There is an old saying that until you write something down, you really don't understand it, so this will improve your understanding of the subject matter as well.

Drucker Lesson Summary

Peter felt strongly that there were other important elements in becoming an effective manager than the traditional functional tracks to the top. He specifically mentioned past proven success and personal readiness for the job. He also emphasized that any manager's preparation for a top job was primarily the responsibility of the individual executive.

Drucker clearly saw that certain abilities were needed by executives at the strategic level which were not developed through challenges at the tactical level, and he hit on a unique way for an executive to develop these abilities. He encouraged us to become experts in at least one field outside of our professions.

Outstanding Performance Is Inconsistent with Fear of Failure

O f all Peter's lessons, this particular one had perhaps the most significant effects on my future professional life. That's probably because the basic concept represented such a departure from the world I had known for so many years.

Most of my background previously had been in the military, except for three years working in the civilian aviation industry in Israel. My military background was probably one of the reasons I had been hired for my first job back in the U.S., as the company developed items partly for the military. Knowing this is important in understanding my interpretation and development of Drucker's wisdom of this lesson and its impact on me. One aspect of career military service is its lengthy tenure of employment. Most career military people can depend on serving at least twenty years. Those reaching the top grades as either an officer or a non-commissioned officer may serve even longer. Those reaching the very top, generals and admirals, or the top non-commissioned officer ranks, can serve even longer yet. As a consequence, when "Japanese management" caught on in the U.S. in the 1980's, and management gurus began to advocate "lifetime employment" as the Japanese supposedly had, Japanese management looked very much like this aspect of a military career.

As a result of this system few in the military fear loss of employment. Of course, this is not necessarily true during reduction in force as occurred in the early 1990's with the end of the Cold War and at various other periods. However, on the day Peter began to lecture about risk-taking and employment, I didn't fully recognize the fear of loss of employment as a problem.

Peter said, "Outstanding performance is inconsistent with fear of failure." I mentally yawned. I thought, "Of course, one does the best one can. If you blow it, you get 'relieved of command.' What's new?" The military does refer to this colloquially as "getting fired." But unless you've done something illegal or immoral or are a senior officer, it is not the end of your career. You are still in the military. They usually just assign you to a new position, generally at some distance geographically and in a totally different environment. Frequently you'll get another chance in a new place, with a new job, and with new responsibilities.

I've known many people to make major mistakes, get a new job, and perform so well that they get promoted. If you read Colin Powell's book *My American Journey* (Random House, 1995), you'll see that this happened to Powell himself, even as a senior officer. He, of course, eventually ended up a four-star general and the chairman of the Joint Chiefs of Staff, the top uniformed job in our armed forces.

In my naiveté, I hadn't given much thought to whether someone of Colin Powell's capabilities could make a mistake, yet avoid being fired in civilian life, although by the time of Peter's lecture I had been in the corporate world for several years and read lots of business books. I should have known better, but I didn't.

As Peter went on, I began to see that he was saying that this wasn't true in the business world at all. You could be fired at any time. You didn't even have to make a serious mistake. Many times bosses had the authority to fire you for just about any reason, and some did. It suddenly dawned on me that what I had considered a peculiar incident two years earlier, when I had first started with an engineering company, was not so peculiar at all.

Sierra was a medium sized company located in the foothills of the San Gabriel Mountains in Sierra Madre, California. The company manufactured various life support and protective products, mostly for the military and for aviation use, but also for civil aviation. I was hired as Director of Research and Development.

As their new boss, I had called all of my project engineers together. I told them that although I liked to consider myself infallible, I knew this was not so. Therefore, in my enthusiasm, it was entirely possible that I would come up with an occasional dumb or otherwise unworkable idea. When this happened, I expected whoever saw this to tell me why the idea was dumb or unworkable in the strongest possible terms right away, and to make sure that I understood the point, even if I got angry with them. I told them my anger would subside and they would not be punished for doing this. If they allowed me to do something stupid without telling me, when they knew better, I told them that they were even dumber than me.

"However," I said, "once I have heard you out, there may be other considerations. If I can and we have time, I will explain these considerations to you. In any case, it's still my decision. If I decide to do what you consider to be a dumb thing anyway, after you know I have understood your argument, I want you to adopt that decision as if it were your own and help me to make it happen the way that I want. Nevertheless, again, I expect you to tell me your opinion and your arguments first."

Everyone agreed that this is what they would do. The only problem was, no one did it . . . at least not right away. It took several months before I actually saw this happening. But finally it did, saving our organization a number of missteps from some of my would-be, out-and-out blunders. I never understood why it took so long for them to start doing this. Listening to Peter's lecture, now I did. As a boss in that company, I had the authority to fire them on the spot. And this wasn't bounced from my organization to someone else's within the company as with the military's "getting fired." This meant out of the company completely. So, they felt less free to say what they actually thought, no matter what I told them to do. In some ways, the ability to instantly discharge people from the company was more authority than I had in the military!

Drucker's Wisdom on an Executive Performance

As I mentioned previously, Peter's lecture was on the manager's need to take risks in his decision-making. I believe his intention was to focus on other aspects of employment, not just job security. However, his statement generated a firestorm of comments from students. I still recall some of these today. They went something like this:

> You cannot ignore how your boss will react to your actions, even if ethically and technically your actions are correct.

> Disregarding the fear of job loss may be okay in theory, but it's a jungle out there. Ignoring the possibility that you could be fired can lead to being fired.

> Fear of losing my job isn't the last thing I think of—it is the first thing.

Peter absorbed these comments, but repeated his earlier statement that fear of job loss was simply incompatible with taking responsibility and exercising the power entrusted to the manager. He concluded that, "If you have this fear, you will improve your performance by ignoring it. Moreover, ethically it is what every manager should do."

At the time, I was surprised that this fear was clearly so prevalent in the middle- and upper-level managers who were my classmates. I did not consider that I had such a fear myself. So I felt there was little for me to do in order to raise my performance by ignoring a fear which I didn't have. As I was to learn shortly it might have been better had I had a little bit of such a fear.

I Am Forced to Resign My Job

I was head of research and development and fortunate in having a great team of engineers to work with, most of whom I had hired myself. Because of these engineers and my rapport with our customers, we had achieved some terrific results during my three years with the company. Research and development sales were ten times what they were when I came aboard. In fact, my team had won the largest research and development contract in this company's forty-year history. They also developed a product that later became the standard in not only the U.S. armed forces, but for many foreign countries. I was particularly proud of this achievement because on my first visit to our Air Force customers after getting the job with this company, I was told that due to a previous research and development problem a couple of years earlier, my new company rated very low in the eyes of the Air Force.

However, despite these and other successes, it became increasingly evident that my boss, the president, wanted me out of the company. Directives began to be given directly to my deputy rather than through me. Two government customers called me to say that he had talked with them and given them instructions directly. They warned me that they thought something was going on. My invitations to have lunch with him and the vice presidents ceased. I had tried to have a "heart-to-heart" conversation with him, but he was evasive and claimed there was no problem.

I was never successful in learning the problem while I was an employee. I knew that my standing with my own people and other senior executives was very high. I could not understand why the company president would not want to reward me, much less why he would encourage me to leave. Of course, with age comes some wisdom, and I understand more now.

This all came to a head at the time of my last annual salary review. I expected that I would get a significant raise, and I did. However, I felt I deserved some more recognition. Aside from research and development, there were three product divisions in the company. One was very small and headed up by a director like myself. However, the other two operating divisions were each led by a vice president. There were two other staff vice presidents. Due to our expansion, my organization was actually larger than one of these two product divisions in sales. I thanked my boss for the salary increase and raised the question of a vice presidency. I didn't want any additional money as a vice president. However, I did feel that I deserved the title. "You're too young," he shot back. "All of my vice presidents are in their fifties. Stick around for another twenty years and I'll make you a vice president."

I didn't even stop to think. "Thank you very much," I said. "But, I prefer to resign. If you want, I'll stay for another month or so while you sort things out and find a replacement."

"Are you serious?" he asked.

"Yes," I replied.

"What will you do?"

"I'll find something."

He stared at me for several seconds and then asked me to agree not to tell anyone else in the company or our customers about this until he was ready. I agreed.

When I left the company, my boss replaced me with one of the vice presidents from one of the product divisions, and he hired another vice president to replace him. I never learned the problem from him, but after my experiences as a headhunter, I saw others in senior management who had encountered similar problems. It was really pretty simple. Bosses are all different and they are all human. Some bosses are more secure than others. I was never disrespectful, but I was young, brash, and much too confident. Without intending to, my attitude threatened my boss. My success in the job, rather than mitigating the problem, probably made it worse.

I didn't suffer from the fear of loss of my job. Maybe I should have. It would have made me more humble and less cocky, and I might have had a better relationship with my boss. He might have even been more inclined to make me a vice president. But that's all speculation, and it is certainly different from the path I took.

This experience gave me an idea of what my classmates had meant when they indicated that the fear of loss of employment was not to be dismissed so lightly.

Why Wasn't I Afraid?

When I had returned from overseas, I had conducted a successful, if somewhat unorthodox, job campaign. It had taken seven weeks from start to finish, and I got the job primarily by what I later learned was called a direct mail campaign to people who never knew I existed, not with a resume, but with a sales letter. My target market consisted of individuals who had the direct authority to hire me, rather than the personnel or human resources manager. After I left my previous company, I became a headhunter for six months and I knew how to run a much better organized campaign because of this experience. I began a new job campaign. At the end of this campaign, I had several companies seeking my services. I got a job in charge of high technology marketing, reporting to the vice president of marketing of a major corporation, McDonnell Douglas Astronautics Company, now a part of the Boeing Corporation.

As I've mentioned previously, I lived in Pasadena, California. McDonnell Douglas was in Huntington Beach and better than an hour's drive south. To avoid boredom, I often listened to tapes in the car. I also thought a lot. One of the things I thought about was Drucker's contention that performance was inconsistent with fear of job loss. I knew he was right. I also knew that the managers who had spoken up in class that day knew what they were talking about, too.

Now I would like to think that managers and executives do the right thing, regardless of personal cost to them or to their careers. However, a potential loss of job can also affect their families. It would be unreasonable to expect that every executive, under all circumstances, would adopt Drucker's philosophy, even if they agreed with it completely. I realized that there had to be some way of dispelling or at least dealing with this fear and resolving these two opposing issues.

So I thought, well, why didn't I have this fear? First, it was due to my ignorance. My work experience had been almost entirely in the military. However, now that I knew the truth, why was I still unafraid? The answer was that I was still self-confident. But based on what? I finally realized that my confidence came from my belief that first, I wouldn't lose my job due to incompetence. More importantly, I felt that if I did lose my job, I knew how to get another. After all, in four years I had done this three times, with successive increases in salary.

I eventually came up with the concept of writing a book for executives that would lay out a specific plan for finding a new job. I reasoned that if an executive was confident that he could find a new job, he would be much less inclined to allow fear of job loss to affect his decisions as an executive.

My First Book

This reasoning process, and Drucker's lecture, led directly to my writing the book, *The Executive's Guide to Finding a Superior Job* (AMACOM, 1978, 1983), which now is no longer in print, and because of the Internet, woefully out of date. This was my first book, and one of my most successful. That's one reason that I "blame" Peter Drucker for what has happened since I was his student. The book was an instant success and a best seller. It got outstanding book reviews all over the country. The *Chicago Tribune* was especially laudatory, saying words to the effect that this was different than any other book of its type.

However, despite the book's success, I caught a lot of flack from two industries. The human resources folks were incensed because I advised readers to bypass them and contact potential new bosses directly. I said, quite truthfully, that human resources managers (or personnel managers, as they were known then) had no authority to hire you unless you wanted to work in human resources; they only had the authority to reject you and block you from reaching the executive who did have the necessary authority to hire.

The other group that was less than happy about what I said in the book consisted of the organizational psychologists. I told readers why they should beat psychological tests and explained how to do it. I pointed out that while psychological tests were good for the company, they may not be good for the individual because they relied on percentages. This meant that a significant number of people who took the tests which said that they wouldn't do very well turned out to be top performers, and I gave examples to prove my point.

One of my first great successes that came from the book was a West Point classmate who was out of work at the time and wanted a job as a vice president at Twentieth Century Fox. He had no experience as a top executive of a major corporation, and no experience in the film industry. Following the concepts in the book, he got the job. If you are thinking I advised lying on his resume, you would be dead wrong. In fact, fudging your resume is the last thing you want to do. For one thing, you will eventually get caught, but more importantly, it is unethical and just plain wrong. And as we'll see in another chapter, ethics count!

Twenty years later, I gave a lecture on my job-finding concepts to my students while teaching a graduate course at my alma mater, by then called Claremont Graduate University. The class met once a week. The week after my lecture, one of my students announced that he had already been invited to fly out for an interview, after using one of my direct-mail techniques updated for the Internet.

Rising above Job Loss—Twice

As I said, Peter taught that fear of job loss was incompatible with executive responsibility. While still his student, I found that he even put this idea in what was our textbook, *Management: Tasks, Responsibilities, Practices*. The exact quote from the book is: "Living in fear of loss of job and income is incompatible with taking responsibility for job and work group, for output and performance."[1]

This is a theory that I believe to be true, but I don't think it's ever been tested. However, one man clearly had no such fear and did demonstrate very high performance. I don't think he ever used my book, and he actually twice lost top executive jobs, but still landed on his feet and achieved great success. Leonard Roberts is his name. His first job loss came at Arby's, a fast-food restaurant franchise then headquartered in Florida.

Roberts became CEO of Arby's at a time when the business was doing very poorly, with sales falling 10 percent to 15 percent a year.

Roberts turned the corporation around by promising service and support to Arby's franchisees with help and money. He delivered, and the franchisees supported him in turn. Sales soared. Eager for even more profits, Arby's then-owner threatened to withdraw the support that Roberts had initiated and he refused to pay bonuses Roberts had promised to his subordinates. Meanwhile, Roberts had been appointed to the board of directors. The first meeting he attended lasted fifteen minutes. He saw that the board was simply a rubber stamp for the owner.

Said Roberts: "I knew what I had to do. I had to take a stand, so I resigned from the board." Roberts also took steps to rectify the situation with his staff bonuses and the franchisees. Roberts had made promises with the full authority of his boss. His boss considered this insubordination. He fired Roberts for supporting the franchisees.[2]

What happened to Leonard Roberts afterwards? Did this finish his career as a CEO? Not quite. In fact, he stumbled right into another situation which eventually led to another unplanned departure. Through a headhunter, he was offered the position of chairman and CEO of a chain of 2,000 restaurants headquartered in Nashville, Tennessee called Shoney's. The situation looked right, so Len Roberts accepted the offer. Only afterwards did he learn that Shoney's was the subject of the largest racial discrimination law suit in history. Questioned by *The Wall Street Journal*, Roberts promised that the suit would be settled without long-term impact on the company.

Unfortunately, this was more easily said than done. This was not some issue of a misunderstanding. The policy of the former chairman was not to hire African-Americans. Moreover, his official policy was to fire any restaurant manager who did! When I spoke with Roberts some years ago he said, "The settlement of that suit was the thing I am most proud of in my life. The former chairman agreed to pay up and settle. This saved the company. But I had to agree to resign after he did so. This was my second time out of work in almost as many years. There was no other way."[3]

So here was a man who achieved high performance while basically ignoring any fear that he would lose his job. And he did the same thing again, even in the wake of losing his job the first time around. Fortunately, Leonard Roberts became the CEO of RadioShack after leaving Shoney's.

A year or so later, *Brandweek Magazine* named him Retail Marketer of the Year. He served more than ten years in top positions at RadioShack, becoming president, CEO, and chairman while building it to more than 7,000 stores nationwide.

Picking Up Where Peter Drucker Left Off

Again, Peter determined that you can't perform your best as an executive if you are fearful of losing your job. If I have learned anything, it is that you can't always depend on the relationship with your boss to sustain you, regardless of your performance or how hard you work. However, there are things you can to do reduce your fear besides working hard and doing great things. These are what I call the "antidotes" to Drucker's observation regarding fear of job loss. They don't even require you to join the military.

You don't think you need to do anything. You just started a new job at a wonderfully stable company and you have the world's best boss. Please. Do yourself a favor. Your boss can get hit by a truck. Your company may be so terrific that another, bigger company gobbles it up. There could be a merger.

The point is, none of us knows the future. You don't want fear of job loss affecting what you do, even if it is just a very tiny worry in your subconscious. Here's what can help you rid yourself of any concern beginning right now:

- Open a special folder on your computer.

- Keep an updated resume on your computer.

- Learn to create focused sales letters.

- Become known in your industry.

- Play the game: "What will I do if I lose my job tomorrow?"

- Work out a rough job campaign plan.

OPEN A SPECIAL FOLDER

What could be easier? Under your word processing program you probably already have a general file labeled "Documents." Under this general file just add a sub-file labeled "Job-Finding Preparation." That's all

you need to do. You have just taken your first step toward freedom from
job loss fear.

THE IMPORTANCE OF A CURRENT RESUME

Through the magic of a computer, it is easy to keep a continuously updated
version of your accomplishments. And this is really important, even if you
won't be sending it to anyone. And I don't recommend sending out
resumes or posting them on the internet. I know that just this statement
will have a lot of folks wanting to know why not. First, why keep a current resume?

Human beings tend to forget. Trying to capture all the great things
we've accomplished under the pressures of having to look for a new job
is daunting and not very effective. Being human, you will forget a lot. It's
much better to get everything down now, and keep adding to it. One of
the insights I've discovered is that some project you may have worked on
for a couple of days can turn out to be more valuable to another company
than one you've been working on for several years.

Don't just write down experience. That's not a very valuable piece of
information. Unfortunately that's what many people do in their resumes.
They write down a job title, the dates they held the job, and a couple of
sentences that describe their responsibilities. That's hardly enough. What
did you actually accomplish during that period? Quantify increases in
sales, profits, awards, etc., and write down exactly what happened making
this so significant. That's what makes all the difference.

The more you document and read about your exploits yourself, the
more you are going to feel what a great candidate you are for any particular job. That's another value to this continuously updated resume which
goes all the way back to the beginnings of your career. It's a tremendous
boost to your self-confidence, and if you are suddenly out of work, it is of
significant value for keeping your thinking positive.

SALES LETTERS ARE BETTER THAN RESUMES

You shouldn't send your resume to everyone. This is one of the most surprising aspects about successful job finding, but it's true. A resume can
actually prevent you from getting more jobs than it will help you to get,
even though we've been brainwashed to think that this is the only way to
get a job. Remember that classmate of mine who got that top job at
Twentieth Century Fox? He didn't submit a resume.

If no resume, what then? In most cases what you want to send to anyone is a sales letter focused not on everything you've done, but on those specific things which support the particular job you are seeking. I tried this myself the first time I sought a job. I mailed out an equal number of resumes and an equal number of sales letters. The sales letters did far better in getting interviews, and without interviews there are no job offers.

With the Internet and all the job sites available, you may think that these problems are solved. They are not. I recently visited an old friend. He was president of the executive recruiting firm where I worked for six months thirty years ago. We've remained friends all these years.

I gave his recruiters a presentation on "Gaining Power and Influence" in exchange for their updating me on the latest Internet techniques used by headhunters. I asked if they used the Internet to find candidates. The answer may surprise you. They said generally not. To illustrate the problem, one recruiter told me this story:

"I usually go to the job sites to locate companies and then contact them to get a job order so that I can submit my own candidates. I almost never use the posted resumes," the recruiter said. "However, a couple months ago, I saw a resume that was almost too good to be true and perfectly fit an ongoing search I had. So I contacted the individual. He told me that he hadn't authorized any other headhunter to submit his name to a company. With this reassurance, I called my client, who asked the name of the individual. When I told him, he responded that I was about the tenth recruiter to contact him about this candidate that week. Many had even submitted this resume without calling. He told me what I already knew: 'If he's that desperate that everyone has his resume, he can't be of the level of individual I am looking for.' It was personally embarrassing," the recruiter said, "but I believe the candidate told me the truth. The problem is that unless the job sought is pretty low level, putting your resume on the 'Net' is not a good idea."

Limitations to the resume are also true in responding to an advertisement for a job, even if a resume is demanded. Don't send it. Why? Because some really great jobs pull in hundreds of resumes. So the first thing that happens is that someone in human resources screens them against a list of requirements. When there are hundreds of resumes to go through, many get eliminated unfairly when it is not easy to determine if a particular requirement is met or not. My advice is that if you are responding to an advertisement for a position, prepare a sales letter that restates each requirement in the advertisement. After each requirement, show by accomplishments and examples, extracted from your resume, how each requirement has been met. Use your resume for the material, but don't send it.

I don't recommend putting a resume in anyone's hands until you know a lot more about what they want. Frequently there are "knock-out factors." If you have one of these in your resume you are automatically eliminated. The problem is that "knock-out factors" can be different in every situation. They may have nothing to do with how well you can do the job. So, delay providing a resume if at all possible until the interview. After the interview is even better. Then you can really put together an effective resume based on what's been discussed during the interview. No one hires from a resume, anyway. They hire as a result of an interview, and once you get to the interview, most "knock-out factors" are irrelevant.

BECOMING KNOWN IN YOUR INDUSTRY

In every industry, there are some excellent people around that few know about outside the company. That doesn't help much if you are looking for a job. There are two ways of getting well known outside of your company. First, get involved in professional organizations. Don't just attend meetings, but become a volunteer for unpaid leadership positions in the organization.

The second way is to write articles read by people in your industry. I mentioned earlier that one of Peter Drucker's earliest boosters was Winston Churchill. Before he became prime minister of England, Churchill wrote a favorable book review about Drucker's first book. That didn't hurt Drucker's writing career any, and probably made it much easier to find teaching jobs once he came to the United States.

PLAY THE GAME: "WHAT WILL I DO IF I LOSE MY JOB TOMORROW?"

It's not much of a game to envision losing your job tomorrow. But just thinking about this possibility can help you to become mentally prepared for some of the tough decisions you'll need to make. Moreover, some of this advance thinking and some of these decisions can be made months or years before you need to face them under the pressures of actual loss of job. When you've thought through everything ahead of time and know what you need to do, a lot of fear will simply go away.

WORK OUT A ROUGH JOB PLAN WHICH YOU CAN IMMEDIATELY IMPLEMENT
According to *The Chicago Tribune*, the fact that I recommended treating a job campaign plan "like a business" in my book was an important new contribution. Peter always stressed the importance of planning followed by action. Although we never talked about this aspect of my book, I'm sure he would have especially supported this idea.

Drucker Lesson Summary
There is little question that eliminating any fear of job loss will impact your own future as a manager and an executive in a very positive fashion. As I said, I feel that this particular Drucker wisdom had more effect on my future professional life than any of Peter's other lessons. First of all, it helped me to understand myself and opened my eyes to concerns I was unaware of but that others had. It was the catalyst which began my career writing business books, and it helped me to advance in the other careers I pursued, in the military and in academia.

The Objective of Marketing Is to Make Selling Unnecessary

*P*eter Drucker was a management professor. He didn't teach marketing as a separate function. At least I didn't think so as he began to lecture one night in the spring of 1976. Outside Harper Hall, it was dark and it was raining. Someone had rearranged the seating, and we were now seated in long tables facing a wall with windows.

I had only recently left my position as the head of research and development at an engineering company, as described in the last chapter. I was then working as an executive recruiter in Sherman Oaks, about twenty miles west of my home in Pasadena. Because of the rain, I left work early. I stopped at home in Pasadena, which was a straight shot on the way to Claremont. I had a cup of coffee with my wife, Nurit, who was getting ready for her own class at California State University, Los Angeles, where three years later I was to become a professor, ironically, initially of marketing.

Although I had actually been practicing marketing for some time, I didn't know it. I had only the vaguest notion of the discipline, or even that it was a discipline. My bachelor's degree in engineering from West Point included no marketing courses. My MBA from the University of Chicago with a specialty in research and development management likewise included no marketing courses.

While working for Israel Aircraft Industries in Israel, I had traveled to Germany and participated in the annual Hannover Air Show. I was given some business cards which identified me as "Chief Sales Engineer." However, my actual duties were to answer questions about and show off Israel's home-designed Arava STOL (short take-off and landing) aircraft to interested parties and direct potential buyers to the real decision makers representing the company at the air show.

As manager of research and development, I was primarily in charge of developing new products, but I also engaged in both marketing and selling, although I didn't realize it. If anyone had asked me if I was doing any marketing while there, I probably would have denied it.

I recall that the president of one of the companies I had interviewed with before I accepted that job had called back to ask whether I would be interested in a senior position in marketing instead of research and development. I told him that I didn't even know what marketing was. This didn't stop him from pressing me further on this issue. I guess he realized that marketing could become closer to some of my interests than I realized at the time.

"Marketing isn't selling," he said. "Oh, right," I thought, but I did not verbalize this as a comment. In any case, my impressions were that he was trying to direct my interests towards marketing, but I wasn't interested. I only half listened to what he said. When he had finished, I thanked him but told him that I would only consider a position managing research and development. That offer eventually came from his company, but I had declined and accepted an offer from elsewhere.

Drucker's Lecture on Marketing

When Peter told us he was going to discuss marketing, I wasn't particularly interested, either. I still thought marketing was the same as selling. Anyway, I didn't much care, so I didn't take time to even consider the difference. Somehow it was a concept I had missed in my attempt to educate myself about business through my off-duty reading of business books.

Moreover, the image I had of a marketer was that of a fast-talking used-car salesman wearing flashy clothes. Although I know today just how inaccurate this image is for most marketers and salespeople, these were my prejudices at the time. This was not how I saw myself, so my mind started to wander at Drucker's mention of the evening's topic. I was more concerned with my new job as a headhunter, anyway. This profession, too, had to do with selling, but I hadn't yet thought about that side of it.

Despite my indifference, however, Peter's opening lines instantly brought me back to earth and got my attention. First, he repeated what the company president had told me four years earlier: "Marketing and selling are not identical." Then he went on to really wake me up. "Selling and marketing are neither synonymous nor complementary," he said. "One could consider them adversarial in some cases. There is no doubt that if marketing were done perfectly, selling, in the actual sense of the word, would be unnecessary." What was Peter saying? He had me. I listened on.

According to Drucker, it was the Japanese who invented real marketing, and not in this century either, but back in the 1600's. A merchant with a different retailing concept came to Tokyo from out in the boondocks and opened what today we would term a retail outlet. Moreover, this merchant had a revolutionary concept of selling. Previously, all selling was done by sellers who made or grew what they sold, whether it was food, clothing, or fighting equipment.

Drucker said that this new merchant was different in two ways. First, he didn't sell a single class of goods. He sold all kinds of goods. Second, he didn't create what he sold. He bought goods from others who had created them. Just like Sears, Macy's, or Wal-Mart today, he saw himself as being a buying agent for what his customers wanted. Consequently, this retailer saw his task not of persuading others to purchase a product which he had already had on hand and therefore must sell, but rather in discovering first what his customers wanted and then getting these desired products from others for resale.

According to Drucker, this concept became so popular in Japan that it led to a conglomeration of retail establishments of this type. Apparently the same concept caught on in the west about the same time, leading first to general stores and, beginning in the early 1800's, to the modern department store. The significance was that this was not simply selling. A smart retailer researched the market to have products that the consumer wanted before he bought them for resale.

The Development of Marketing According to Drucker

Before this retailing breakthrough could occur, innovation and technology had led to the availability of formerly scarce products, so that these new retailers could offer to their customers many products that could be mass-produced. For example, before the invention of the Gutenberg printing press, books were painstakingly written by hand. One error could cause the destruction of many weeks' work since an entire page would need to be redone. To complete a single book might take a year or more of labor by trained specialists, most of whom were monks.

Under these conditions, the very limited supply of these books could never fully satisfy the demand for them. Consequently, it was not necessary to persuade others to purchase one of these handmade books. The market already existed and potential buyers came running to bid for every one that became available. Of course, only the extremely wealthy could afford a single book, much less collect many for a library. Then came Gutenberg's printing press and everything changed.

In the west, the process of excessive supply was accelerated with the advent of the industrial revolution. Products of all types that had been extremely scarce and expensive could now be mass produced. As a result, they could be sold at a much more reasonable cost, making them available to not only the moderately wealthy, but also to the middle classes, and, for some products, even the poor.

However, this success in production eventually led to another problem for the producer. A manufacturer focused on producing a product in order to achieve the lowest price in order to sell the maximum amount of product to the greatest number of people. This meant that the amount of product available after manufacture frequently exceeded the number of potential buyers and the amount of product sought. Some kind of additional inducement to purchase was necessary. Potential customers needed once again to be persuaded to buy. So persuasion remained important. Through persuasive selling, additional prospects could be made aware of the product, as well as the benefits of ownership and the advantage of the product over those produced by competitors.

The result was that manufacturers and merchants all began to develop sales departments whose responsibilities were to sell whatever was produced. The emphasis was on the product and persuading prospects to buy it, whether through face-to-face selling, advertising, sales promotion, or some other means. They were all part of selling as distinct from marketing.

The innovation introduced by the Japanese retailer in the 17th century was significant in that for the first time, the emphasis was not on the product, but rather on the customer. Again, under this new concept, the seller had products that the customer already wanted, rather than trying to sell what the merchant had on hand and therefore had to unload in order to make a profit.

To do this, the retailer, manufacturer, or producer had to first discover what it was that customers wanted. This led to new techniques and methods of researching the market. For the first time, the emphasis was on the customer and not the product. As direct marketer Freeman Gosden, Jr. once told one of my classes in marketing, "It's not what you want to sell, it's what your customer wants to buy."

Recently I was watching an interview with one of the judges on *American Idol*. He was asked to comment on the decline in sales in the recording industry at the same time that *American Idol* and its alumni are having such success. "That's easy," he said. "The recording studios have been trying to give the public what they think the public wants. We let the public decide, and then we give it to them."

Marketing Is the Basis of Any Business

Drucker went on to explain that marketing was more than just an important business function. In fact, he said it wasn't a business function at all, but rather the basis of any business. It was a mistake to consider marketing on an equal basis with other functionary areas such as manufacturing, because marketing permeated every aspect of the business. He continued that marketing's importance was at last recognized when companies began to add marketing departments to their organizations. However, Peter pointed out that, although many corporations agreed with "the marketing concept," which primarily emphasized the customer and paid lip service to it, in practice many, if not most, companies ignored this reality.

Drucker said that companies struggled to adopt the marketing concept organizationally in several ways. Some companies added a separate department which was responsible for either marketing research or marketing strategy, but they really functioned as staff to top management, production divisions, or a separate sales division. Others combined marketing and sales into a single department; sometimes with marketing in charge, sometimes with sales in charge. Few companies gave much thought to the idea of the basic marketing concept as driving the business, which was far more important. According to Drucker, this concept would drastically challenge the position of marketing in many companies, despite the considerable evidence that this was clearly what should happen. In Drucker's view, marketing drove the business and needed authority in a business to market correctly.

Peter used IBM as an example of the power of marketing. He said that the reason that this company had successfully overcome the competition in the early days of computer development was that IBM looked first at its potential customers and asked what these customers wanted. Univac, RCA, and GE, IBM's competitor company, were driven not by marketing, but by technology. As a result, their emphasis was on how they thought the product should be, and not guided by their customer's wants and needs. IBM, by pursuing a marketing approach, came to dominate the market.

Not long after I graduated from Claremont, IBM stumbled and provided a cautionary tale to the practice of marketing. Several years earlier it had asked the wrong question of its potential customers and concluded that only 1,000 personal computers could be sold every year if a personal computer were developed. Based on this flawed analysis, IBM halted PC development. This decision allowed Steve Jobs and Steve Wozniak to start a revolution in their garage by realizing that there were millions of potential customers who were ready to purchase an *affordable* "PC". Their company, Apple, was able to fulfill the needs of this market almost unopposed. However, IBM recovered quickly when it recognized that encouraging, rather than prohibiting, independents to develop software for their operating system would best satisfy what the customer wanted. Marketing, again. There is no question about marketing's power.

My experience in an aerospace company about a year after Peter's lecture seemed to confirm his conclusions regarding the weak position of marketing in many high-technology companies. At McDonnell Douglas Astronautics Company, success came from bidding against competitors, usually on a combination of low price and technological innovation. However, the primary criteria were government specifications which had to be met. Why waste resources on marketing and marketing research in unearthing what the customer wanted when the customer would tell all competitors exactly what was desired anyway?

All aerospace companies seemed to operate the same way in those days in selling to government. All had marketing departments. However, in each case it operated as staff to the senior project managers, all of whom were engineers. In fact, virtually all of those involved in marketing in these companies were professional engineers, not professional marketers. These marketing departments provided insights into what the customer might want, managing relationships between project personnel, etc. They did not operate as the central dimension of the business. I recall one senior engineering manager saying proudly just before a major loss to a competitor, "Marketing doesn't have much clout around here."

My Research into Marketing

My work led to dissertation research in this area. My boss was Paul Smith, then legendary vice president of marketing for McDonnell Douglas Astronautics Company. My assignment was as a marketing manager to one of two divisions of our high technology. In this I supported several hundred people, mostly PhDs, in their bidding research and development contracts, generally under three million dollars, with a variety of government agencies.

In most cases we responded to Requests for Proposals (RFPs) in which the government specified the technical objectives, some criteria that must be met, and due dates. We responded with a proposal detailing how we would do it, and what it would cost. My input as a marketing manager was advisory only. Engineering called the shots. The conventional wisdom at the time was that we won against our competition by being the low bidder or because of our technological wizardry or some combination thereof. I wasn't so sure.

Paul Smith gave me permission to do the research, to use the resources of the company to complete my dissertation, and to investigate the influence of marketing in these bidding results. I investigated all wins and losses over the previous year. I examined records of phone calls, travel, and all other contacts with the customer by the PhDs who later bid the contracts. Through interviews, I identified who each government engineer met with and why, noted what was discussed, the objectives of the contact, and the outcome and perceived quality of the meeting.

I discovered that the total number of contacts was a far better predictor of success or failure in winning these contracts than either the price bid or the technological innovation, or even how well the engineer thought the meeting went! To note the extreme, there were a few bids where there was no prior contact with the customer in the preceding year. Even if our bid was the lowest and we had a technological breakthrough which we felt offered many benefits which were fully explained in the proposal, not a single win resulted.

The reasons for these results were not hard to uncover. During these visits, our engineers and scientists traded information with the customers. They found out what the customer wanted and why. If there were aspects which could affect the customer's programs we were working on, our people were able to explain them. If one approach was particularly promising, but also expensive, that cost could be discussed and justified. Or if it was more money than the customer was willing to pay, a search could be made for a more economical route long before bidding started.

In effect, invaluable marketing research was accomplished during these visits with customers, and the secret to winning more contracts was not lower bids or even more money allocated to our internal research budgets, but more personal contacts prior to bidding. In this way, we could better have what the customer wanted in our proposal. However, such visits were prohibited under government regulations once a Request for Proposal (RFP) was published by the government. So once the RFP was published, these contacts could not be made. The bottom line was that pre-proposal marketing was essential, and Drucker's theory was confirmed for these bids.

Drucker Thought Marketing and Selling Were Adversarial

Like many of Drucker's concepts, one had to think about them deeply to understand them fully and apply them correctly. In the opening to his lecture, Drucker had stated that marketing and selling were neither complementary nor supplementary and were almost opposites. This idea is certainly counterintuitive. Even today, most marketing theorists envision selling as a subset of marketing. Currently accepted marketing theory goes something like this:

Corporate Strategy. At the top sits corporate strategy. Marketing strategy is one level down and must support the strategy decided on by the corporation.

Market Positioning Strategy. One discrete marketing strategy is positioning. This means emphasizing where your product is relative to competitive products in the mind of the buyer. Jaguar, Porsche, Mercedes-Benz, BMW, and many other automobile manufacturers all sell sports cars.

However, each sports car model is seen differently by the consumer, even if two models are priced similarly. That's not an accident. It's a marketing strategy intended by these companies after marketing research and analysis. It's a way of differentiating a product from a competitor in a very positive way.

Niche Marketing Strategy. Another discrete strategy is niching, or focusing on a small portion of the overall market. There are an infinite number of marketing strategies. What is important to understand is that these strategies must be again supported and implemented by the next level down. This level is generally referred to as tactics. These tactical variables are frequently called "the Four P's."

Marketing Tactics. Professor Jerry McCarthy of Michigan State University conceptualized "the Four P's" back in 1960 to make some order out of a multitude of sales and promotional actions supporting a marketing strategy. The Four P's are product, price, place (or distribution), and promotion. Promotion is further subdivided into categories: advertising, sales promotion, public relations, and personal selling. However, all of these have to do with selling.

From this we can see that selling, once thought to be the only way for a manufacturer to dispose of a product profitably, is now a tactic that must be employed to implement a strategy.

For a long time I did not understand why Drucker claimed that selling and marketing were not complementary or supplementary and in fact were in an almost adversarial relationship. I thought perhaps that Drucker had misspoken. In 1985, I began research for a textbook on marketing and I came to understand exactly what Peter meant and the importance of his concept.

In a 1984 article in *Harvard Business Review,* a Harvard Professor explained a strategy/tactics matrix he had developed.[1] On the vertical axis, marketing implementation was shown increasing upward from poor to excellent. The horizontal axis increased from right to left from inappropriate to appropriate. It was labeled strategy/tactics. The matrix was divided into four cells: 1. success, 2. failure, 3. trouble or failure, and 4. possible short term success, but ultimate failure.

The article and the concept contained in it were both excellent. However, the professor made a statement to the effect that good implementation could overcome poor strategy/tactics. Since strategy is frequently divided into three levels (corporate strategy, marketing strategy, and marketing tactics), with tactics being tied to implementation, by inference he was saying that good actions at one lower level could overcome a poor decision at a higher level, i.e. that good marketing tactics could overcome a poor marketing strategy; that a particularly successful implementation could overcome the decision to adopt "inappropriate" higher level marketing strategy/tactics. I knew from my own study of strategy that couldn't possibly be correct. In fact, the exact opposite is true.

You may remember the short-lived XFL football league, which lasted only one season back in 2001. The XFL itself was the brainchild of Vince McMahon, World Wrestling Federation's Chairman. The idea was to combine sport with spectacle and duplicate the success of professional wrestling while presenting "off-season football," which would not compete with the regular game. That was the strategy. The problem was that the strategy was wrong. McMahon was ridiculed by mainstream sports journalists due to the stigma attached to professional wrestling's image as being "fake." Some journalists speculated, only half-jokingly, whether any of the league's games were rigged for one side or the other. For the same reason, football fans were not convinced from the start. The tactics were pretty good. Good TV coverage, including NBC, who was a partner, no penalties for roughness, and fewer rules in general. The teams played their hearts out, and many of the players went on (or back) to the NFL once the league broke up. But that's all tactics. Despite good tactics, the XFL could not overcome the strategy, and it lasted only one season.

Drucker's Principle Holds

I knew that "selling" was one of the tactics of "the Four P's". It was basic that it had to support whatever marketing strategy was decided on. In other words, if your strategy was to niche the market and sell only to high-end customers, it made little sense to initiate a low-price tactic. It was incongruent with what the market expected to pay and it affected the image of the product to your prospects. In a high-end customer strategy, you would distribute a retail product through Neiman Marcus, not K-Mart.

All of your tactics have to be lined up to support whatever strategy, target market, etc. that you select. With high-end customers, your price would tend to be relatively high, you would distribute in ways that would best reach your market, and the product would be of a quality to match the higher price you associated with it. Of course, your advertising would be in channels most likely to reach this segment of the overall market.

But let's shift gears somewhat. Let's say you have a totally new innovation. You could introduce the product into the mass market instead of concentrating on a niche. You are the first to market and know that all segments of the market would be interested in purchasing your product. However, you make the decision to go to the high end only, because there you will have higher profit margins due to the much higher price which you can charge. So, you enter this market as planned.

However, let's assume it would have been much better to adopt a mass marketing strategy. Maybe you would have sold so much of the product that it would have made up for the lower per-unit margin and, moreover, you would have captured most of the market. Anyone else entering the market would have been perceived as number two. It would have been difficult for anyone to take the lead from you. Those could be critical elements.

If you proceeded with your poor strategy and your tactics weren't too good, you probably would take another look. You might even re-enter with "the correct" mass marketing strategy. If your implementation and lower-level tactics were really good with the niche, segmentation strategy you adopted, you would probably continue profitable, but not taking full advantage of your lead in the marketplace.

Now let's say that a year or so later, a competitor enters the market with the correct strategy that you should have adopted in the first place. Through mass marketing, the competitor takes over the market and becomes number one, and now you may not ever be able to break out of your niche. This happens. This competitor eventually may even take your niche market from you as well. In this sense, marketing and selling are adversarial.

Another Look at Ford's Early Success

Henry Ford did not establish the first successful automobile company. That would be Oldsmobile, which was founded in 1897 by Ransom E. Olds. Cadillac was founded in 1902 by Henry M. Leland. It too was a successful brand. Henry Ford didn't create the Ford Motor Company until 1903. Ford's genius wasn't the assembly line, which had already been introduced in the meat-packing business, but the fact that first he made a marketing strategy decision to produce cars for the masses and then he adopted the assembly line.

The assembly line, especially the moving assembly line, was important as a tactic to enable low prices in supporting Ford's strategy. As a result, the famous Model T dominated the industry for several decades and was arguably the most successful automobile of all time. Only later did Ford go after other mid-priced and later high-priced market segments. However, had Ford selected a different strategy to serve high-end customers, as did Cadillac and Oldsmobile, an assembly-line tactic would have been incongruent with this strategy. No matter how well implemented his assembly line, the overproduction and lack of uniqueness and exclusiveness would not have been attractive to wealthy prospects.

Clearly, strategy is more important than tactics. While it is desirable to be on target with both, it is far better to be pursuing the right marketing strategy with less than optimal selling than vice versa.

Drucker Lesson Summary

Here are some of the key aspects of Drucker's theory on the relationship between marketing and selling:

- A poor marketing strategy cannot be overcome by good implementation or marketing tactics; marketing strategy is the governing aspect.

- Marketing and selling are neither synonymous nor necessarily complementary.

- The objective of marketing (and therefore marketing strategy) is to make selling superfluous.

- Selling and marketing can be adversarial.

Drucker did not intend to negate the importance of selling. Advertising, distribution, and face-to-face selling are all critical functions. Drucker wanted us to understand that marketing was the governing factor of any business and was so central to all business that its goal was to make selling unnecessary, even if this objective could never be attained in the real world.

Ethics, Honor, Integrity, and the Law

I consider Drucker's lessons on the subject of ethics, honor, and integrity to be among his most important and relevant. This is even more important today because the world has shrunk so much that most businesses must deal with foreign cultures with very different beliefs and value systems from our own.

In the 1970's the United States had gone through a number of national scandals. First there was Watergate, which eventually resulted in Richard Nixon's resignation from the presidency, and there were corporate scandals. In some respects, these scandals and others rivaled those we have seen in recent years. They certainly got our attention.

Lockheed Aircraft bribed the Japanese government to subsidize the purchase of the L-1011 aircraft. The resulting scandal led to the arrest of Japanese Prime Minister Tanaka Kakuei after his resignation due to a different scandal. Lockheed board chairman Daniel Haughton and vice chairman and president Carl Kotchian resigned from their posts.

Meanwhile, in the Netherlands there was another Lockheed scandal related to the purchase of Lockheed F-104G Starfighters aircraft for the Dutch Air Force, again involving bribes from Lockheed. The scandal gave rise to the American Foreign Corrupt Practices Act of 1977, which made it illegal for American persons and their representatives to bribe foreign government officials.

In 1976, we elected a new president, Jimmy Carter. Even many of his opponents felt that President Carter's well-known religious beliefs would guide the country in a way that would lead to a higher moral tone in government and business.

An informal discussion on this subject had started before class had actually begun. Peter arrived early and he got right in the middle of it. When the time came for class to begin, we took our seats, but continued to discuss ethics and moral leadership. Peter stated that having a president expressing high ethical values did not guarantee an ethical outcome because perception of what is ethical and what is not varied in different cultures. Peter then launched into one of his stories to illustrate his point.

A Japanese Executive Is Shocked at U.S. Laws

"A large Japanese corporation decided to open an American manufacturing plant," Peter began. "This plant would bring many jobs to whatever area was chosen; so many states and city locations vied for the opportunity. The Japanese company investigated various locations in several different states, considered a number of proposals, and finally, decided on a particular site. After negotiation with local and state officials, the announcement was made. So significant was this event that the president of the Japanese corporation flew in from Japan for the ground breaking. The local government scheduled an elaborate ceremony with attendant publicity. They invited the state's governor and many other senior state officials, as well as company officers and other dignitaries.

"The Japanese executive spoke English. However, to ensure that everything he said would be understood, the company hired a *Nisei*, or second-generation American of Japanese descent. This woman held an advanced business degree and was fluent in both Japanese and English. She would translate his speech into English as he spoke.

"With dignity and measured tones, the Japanese president began to speak, noting the great honor it was for his company to be able to open its plant at this particular locale in the United States. He would speak a couple of paragraphs, and then the interpreter would translate his remarks into English. The Japanese executive noted the mutual benefits to his company, to the area's citizens, to the local economy, and to Japanese-American friendship. Then, nodding in the direction of the governor and other state and local officials present, he said: 'Furthermore, Mr. Governor and high officials, please understand that our company knows its ethical duty. When the time comes that you retire from your honored positions, my corporation will not forget what you have done and will repay you for the efforts which you have expended in our behalf by giving us this opportunity.'

"The Japanese-American interpreter was horrified," Peter explained. "She made an instantaneous decision and omitted these remarks in her English translation. The Japanese president, who understood enough English to realize what she had done, but did not know why, continued his speech as if nothing had happened. Later, when the two were alone, the president asked his interpreter, 'How could you exclude my reassurances to the governor and other officials regarding our ethical duty? Why did you leave this important statement out of my speech?' Only then could she explain, to his amazement, that what is considered ethical, even a duty, in Japan is considered unethical and even corruption in the United States."

Peter paused for effect. Then he asked, "Please tell me whether you consider the Japanese interpretation of their duty to be ethical or not." Many hands went up.

When in Rome . . .

The general response from students was that the Japanese approach was not ethical and was, in fact, corrupt. It was an opportunity for a company to buy favors with the promise of future rewards. As proof of its being unethical, one student cited the fact that what the Japanese corporation did was against the law. It could be considered a form of bribery, and, in fact, the L-1011 scandal had resulted in the arrest of the Japanese prime minister.

Drucker responded: "Let me tell you why this is considered an ethical duty and neither unethical nor necessarily unlawful in Japan. In Japan, government officials are paid very little. They can live on what they receive in retirement only with great difficulty. It is therefore expected that when they retire, companies which have benefited from their actions during their tenure will assist them, financially and otherwise. Since they could barely get by in their retirement, this is considered the only right and ethical thing to do."

This left most of us somewhat perplexed. We had never looked at this sort of thing in quite this light. In fact, we had been warned by Drucker and others about "situational ethics." He seemed to be saying that there were geographical or cultural ethics that must be taken into account. Nevertheless, we were all in agreement that regardless of what went on in Japan, when doing business in the United States, Japan or any other country had to play by American rules and abide by American law.

"That's very interesting," Drucker continued. "So you feel that when doing business in the United States, a foreign country must follow our laws, ethics, and ways of doing business." All agreed that this was so.

"This, in fact, is exactly what the Japanese executive did," Peter said. "He congratulated his interpreter and thanked her for taking the responsibility for excluding this statement from his speech. 'Because it is against the law here, we will absolutely not do it,' he told her. 'Moreover, because it is considered unethical here, it would be improper. It would be considered in the form of a bribe.'"

Drucker Looks at Bribery

"One should not take bribes," Peter continued. "In fact, most countries have laws against bribery. Yet it is a fact that bribery, as we define it, is routine and expected in some of these countries. Many would perceive that the promise of the Japanese CEO—that his company would reward government officials who helped his company while they were in office—to be a form of bribery. But everyone understands in Japan, or in other countries that expect "*baksheesh*," that this is the traditional way of doing business in their country.

"Most companies doing business in countries where bribery, as we define it, is the norm understand this fact," he said. "They ignore any laws that may have been enacted as 'window dressing'. Some of you said earlier that the fact that a law was broken was itself evidence that what the Japanese corporate president wanted to do was unethical. Do you consider breaking a law concerning bribery, or any law for that matter, to be unethical?"

Hands shot up. Most responses to Peter's question were to the effect that bribery was indeed, unethical. The reason given by students was that it was "wrong," but when pressed, these students said that it was wrong because it was against the law.

The Law Versus Ethics

"You are saying that something is unethical because it is illegal. You are confusing the law and ethics," Drucker said. "Until the 1860's, slavery was legal in the United States. Moreover, in the Dred Scott decision of the late 1850's, the Supreme Court ruled that no African-Americans, not even free blacks, could ever become citizens of the United States. According to the law, the Declaration of Independence did not refer to them, nor did the U.S. Constitution offer them any protection. So, if you maintain that the law and ethics are the same, you would have to say that if you in any way attempted to subvert the law to award Constitutional rights to African-Americans in those days, you would not only be in violation of the law, you would be unethical."

Drucker gave another example. "In this century," he said, "Hitler's Germany passed the Nuremberg Laws, which denied German Jews the rights of German citizenship, and passed other restrictions on them. As a German citizen, if you attempted to circumvent these laws or violate them directly—say, by marrying a Jew, officiating at such a marriage, observing a Jew practicing a profession, or failing to report any violation of the laws to the authorities, you would be sent to prison or worse. Were those who violated these laws unethical? Of course not! We can expect to be punished if we fail to obey a law whether it is a good law or a bad one, but it has nothing to do with ethics."

The Legal Dilemma

"But let's return to our earlier discussion," Peter went on. "I asked if you felt that a company doing business in another country must follow their practices and laws, since clearly the view of what is and what is not ethics may vary from culture to culture and country to country. You agreed that they must. That, for example, the Japanese president must not provide rewards to U.S. government officials after their retirement from government service, as he himself decided, because of our laws and ethical values. Then, by the same logic, shouldn't American companies "bribe" foreign officials to obtain contracts, when this is expected and is the custom and is not considered unethical?"

There was silence at first in the room. No one seemed particularly eager to respond. Finally, someone said, "But this is our law."

"Correct," responded Drucker, "and because it is our law, we Americans must obey it, even though it may not be considered unethical or be against the law in a foreign country."

The students reluctantly nodded their assent.

"Now let us put ourselves in the position of an American company executive who is trying to win a contract in one of these countries in which bribery is both expected and is the norm. By our definition, bribery is against the law in the United States, and the use of bribes to assist in obtaining contracts in foreign countries is specifically forbidden. However, it is not against the law in various countries in which some of your competitors are located, or if it is, these laws may not be enforced. You know that these foreign competitors will be employing bribes. How do you deal with this situation?" he asked.

There really was no good solution to the problem Peter posed, and I think he knew it. He concluded that no one should take bribes. However, this particular U.S. law confused ethics with the perception of what was and what was not a bribe and therefore ethical in different cultures. He predicted continued violations and problems with enforcement of this law, which had been recently strengthened, when American companies attempted to compete in countries in which bribes were expected and were not considered unethical or illegal.

Drucker's prediction came true. A 2002 article in WorldTribune.com pointed out that the U.S. government ignored a record of bribery connected to defense contracts in the Middle East, when by its own policy it should not be dealing with U.S. defense contractors with a record of bribery. It reported: "The Washington-based Project On Government Oversight said the government has violated its policies that contracts be awarded only to responsible contractors that have a satisfactory record of integrity and business ethics. But the report said 16 of the top 43 contractors chosen during fiscal 1999 have been fined billions of dollars for violations."[1] All were major U.S. corporations. With such a high percentage, one wonders whether there weren't more violators that were not caught.

Business Ethics and Honor

Peter continued his lesson by saying that much that was claimed to be business ethics had little to do with ethics at all. Ethics had to do with adherence to a moral code. However, there was not one single moral code in the world, but many. "Hiring call girls to entertain visiting business executives does not make you unethical," he said. "It just makes you a pimp. Cheating on your expense account may make you a thief and untrustworthy, but only arguably unethical."

I raised my hand. "Where does honor fit in?" I asked.

"Honor," Peter said, "is demonstrable integrity and honesty. In other words, an honorable man stands by his principles. However, again, these principles might vary from society to society."

I was amazed at this entire evening's discussion. I had never before considered ethics in this light. Because of the teaching style he used that evening, but mostly because of the West Point concept of honor, which was such a part of my own experience, this evening and its events stands out in my mind.

At this point, I described for Drucker and the class the West Point Code of Honor and the lifetime commitment to it by most graduates.

The West Point Honor System

If you think of West Point, you probably think of it primarily as a training ground for military officers. You may recall Grant, Lee, Eisenhower, MacArthur, Schwarzkopf, and others. But West Point is much more. It was the first engineering school in the country and it was the first establishment in the United States to institutionalize honor. Its stringent code is very much a part of every West Point graduate. That is why Drucker's lesson on this topic immediately captured my full attention. It coincided with what I considered an important part of the way I tried to live my life, both personal and professional.

The basic requirements of the West Point honor system are extremely simple: "A cadet will not lie, cheat, or steal nor tolerate anyone who does." The non-toleration clause, perhaps the code's most controversial aspect, sets it apart from many other academic institutions having an honor system. It requires cadets to report honor violations they observe or learn about, or they themselves will be considered equally guilty. Despite its strictness, it is overwhelmingly endorsed and applied by cadets, it is run entirely by cadets, and it works, although there have been two scandals in the last half century involving widespread violations.

Moreover, while most honor codes in academic institutions are focused on cheating in academics, West Point's code is focused on day-to-day living and honor and integrity as a way of life.

Honor Versus a Violation of Regulation

The difference between honor violations and a simple violation of cadet regulations is made absolutely clear from the first lesson on honor given to new cadets. During the cadet's first two months, he or she receives considerable instructions in the code, but the cadet is not subject to its conditions, until all aspects are thoroughly understood.

Central to understanding the code is the fact that a cadet can violate regulations without compromising his honor. Of course, if a cadet violates a rule and gets caught, he or she must pay the penalty. There are usually demerits, or for more serious offenses confinement to quarters, loss of various types of privileges, and at various times in West Point's history doing "penalty tours" (walking back and forth along a prescribed path while carrying a shouldered rifle). At the extreme, the most serious violations of regulations, or repeated violations, can lead to dismissal. However, no matter how serious the violation of cadet regulations, this is never considered an honor violation. An honor violation, no matter how minor, originally merited only one punishment under all conditions: dismissal from the Academy, even if the violation was self-reported.

Because of the honor system, both officers and other cadets will always accept a cadet's word without question. General H. Norman Schwarzkopf wrote about West Point's honor system in his book, *It Doesn't Take a Hero*. General Schwarzkopf said, "The most important lesson drilled into us during those first weeks was the honor code."

During his first year at West Point, there was a parade going on near his barracks. A classmate whose room was on the other side of the building asked if he could watch from Schwarzkopf's window, even though this was against the rules. Schwarzkopf said, "It's your neck. If you want to do it, it's fine with me."

After the parade, a First Classman burst into his room. This was a cadet who didn't like Schwarzkopf, and had told him so. If fact, he had threatened to drive Schwarzkopf out of West Point if he could!

The cadet stood Schwarzkopf at attention and criticized him for looking out of the window during the parade. He told Schwarzkopf that he was going to pay a terrible price. Schwarzkopf related the following exchange in his book:

"Sir, I did not watch the review."

"I saw you standing on that chair! Who do you think you're trying to fool?"

"Sir, I did not watch the review."

"You didn't?"

"No, sir."

"'All right,' he said and walked out the door. That was the end of the matter. Because of the honor code, despite his dislike of me, he accepted my word. And I was not expected to report the guy who had actually watched from my window, because that was a regulatory breach, not an honor violation."[2]

This, then, is the background from which I personally received Drucker's lessons on this subject.

Drucker's Reaction to the Honor Code

Peter asked me how the West Point honor code would apply for a "white lie." That is, what if you have a parent who was seriously ill. The doctor tells you that there is no chance of the patient surviving, but that you should do everything possible to maintain your parent's morale. "If your parent asks you what the doctor said about his chances, is it dishonorable for you to tell him that all would be well?" Peter asked. I had to agree that this would not be dishonorable.

Peter mentioned other situations in which the honor code, good as it might be, might not apply. He noted that the code did not apply to moral values, which was an individual thing. "A man could be a womanizer, a drunkard, not take proper care of his family, and still be considered honorable by the West Point code," he said. Again, I had to agree that Peter was correct, although I pointed out that it was not only the words of the code that were important, but its spirit.

Peter agreed and again noted the differing definitions of bribery within differing cultures. He went on to say that the West Point honor code had stood the test of time and was worthy as a test of honor whether at West Point, or anywhere else in our culture. But once again he cautioned that one should not confuse honor with ethics, integrity, or the law, even though there was clearly a relationship among them. He reiterated that different interpretations of what was and what was not honorable might prevail in different cultures.

Later, I thought of other examples in which the Code of Honor did not apply. One was negotiations, during which verbally exaggerating or minimizing some things is considered normal. However, once an agreement is reached, both parties are expected to abide by the terms. Thus, as a result, one needs to pay particular attention to what is actually written down, no matter how honorable or ethical one's negotiating partner.

A friend who teaches negotiation once noted that in labor negotiations or negotiations of international disputes, one side or the other might immediately refer to a proposal presented by the other side as "totally unacceptable." Yet frequently this very same "totally unacceptable" proposal would be accepted a short time later. Both sides knew that the proposal made by one side was not necessarily "totally unacceptable" at the time it was made. It was an exaggeration stated as fact and was understood to be a negotiating position. My friends comment was, "a lie is not a lie when the truth is not expected."

Finally, the realization that ethics, and therefore integrity and honor, might differ in different cultures surprised me. Somehow I had always assumed that these were universal constants. I should have known better. Since the examples that night centered on the Japanese, I remembered that the Japanese considered surrender in battle to be dishonorable. If capture were inevitable, Japanese soldiers were expected to commit suicide. And they considered an enemy who surrendered in battle to be without honor. This was one reason for the inhuman treatment that the Japanese meted out to prisoners of war. Americans clearly have different ideas about honor and surrender.

To me, it would seem that spies violate the honor code in everything they do. They lie, cheat, and steal as a way of life. Yet spies have been employed, especially in warfare, since time immemorial, and spying has not generally been considered dishonorable.

Unfortunately, the concept of spying has been extended to civilian practice. Twenty-five years ago, I attended a seminar for professional researchers. Teaching marketing research in the university, I was intensely interested in what was currently being done in industry.

The Ethics of Business Research

Washington Researchers is a consulting firm that conducted competitive research on companies, products, and strategies. It also conducted seminars around the country on how to accomplish various types of competitive research.

I had the good fortune to attend one of these seminars. As a part of the seminar, all attendees participated in a survey of information-gathering techniques. This survey was developed originally because participants had asked the company for judgments about the ethics of various means of information gathering. Washington Researchers decided that the issues were too complex to allow for easy answers. So they decided to conduct this survey as a simple measurement of individual and company practices.

On a confidential survey form, they asked participants to assume that each was asked to find out everything they could about the finances, products, marketing strategies, etc. of their company's closest competitor. Several research techniques were suggested, all of questionable ethics. The participants were to respond either "yes" or "no" to each of seven questions.

Here are the questions posed by Washington Researchers. The percentages listed are based on several hundred responses received up to the time when I asked and got their permission to use the material in a previous book.

1. Researcher poses as graduate student working on thesis. Researcher tells source that dorm phones are very busy, so researcher will call back rather than having phone calls returned. In this way, researcher's real identity is protected.

   a. Would your company use this technique?   Yes / 39%

   b. Would you personally use this technique?   Yes / 46%

   c. Do other companies use this technique?   Yes / 86%

2. Researcher calls the VP while s/he is at lunch, hoping to find the secretary who may have some information but is likely to be less suspicious about researcher's motives.

   a. Would your company use this technique?   Yes / 63%

   b. Would you personally use this technique?   Yes / 65%

   c. Do other companies use this technique?   Yes / 86%

3. Researcher calls competitor's suppliers and distributors, pretending to do a study of the entire industry. Researcher poses as a representative of a private research firm and works at home during the project so that the company's identity is protected.

   a. Would your company use this technique?   Yes / 41%

   b. Would you personally use this technique?   Yes / 47%

   c. Do other companies use this technique?   Yes / 88%

4. The competitor's representative is coming to a local college to recruit employees. Researcher poses as a student job-seeker in order to learn recruiting practices and some other general information about the competitor.

   a. Would your company use this technique?   Yes / 33%

   b. Would you personally use this technique?   Yes / 38%

   c. Do other companies use this technique?   Yes / 81%

5. The researcher is asked to verify rumors that the competitor is planning to open a new plant in a small southern town. The researcher poses as an agent from a manufacturer looking for a site similar to the one that the competitor supposedly would need. Researcher uses this cover to become friendly with local representatives of the Chamber of Commerce, newspapers, realtors, etc.

   a. Would your company use this technique?   Yes / 36%

   b. Would you personally use this technique?   Yes / 36%

   c. Do other companies use this technique?   Yes / 80%

6. Researcher corners a competitor's employee at a national conference, such as the one sponsored by the American Marketing Association, and offers to buy drinks at the hotel bar. Several drinks later, the researcher asks the hard questions.

   a. Would your company use this technique?   Yes / 63%

   b. Would you personally use this technique?   Yes / 60%

   c. Do other companies use this technique?   Yes / 91%

7. Researcher finds an individual who works for the competitor to serve as informant to researcher's company.

   a. Would your company use this technique?   Yes / 35%

   b. Would you personally use this technique?   Yes / 36%

   c. Do other companies use this technique?   Yes / 80%[3]

Without doubt, a great many of these techniques were being used twenty-five years ago. These techniques, called "pretexting," were all considered legal at the time. However, in the Hewlett-Packard case of 2006, the Chairwoman, Patricia Dunn, discovered that pretexting might not only be considered an ethical violation, it might also be illegal. Dunn was accused of spying on some of her employees.

The scandal erupted after Dunn assigned a team to investigate boardroom leaks to journalists. She gave them permission to use false identities and other questionable tactics to obtain personal information of directors, employees, and reporters. Dunn had questioned supposed experts and was told it was legal, even routine. As you might imagine, HP's ethics chief was also fired.

The Hewlett-Packard case led to a number of other actions. The Federal Trade Commission and several state attorneys general eventually got involved and brought enforcement actions against pretexters for allegedly violating federal and state laws on fraud, misrepresentation, and unfair competition.[4]

What this case seems to say is that while government spies may lie, cheat, and steal, industrial spies may not.

Drucker's First Test of Ethics

I think this discussion on ethics lasted far longer than Peter intended, and it was just about time for a break. He wrapped up the discussion by a summary. "Ethics and integrity should be measured primarily by the oath of the Greek physician Hippocrates," continued Drucker. "Primum non nocere—First, do no harm."

Drucker Lesson Summary

Drucker's lecture did not resolve everything, where countless books on the subject of ethics, honor, and integrity had failed. He did, however, help me to make certain distinctions. The concepts of ethics, honor, and integrity all have to do with right behavior according to our values. But because these values may differ in differing cultures or society, not all are universal. What we consider universal may be universal, only to us. Moreover, the law is separate from these values. One can be ethical, honorable, and of high integrity, and still be in violation of the law and land in jail. Conversely, someone could be an all-around sleaze and not be violating any laws.

The first guideline for ethics in business, according to Peter, and this does seem to be of universal application, should be to do no harm. If you take the time to think through any potential situation using this criterion, you will not go very far astray. Like many such valuable insights from Peter, it is a simple exhortation—but it is up to us to think through and apply it.

CHAPTER ELEVEN

You Can't Predict the Future, But You Can Create It

Some of Drucker's lessons were repeated by him again and again at different times and in different courses. His admonition that you cannot predict the future is a good example. I don't remember the first time Peter spoke about creating the future. However, my recollection was that he did so in just about every course.

I heard this message not long after beginning my classes at Claremont. Clearly, this was something that he believed in strongly. The first time he spoke of this, however, I missed it completely. I heard about it only second-hand. This was because I walked out of Peter's class.

I Walk Out of Peter's Class

Peter didn't always pay attention to the clock, with the possible exception of the mid-course break in the evening. He was constrained then because there were so many students in the various classes that break times were staggered for the purpose of dinner and socialization at the faculty club. Also, he realized that he could easily pick up on the subject matter wherever he left off after the evening meal. After class, this was a little more difficult, since the class met only once a week. Therefore, at what was supposed to be the end of class, he did not always stop when the clock said that the class was over. He stopped when he felt his lecture was complete and not before. Usually he managed to complete on time, but not always.

The first time this occurred, I was aghast. At ten o'clock in the evening when the class was scheduled to end, he was still in the middle of a lecture. At first, I was not too disturbed. I thought that he would tie things together and quickly wrap things up. All of his students were rabid Drucker fans. However, on this particular evening at 10:15, he was still at it. And he didn't stop at 10:30.

I was tired. I had worked all day and was I eager to get home to my family. Pasadena was still a 30–40 minute drive away. In the morning, I had to get up early to go to work. Fortunately, at the time I was still working as Director of Research and Development for a company only a few miles away from my home. As I noted in a previous chapter, I was to leave this job several months later.

As the boss of my research and development domain, I was the first to arrive in the morning. I had an important meeting scheduled with my immediate superior, the company president, for shortly after 8:00 AM But Peter lectured on. I was sitting right up front in the first row. Were it any other professor, I would have left as quietly and inconspicuously as I could, first row, or not. But how could I possibly get up and walk out on Peter Drucker? Not one of the other fifty or sixty students got up and left either. Finally, a little after 11:00 PM, Peter concluded his lecture. He finalized his points and the class was over. I arrived home about 11:45. I suffered a mild chiding from my wife and vowed never to sit quietly past the time for the end of course again, regardless of whether or not it was Drucker lecturing and regardless of what he or anyone else thought about my getting up and leaving.

A few weeks later, the same thing occurred. Peter continued to lecture past the end of the class. I gave him until 10:05. Then I arose from my front row seat as quietly as I could; I gathered together my notebook and other class materials, and stuffed them in my briefcase. I nodded good-bye to Peter. He nodded back and I left. Seeing me leaving, a number of other students followed my example.

I was concerned, and the next day I called one of my classmates by telephone. "Was my leaving noticed?" I asked. "Oh, yeah," he said. "And I'm sure you noticed that you took some others with you."

"Did Peter say anything?"

"No, but you missed something interesting."

"What was that?" I asked.

"You missed one of Peter's truly poignant comments. We were talking about planning. He said that it was important that your plan and its strategy fit the environment. Someone asked how you could predict the future, since even if you started to implement your plan today, the environment was bound to change as you proceeded."

I knew by "the environment" my classmate was talking about the situational environment that a company would encounter at the time of implementation, including technology, economic, and political conditions, and so forth.

My classmate continued: "Peter answered that you couldn't predict the environment of the future. However, what you could do is create the future."

"How in the world would you do that?" I asked.

"I don't know. We asked him that. Since it was almost an hour after the time when the class should have been over, and less than half the class was still present, Peter promised to tell us next week."

From then on, if Peter went past the hour, I let my schedule and my interest in a particular lecture be my guide. And if I did leave, the next day I always asked a classmate who remained what went on. Despite this, I probably missed some of Peter's important lessons anyway. Of course, I regretted this, even more once I graduated. After I graduated, however, Peter was generous enough to tell me that I was always welcome to return to his class as a visitor and later extended the same rights to my son Nim when he became an MBA student at Claremont.

I truly regret missing anything Peter talked about. Couldn't I have managed to get by on a little less sleep every so often? But you can never redo the past, no matter how much you would like to. On Peter's side, he understood that his students were full-time employees traveling some distance to hear him lecture. He continued to lecture so long as he felt that he still had something worthwhile to contribute on the subject. But he didn't hold it against us if we had to leave at the scheduled end of class time, even if we sat in the first row. This was another tribute to his character, and it never affected the grade he later awarded or his friendship. I tried to remember things like that later, when I became a professor.

You Can Create Your Own Future

As promised, the week following my first disappearance from his class, Peter gave his lecture about dealing with the future. The future, Drucker said again, is unpredictable, but can be created. In his lecture, Peter emphasized that while planning, especially strategic planning, was difficult and risky, it was one of management's primary responsibilities. "Strategic planning is not about making decisions in the future," he said, since decisions could only be made now, in the present. So what he was really talking about was making decisions now to create a desired future for our companies. This implied reaching the goals or objectives we set, regardless of the environmental conditions we might later encounter. However, it was crucial to start with our objectives. What exactly did we want to do? Only then could we decide on the actions we needed to take now, in the present, to realize these goals.

Applying Peter's Lesson to My Own Problem

I paid particular attention to Drucker's lecture because at the time I was faced with a challenging problem at work. Our company's business was mostly with the government. Unfortunately, the government placed most of its orders at the beginning of its fiscal year in September. We bid production contracts, won all we could, and then bought the materials and started manufacturing the products for our government customers. When we were done, our machines and labor force were generally idle until the next cycle. So we went through a year of peaks and valleys. We were losing a lot of money due to the wasted overhead when there was no work for a good many of our employees.

The president of our company had asked me to look into this problem and to recommend a non-U.S. governmental product which would use the same machinery, labor, and somewhat similar marketing methods. I had investigated the problem, and made a presentation of my findings to top management. As a result, I was told to put together a five-year plan for this business. Some people may not call this a strategic plan, but it was strategic enough for me. I couldn't predict the future either, but I certainly wanted to create a viable future for my company in this business.

Though Peter was unambiguous on this subject, I think Peter's lecture made most of us who were seriously engaged with the issue feel very uncomfortable. The idea of creating a real plan without knowing the future was just plain disquieting. However, Drucker told us the secret was not to create a plan cast in iron, but to review it frequently and make adjustments as required as time went on.

I used Drucker's ideas to develop my first plan for this product line. Later I developed the concept further, and the ideas have been incorporated into my books on planning and strategy and my lectures on strategic planning, marketing planning, time management, and more. I realized that the key to Drucker's mandate that we must create our future was that a plan must consider and specify alternatives. And you must get feedback and refer to the plan frequently over the entire period that the plan is being implemented.

Implementation and action were considered of prime importance. Peter's lecture made me realize that, to a large extent, almost anyone could create the future that they desired for both themselves and their companies. In fact, many were already doing this on a personal basis. For example, the heads of smaller companies were doing this in growing their companies. In some cases they were accomplishing what any rational person considering the facts might believe to be unattainable. Yet, on both a personal and professional level, they were creating their futures. Sometimes the futures they created, considering where they started, appeared impossible.

The "Impossible" Story of a Bodybuilder (Not Arnold)

Angelo Siciliano was a boy from a poor Italian family whose parents immigrated to the U.S. from Italy. Skinny and shy, Siciliano was bullied by bigger and stronger boys. One day he stood up to them and in return they gave him a bad beating. Siciliano vowed that this would never happen again. He was determined to create his own future and become not just strong enough to defend himself and ward off their bullying, but to become impressively strong. This was the definite goal that Drucker said must be the starting point of all planning.

For months, Siciliano avoided everyone. Even friends wondered what had happened to him. In secret, he borrowed books on bodybuilding from the library. Unable to afford the weights most of them recommended for building muscle, he made a close study of all bodybuilding methods. He recognized that muscles were enlarged by working each muscle against increasingly greater resistance. He saw that such resistance could come from other sources besides the use of weights. Conducting his own experiments and using his own body as a subject, he took action and put his ideas into practice without the use of the weights and the other equipment which he could not afford.

Working his muscles daily and applying his methods, he gained the strength and muscles he sought. Finally, he was ready to meet his tormentors. He actually sought them out. They wanted no part of him. Rather than fight the strong man the former weakling had become, they fled.

Angelo Siciliano, however, continued to develop his body. As many reached a goal after working a plan, he set a new goal. His success as a bodybuilder led him to enter bodybuilding contests. At first, he did poorly. But as he continued, and with the future he was creating constantly in mind, he got better and better. Finally came the day that he won a major bodybuilding title: "The World's Most Perfectly Developed Man." Angelo Siciliano had created his own future in a big way, but he still wasn't done.

Now Siciliano set a new goal. He had a vision of strong young men who had once been weak, all changed by his methods, which he called "dynamic tension." He put together a bodybuilding course which he sold through the mail. That course made Siciliano a multi-millionaire. Over the next fifty years, tens of thousands of his mail-order students benefited from it. So powerful was the course that he envisioned that it still sells today, more than thirty years after his death. If you are a male, you will probably recognize the name he adopted, for long ago Siciliano changed his name to better reflect who and what he had become. The name the world came to know him by is "Charles Atlas."

In every field, there are those like Charles Atlas that may have few resources to begin with. They create their own futures. They may not have strength or wealth or education or anything that you think may be necessary for success in any given field of human endeavor. Yet they create billion-dollar corporations and even whole new industries. And they attain other goals as well.

For example, Madonna is world famous as a singer and performer, yet she never took singing lessons. She actually moved from her native Michigan in 1977 to New York with dreams of becoming a ballet dancer, but she soon changed her mind. She wanted to sing. To create this future, she formed a band called "The Breakfast Club" with a partner. However, her singing abilities were not yet developed. So she started out playing drums for the band, but soon developed her voice sufficiently to become lead singer. She saw to it that a demo tape she had made fell into the right hands. In 1982, she made her first single, "Everybody," which became a hit. She kept working until the future she created was realized, and then continued to set higher and higher goals for herself. She couldn't predict her future, but she could create it—and so she did.

It is clear that regardless of your age, background, or wealth, nothing seems to matter very much if you commit to creating a future—either your own or a company's. Somehow you will find a way of getting the job done.

The Process of Creating Your Future

Peter made it very clear that the process of creating your future, anybody's future, begins with your goals and objectives. These need to be crystal-clear. Then you need to determine the actions that must be taken today to achieve these objectives in the future. Drucker said there was danger in assuming that today's trends, whatever they are, will continue into the future. This is where things become a bit tricky. How do you start and yet forget the past?

In analyzing my notes on Peter's concepts sometime later, I realized that Drucker wasn't saying what I had first thought. He was not saying that the planner should forget the past, but rather that one should not assume that the past or present would continue in the future. Peter wanted us to focus on future goals first. Then consider what we face today and take the necessary actions that will point us toward reaching those goals in the future. As we progress, the environment and conditions are going to change. We can't predict these changes. In fact, if we hold to those initial actions and stay the course, we're never going to reach the future we are intent on creating. However, we can and must take new actions to enable us to make progress toward and reach these future goals.

Consider the astronauts heading for the moon. The astronauts didn't calculate a course to the moon and hold that single course the entire 240,000 miles. If they had held to a single course, they would never have reached the moon. Instead, they made a mid-course correction, and they were prepared to take other actions and make corrections to get them to their goal as required.

My Corollary to Drucker's Process

As Drucker saw it, one made necessary decisions and continued to focus on the end objective. You didn't stay tied to old products, services, customs, or ways of doing business. Given that no trend could be extrapolated forever, he knew that "mid-course" corrections were essential. While future goals might remain constant, strategies needed to reach those goals did not. With my aviation background, it was easy to relate to Peter's theory. However, based on my experiences flying aircraft, I added a corollary to his basic thesis. I think Peter would have agreed with it. I call it "Plan B." The Plan B Corollary says that as you note changes that require new actions, you should ask yourself some "what if" questions.

These "what if" questions define potential problems, opportunities, and threats that might occur in the coming leg of your journey toward your eventual goals. What if an industry you depend on collapses? What if you can't get raw materials? What if there is a major war? What if the demand suddenly quadruples? I don't mean that you need to consider every possibility of every single change occurring—only those that are most relevant. For each of these occurrences, whether problem, opportunity, or threat, you need to decide what you are going to do. That's your Plan B.

In flying, you develop a flight plan from point A to point B. The wind changes and that blows you off course. So you need to make the directional corrections to keep you pointed toward your destination. That's analogous to the monitoring of the situation Peter was talking about, and the need to keep making corrections and to not rely on the past. But what if you have an in-flight emergency? You have a fuel leak and can't make it all the way. You have a landing gear that won't retract. You lose all your communications.

The point is that under these conditions, you don't have the time to start planning anew. These things should be thought through ahead of time. And in fact, they are. Every airplane I flew had what was called "the red-bordered pages" in the flight manual. These were emergency aircraft procedures that had already been worked out. You had to commit these to memory, because in many situations there wouldn't be time in the air to look them up if you encountered them. In some cases, your actions had to be immediate and almost instinctive. Some of these procedures could only be calculated once you knew where you were going and after you had considered other conditions. For example, if you needed to land fast, what was the nearest landing site which was suitable for your type of aircraft?

In business, the same is frequently true. You don't want to be struggling when something happens in your environment, a competitor's action, a new regulatory requirement, a foreign embargo, or anything else which could affect your strategies which could not be predicted. You must be ready ahead of time to avoid the threats, handle the problems, and take advantage of the opportunities. Thus Plan B.

It is important to remember that while you start the analysis for your plan with the current situation and past trends, you are not going to assume that they will continue forever into the future. This is a starting point only. All these will change as time passes, and as conditions change, you will make new decisions and introduce new strategies to keep you moving toward your future goals and objectives, which is your constant focus.

Current Situation Analysis

The whole process begins with a current situation analysis. I have heard this process called "environmental scanning." I like to approach the situational analysis by dividing the analysis into four categories. I call them the environs of the situation: situational environs, neutral environs, competitor environs, and company environs. Let's look at each in turn, and then we'll look at how you pick your target markets based on your situational analysis.

SITUATIONAL ENVIRONS

As I see it, the situational environs are those peculiar to the individual situation. They include current demand and demand trends for your product or service. Is this demand growing, is it declining, or has it leveled off? Are there certain groups in which the demand is growing and others in which demand is declining? Who are the decision makers regarding purchase of the product, and who are the purchase agents? Sometimes the decision maker and purchase agent are the same, but often they are not.

For example, one member of a family may be the decision maker with regard to purchasing a certain product, say, a brand of soft drink. But the individual who actually makes the purchase may be another family member. Who influences this decision? How, when, where, what, and why do these potential customers purchase? What are the social and cultural factors? Are demographics of consumers important? Then, maybe you need to analyze educational backgrounds, income, age, and similar factors. What are the economic conditions during the period covered by the marketing plan? Is business good or is it bad?

High demand can occur in both a good or bad business climate, depending on the product or service offered. What is the state of technology for this class of product? Is your product high-tech and state-of-the-art? Are newer products frequently succeeding older ones, thus indicating a shorter product life cycle? In sum, how is technology affecting the product or service and the marketing for this product or service?

Are politics, current or otherwise, in any way affecting this product or service? What potential dangers or threats do the politics in the situation portend? Or do the politics provide opportunities? What laws or regulations are relevant to the marketing of this product or service?

What conditions exist in the industry that are favorable or unfavorable? It is important to document these in our plan, for they will not necessarily be true in the future. As we adjust our plan, we want to recall the then known facts and assumptions on which it is based.

NEUTRAL ENVIRONS

Neutral environs are groups or organizations that have the capability of helping or hurting your plan. In doing this part of the analysis, you want to analyze which is likely. Government may have an impact. Is legislation on the state, federal, or local level likely to affect the demand or marketing of the product or service? What's happening in the media? Does current publicity or public opinion favor your project or does it make any difference? Look at special interest groups. Might they have some impact? Are any influential groups (e.g., consumer organizations) likely to affect your plans for marketing this product or service?

COMPETITOR ENVIRONS

There are those organizations that compete against you. They are especially important because they are the only elements of the environment that may intentionally act against your interests and therefore respond to any actions that you take. In this part of the situational analysis, analyze in detail your main competitors, the products they offer, their plans, experience, know-how, suppliers, and financial, human, and capital resources, and suppliers. Discuss their current and future strategies. Note whether your competitors enjoy favor with their customers or not, and why. Investigate your competitors' strengths and weaknesses, what marketing channels they use to reach the customer, and anything else that you feel is relevant to the situation.

COMPANY ENVIRONS

Company environs describe the situation within your organization and with the resources that you have available. Note your current products, experience, and know-how, financial, human, and capital resources, suppliers, and other factors as you did the previous environs. Do you enjoy favor with your customers or potential customers and why? Summarize your strengths and weaknesses as they apply to your project. In many ways, this section of your analysis is about the same items as the competitor environs section.

Picking Target Markets

Knowing your customers is as important as knowing yourself (the company environs), your competitors (the competitor environs), and the other environs that you have analyzed (neutral and situational). Identifying key aspects helps you to correctly identify the decisive point or points to concentrate your resources.

Not everyone is a worthwhile potential customer, even though anyone might be able to make use of anything that you may introduce into the marketplace in the future. Some segments of the total market are far more likely candidates than others. If you attempt to serve every single potential customer segment, you cannot satisfy those that are most likely to buy as well as you should. Furthermore, you will dissipate your resources by trying to reach them all. If you pick the most likely target market, or markets, you can devote the maximum amount of money to advertising your product or service in a message that your most likely customers can best understand.

The basic concept of all strategy is to concentrate your scarce resources at the decisive points in the situation. Your target markets represent one application of this concept. You usually cannot be strong everywhere. You must be strong where it counts, in this case, in the markets you target.

How will you define your target markets? Start by defining them in terms of:

- demographics (i.e., such vital statistics as age, income, and education);

- geography (i.e., their location);

- psychographics (i.e., how they think); and

- lifestyle (i.e., their activities, interests, and opinions).

There are an infinite number of ways of describing and segmenting your market.

Again, all these factors may change in the future from what they are today. However, as long as you keep track of changes as you progress and keep focused on your future objectives, you will be on the way to creating your future, just as Drucker indicated you could.

What Next?

Once you have completed this analysis, you are in a better position to see your problems, opportunites, and threats. As you proceeed, you will note that your strengths and weaknesses must figure closely in the strategy that you formulate. One part of your strengths analysis is especially important to consider. It is called a competitive advantage or differential advantage. It means, essentially, what do you have that others do not, and which are important in this specific situation?

After assembling this information, you are in a position to develop the strategies which will lead you to create the future you want and to take the necessary decisions to implement them.

There is, however, one more step. How do you determine whether you are getting there or not? As you take action you should determine if you are moving closer and closer to these future objectives. To make this determination, you need to establish metrics.

Metrics are objective measurements which tell the tale. If the future you are creating has to do with becoming a major force in your industry, what metrics can you look at every year to see how you are doing? Sales might be one, percentage of the market served another, innovations introduced could be a third. You need to work these out depending on your future. I think Charles Atlas probably used a tape measure to see whether he was developing muscles or not. Later, he probably noted his success in bodybuilding competitions, and later yet, the sales or number of students who bought his courses.

Drucker Lesson Summary

As Peter often said, you can't predict your future, but you can create it. Quit worrying about your future environment. No one can predict it. Especially don't focus on why you can't do something. Instead, decide what your objectives are, look at the resources you need, and do a situational analysis. Then go from there and take action. Others have created their futures, and so can you!

We're All Accountable

*P*eter had a good sense of humor. I don't mean to describe him as so jocular that he was always cracking jokes. That wouldn't be true. Still, he was far from humorless or uptight. I was not surprised when I read in Doris Drucker's memoirs, *Invent Radium or I'll Pull Your Hair* (The University of Chicago Press, 2004), to hear that the future Mrs. Drucker's mother referred to him not necessarily very flatteringly as "that happy-go-lucky Austrian, Peter Drucker." Her mother can probably be forgiven. Peter was not well-known in those days and she wanted her daughter to marry a Rothschild.

By the end of my second year at Claremont, I had decided that on earning my doctorate, I would leave business and join academia. This was because of Peter and a marketing professor, Professor Leonard Parsons, from whom I had taken a course in marketing management. Of course, one doesn't typically give two years' notice in a business, and by then I was a senior manager reporting to the vice president of a major corporation. So this bit of information was highly confidential, which I, perhaps foolishly, had shared with several classmates.

As noted in previous chapters, the routine was that Drucker's class began at about 4:30 PM. We were in class for an hour and a half to two hours. Then we had an hour break at the faculty club, during which we socialized and shared a meal with our classmates and faculty. After this, we returned to class for another couple of hours of class work.

One evening I was sitting at a table for six at this evening meal break from our classroom instruction. I sat in the middle on one side of a rectangular table, with Peter sitting on my right. My classmate sitting on my left introduced me to a new student sitting opposite him. "Bill, this is Joe Smith. He's a vice president at your sister company, Douglas Aircraft."

Douglas Aircraft Company was located in Long Beach, California, only a few miles away from McDonnell Douglas Astronautics Company where I worked, and all the senior executives from both divisions knew one another. This new executive student was a colleague and at the same level in the chain of command as my boss, Paul Smith. Paul was vice president of marketing. Although some months before leaving I did tell Paul of my plans, this was two years before my potential graduation and I had told no one in my company.

Without pausing, my classmate turned to the newcomer and said, "Bill works for the vice president of marketing at your sister company, McDonnell Douglas Astronautics. However, Bill intends to quit and become a professor as soon as he has his doctorate."

I mentally sunk into my chair. I could have decked my big-mouth classmate on the spot. Instead, I straightened up and managed a smile. My hand shot out almost automatically. I shook the newcomer's hand warmly and said: "Hi, I'm Bill Drucker, Peter's son." Peter was talking to another student sitting to his right and I didn't think he even heard what was going on, or my surprising statement claiming to be his progeny.

Peter completed his conversation with the other student. Then, he turned slowly to me and said, "Bill, you may be my son, but I am not your father."

I was embarrassed, although I knew Peter had not taken my comment seriously, nor was he offended by it. On the way back to class, I explained what had occurred and why I had tried to claim a relationship as one of his offspring.

"I was not offended," he told me, "but you were careless in telling someone of your future intentions who did not keep this information confidential. However, it was your error, and it is you who are fully accountable for it. We are, in fact, all accountable—management, employees, labor, and subordinates—and we must all be held accountable for not only what we say, but the actions and decisions which we take or fail to take."

I do not remember the general topic of that week's lesson. However, when we returned to class, Peter lectured on accountability, and a valuable lesson it was.

Drucker on Responsibility and Accountability

On our return to the classroom Peter began to talk about responsibilities and accountability, not just of managers, but of employees as well. The idea, as I remember it, was that everyone is responsible in one way or another for the success of an enterprise, and that it followed that everyone concerned had to be held accountable for what he was responsible for.

Drucker used executive salaries as his prime example. He said that executive salaries at the top were clearly out of line with the responsibilities of those holding these positions. He said that the ratios of the compensation of American top managers to the lowest-paid workers were the highest in the world. In addition, he said that this difference wasn't slight, but differed by magnitudes and that we would end up paying a tremendous price for this. I don't believe that Peter was specific in quoting ratios, but I do know that by one analysis, the ratio of average CEO compensation in the U.S. to average pay of a non-management employee in the U.S. hit a high in 2001 of 525 to one.[1] Drucker's recommendation was that the ratio needed to be something less than 20 to one.

He went on to debunk the main arguments for such pay differentials: that top executives deserved these salaries due to the performance of the corporations they headed, or that such salaries were necessary to attract the most qualified executives. He stated flatly that they were nonsense.

He pointed out that top executives in many corporations were paid these ridiculous salaries even when their documented performance was far below par or even as they drove the organizations for which they were responsible into serious financial problems or even bankruptcy.

As far as these salaries being needed to attract the most qualified executives, he gave us examples of several well-known companies which were performing very well, but whose chief executives were paid much more modest salaries. The only one I can recall now was Robert Townsend, who had been president of Avis-Rent-A-Car. He was well-known for instituting the "We Try Harder" advertising campaign several years earlier and had had a major effect on Avis' success during his tenure as president.

Drucker concluded that it was the executive himself who was responsible and accountable for his own salary. He said that Robert Townsend had refused a salary increase after his success at Avis on the grounds that it was simply poor leadership for what he was trying to accomplish. He also told us that many of the most effective executives took salary cuts in time of trouble.

I read an account of Townsend's rejection of a salary increase in his book, *Up the Organization* (Fawcett, 1983). During a board meeting at which his stunning successes over the previous year had been reported, the chairman of the board asked Townsend to leave the room. Townsend refused saying, "If I do, you'll raise my salary, and this would be counterproductive to everything I'm trying to accomplish."

Peter also noted the U.S. military, where a top general was frequently responsible for life-and-death decisions, and who in time of war, might have several hundred thousand, or even a million or more subordinates, and millions of dollars of stores and equipment. Such an individual was paid $100,000 a year, with no bonuses. Of course, inflation has taken its toll. Today, the top of the scale for a full general with the maximum year's service is $169,995.56, whereas the newest and lowest ranking private makes $14,137.20. The pay ratio of top general officer to newly enlisted private is 12:1. What is the ratio of the CEO's salary to the newest and lowest ranking employee in your company?

Unfortunately, I failed to write down some of Drucker's other examples, but surely few executives can equal that of Ken Iverson, once CEO of the then multi-billion dollar Nucor Corporation, one of the three largest companies then producing steel in the U.S.

The Kind of Executive Drucker Meant

Ken Iverson has long since retired. In fact, he passed away in 2002. However, when Iverson was CEO of Nucor, this steel company, the third largest in the nation, consistently racked up high profits in what can only be termed a declining industry. Nucor's 7,000 employees were the best-paid workers in the steel business, yet they had the industry's lowest labor costs per ton of steel produced. Although a Fortune 500 company, only twenty-four people were assigned to corporate headquarters, and there were only four layers of management between the CEO to the front-line worker.

When Iverson first became CEO, the business was failing. He built Nucor into a profitable giant, and some indication as to his methods relate exactly to Drucker's point about executive salaries relative to that of the workers. When the steel industry almost went under in 1982, the total number of steelworkers in the industry dropped practically overnight from 400,000 to 200,000.

At Nucor, they had to cut production in half. Iverson did not, however, "downsize" anyone. How did he avoid doing what every other steel company did? Iverson insisted that management take large pay cuts. Department heads took pay cuts of up to 40 percent. For top management, Iverson insisted that company officers cut their salaries up to 60 percent. At a time when Fortune 500 CEOs were taking home millions of dollars in compensation, Iverson cut his own pay from $450,000 to $110,000, a salary cut of more than 75 percent.

When that wasn't sufficient, Iverson cut back work weeks from five to four days, and then, to three days a week. This meant that, on average, his workers suffered a 25 percent cut in pay. "You know that had to hurt," said Iverson. "Still, as I walked through our mills and plants, I never heard one employee complain about it. Not one."[2] That's not too surprising when those workers fully understood that their leaders were taking significant cuts also.

According to Iverson, "It was the only right thing to do. Of course, nothing is written in stone. If we have to lay people off some day to save Nucor, we'll do it. But not before we try everything else first. We call that 'pain sharing.' When times are good, we share the benefits, and when times are bad, leaders have to share that as well. For all of us, but leaders especially, there is a duty that comes before personal interest, and certainly before my personal interest."[3]

On his part, Peter Drucker set the example in his own behavior. There is no doubt that his genius and its application in consulting to corporations, and his writing, made him a wealthy man. Yet he lived simply in a modest house in a middle-class neighborhood in Claremont. As someone once pointed out, he could have started "the Drucker Group," cloned himself, and leveraged his name to become perhaps the largest consulting firm in the world. He didn't, because he knew what he wanted to do and the contributions he wanted to make in life. Such wealth as he attained was only a by-product of his contributions and the main goal he set for himself.

The Responsibilities of the Leader

His lecture well represented what Drucker was trying to teach us about the responsibilities and accountability of management and of any leader. He could not understand how any top executive could be earning high compensation while the business was performing poorly or if there was a need for layoffs.

Actually, this example of the accountability of the leader was but one of many examples that Drucker gave during this lecture and others. However, what stuck with me was that this particular example emphasized that the leader or company executive was always responsible, even for actions that he did not personally initiate, such as having his own salary raised.

In many ways, Drucker's lecture on the accountability of management emphasized something I was taught early on in my own career. I believe leaders in all organizations, including those in business, should adopt it without qualification. Namely, this is that a leader is responsible for everything that his or her organization accomplishes or fails to accomplish, regardless of other factors, including the business or economic climate or anything else. It is the leader who is always responsible!

In reviewing my own experiences as a leader over the years, in the military, in business, and in academia, I cannot think of a single failure in which some action or lack of action on my part was not the root cause or a major contributing factor to a less-than-desirable outcome. Executive salaries, which Drucker used as his prime example, were but representative of all executive actions or inactions for which an executive is ultimately and always responsible and accountable.

Union Accountability

Leaving top management, Drucker then turned to labor, and especially the unions. He told us that there was a time when management ruthlessly exploited workers, and unions were formed to protect the worker from this mistreatment. So the formation of unions to protect the worker was well justified. However, in the United States and many other countries, labor laws now largely protected workers from unfair practices. The problem was that most unions saw themselves as accountable only for worker welfare.

They did not in any way consider themselves accountable for worker performance or productivity.

According to Peter, unions had become accustomed to demanding more benefits every time a new labor contract was negotiated. The union membership expected this. In fact, the norm was to make demands that everyone knew would not be met, but then the final terms would be better yet than the previous contract. The problem was clearly that while the unions were gaining more compensation and more favorable working conditions for their membership, they were not accountable for worker productivity or manufacturing costs, and therefore any negative impact on the corporation was simply viewed as management's responsibility. The unions' view, of course, was that since management was pulling down salaries that weren't commensurate with their contribution, why should workers do otherwise? This view reflected back on what Drucker saw as management's accountability and responsibilities and how they were related.

As Drucker saw it, labor had to be held accountable just as did management. Adding benefits without increasing productivity just meant that workers were increasingly less productive and that the company was increasingly less competitive in the world marketplace. For a start, Drucker thought that boards of directors should include union representatives who were full and voting members. This wasn't the practice in those days.

What Peter was stressing was that in an internationally competitive environment, the time was long past when management and unions in a company should consider themselves as adversaries on the opposite side of the fence. Company managers and workers were not in competition; they were both on the same side.

After this lecture, one of my doctoral classmates, the vice president of a division of a major corporation, showed me a book that had been given to all senior divisional managers in his corporation. The title was something to the effect of "Keeping the Union Out and Minimizing Its Effect." Certainly this was clear evidence that at least this major corporation considered the relationship adversarial.

Former astronaut Frank Borman later served as CEO of Eastern Airlines. I had known Frank since the time I was a cadet at West Point. When he was a young Air Force captain, Frank had been my professor of Thermodynamics. Frank was a book author as well. In his book *Countdown: An Autobiography* (Silver Arrow Books, 1988), he speaks of flying with Eastern Airlines pilots for the first time after he became CEO.

As a pilot and former test pilot, he thought he would have much in common with them. He was extremely disappointed to discover that rather than the close relationship and rapport he anticipated as one pilot to another, his pilots took the attitude that he was management, they were labor. They considered themselves adversaries, not fellow members of Eastern Airlines with common flying backgrounds working toward the same goals in the same organization.

The Kind of Thing You'd Like to See

For a number of years I worked with a company called Vector Marketing. Vector Marketing used almost entirely college students as their door-to-door salespeople who sold some of the highest-quality kitchen knives in the world under the brand name "CUTCO." During World War II, one division introduced the famous K-bar knife, the official knife of the U.S. Marine Corps. As a university professor, I was a strong supporter since I felt that the experience that these young students gained from Vector taught them great lessons in leadership, business, hard work, and a lot more.

Erick Laine is chairman of the board of Alcas, Inc., the company which oversees manufacturing, marketing, and sales of CUTCO products world-wide. But when Laine took over as CEO in 1982, sales were only $5 million. Vector sales today are over $200 million worldwide. That's a 4,000 percent increase in a field that older, established brands from Europe have dominated on the high end.

When Erick became CEO of Alcas, his manufacturing arm was in disarray. In a nine-year period prior to his becoming boss, there wasn't a single contract that was settled without a strike. There were no less than 270 outstanding grievances on the books!

Now, in addition to integrity, Laine is tough. He was born in Finland, and his parents taught him something that doesn't translate easily into English. The word in Finnish is "*Sisu,*" which means a sort of stubborn persistence wrapped up with sheer guts. He knows what he is doing, and he is no pushover. But he truly cares about his people and he insists on treating them fairly. They aren't only union members; they are part of the Alcas team.

So Laine met with his union in a spirit of openness and listened. And when the union was right, he acknowledged it. And when he thought they were full of bologna, he told them that, too. But then, a strange thing happened. They proceeded to work things through together. Over a period of years they developed great trust, and when management and the union had a problem, they worked together to solve it.

Does your union present you with a yearly gift of cash collected from your workers? I don't know whether this is still done or not, but for a number of years, every year at Christmastime, a very unique thing happened at Alcas. It was not mandated, and neither Erick Laine nor any of his managers thought it up. No, this idea originated with his workers and their union. The union leaders would call Erick and request a meeting with him. At the meeting, the union representatives presented cash to their management . . . money they had collected from the workers on a volunteer basis. Erick always accepted the money on behalf of management, but then he always used the money to purchase something that would benefit the workers, like a TV for the cafeteria or a clock . . . that type of thing.[4]

Now why do you think the workers and their union did this? Obviously, they could have just collected the money and gone out and bought something for themselves. Erick Laine didn't tell me this, but I believe this informal and unusual ceremony occurred because it was a symbol of the trust between Alcas's union and management, between the company leaders and their workers. It is rare and unprecedented. It happened only because Erick Laine really cared about his workers and because the union and management were part of the same team.

This is the sort of story that Drucker would have liked. It was a sure sign that both labor and management had accepted responsibilities and worked toward the same goals. It was a sign that labor understood that increasing wages and benefits without increasing productivity was detrimental to the corporation, both labor and management, and it was a symbol to management of an almost sacred trust that they must not break by foolishly increasing their own salaries, benefits, and perquisites without granting similar benefits to their employees.

The Right Attitude

I think it was one of my seminar students, and not Peter, who told me this story. Nevertheless, I like it so well that I have often repeated it, although I have long since forgotten the source. I continue to tell it because it is an excellent example of the right attitude on the part of a chief executive to encourage a similar right attitude on the part of labor.

Anyway, the story goes like this. A CEO took an extended vacation in Europe. For whatever reason, a conflict between labor and management arose during his absence and his workers went out on strike. I don't know why the CEO wasn't informed of the impending problem as it occurred, or at least prior to the action of the union, but apparently he was not. In any case, he immediately cut short his trip and flew back to his embattled company. He found all work stopped, his employees on the picket line, and union and management not even talking with one another. He took the following actions immediately on arrival:

1. A temporary shelter was erected along with refreshments near the picket line for the benefit of his striking workers.

2. Baseball bats, balls, and gloves were made available on loan, and a nearby vacant lot was prepared, so that those employees not currently on the picket line could play baseball if they wished.

3. The company set up a day-care center to take of the children of striking employees who needed these services because of the strike.

Other services to accommodate striking employees were also implemented. The clear message was that these employees may be on strike due to a grievance with the company, but they are *our* employees. As you might imagine, the strike was soon settled.

Joint Responsibility

Peter felt strongly that management and employees had a joint responsibility for performance. He said that both the boss and subordinates needed to get things right. "Too many bosses," he said, "assume that what they want done is obvious or easily understood." In fact, the opposite is usually true. "Frequently," he said, "it is communication which is the problem. However, sometimes there is no communication at all."

This comment reminded me of a graduate student I knew who had interned with a well-known consulting company. The student's boss was known to be brilliant, but she couldn't seem to retain subordinates for very long, whether they were full-time or interns. This executive traveled frequently. She instructed her intern to prepare a presentation on a certain subject and to have it ready on her return, as she would be leaving again the following day. She was called out of the room during her discussion with the student, and left town without him being able to speak with her or her contacting him further.

The student tried without success to communicate with his boss during her trip, by both telephone and e-mail. She was always unavailable when he called and never returned his calls. He asked others, and even her boss, about the assignment. No one knew anything more about the presentation than the information the student had already been given. Knowing that his boss expected a completed presentation ready to go, he did the best that he could with the sparse information he had.

His boss returned and immediately asked to be briefed on the presentation. He went over the presentation with his boss. "This is a terrible job," she said. "This isn't what I wanted at all. I'm leaving tomorrow morning. Now I'll need to stay up the entire evening putting together a presentation myself."

The student resigned from his internship on his boss's return from this second trip. "I admire the fact that you know when you are in over your head," his boss said.

On graduation, the student got a job with another company where he was a great success. When last heard of, he had gained early promotion to vice president.

Peter told us a similar story. Then he added: "I wish I could say that such instances of subordinates being treated grossly unfairly were rare, but unfortunately they are not."

I raised my hand. "I believe I can top your story," I said. Peter looked at me. This was unusual. I rarely volunteered myself in this way. "Proceed," he directed.

How Miscommunication Got an Engineer Unfairly Fired

The story I told in class that day involved my then new job at McDonnell Douglas Astronautics Company. My job as a marketing manager was to support our high-technology engineers and scientists in marketing to the U.S. government. I set up appointments with each of the chief engineers and introduced myself so that I could meet each one personally. They would know me better and I could gain some immediate understanding of their problems in the area I was going to be responsible for.

John Fletcher, one of the chief engineers, told me the account of his first day of work as an engineer back in 1940. This was the story I told

Peter and his class. Fletcher had just graduated from engineering school prior to World War II and was immediately hired by the Boeing Aircraft Company in Seattle, Washington. He was one of five brand-new engineers to show up at work that day. They were all assigned to one particular chief engineer for duties. The chief engineer gave each of them a job to be completed by the end of the day.

One of John's fellow new hires was given a number of large aluminum sheets, which were dirty with black ink and from much use. These were "blueprints" of the B-17, which was being manufactured for the Army Air Force by Boeing. However, instead of the blueprints being made of paper, these were sheets of aluminum on which the lines of the drawings were permanently etched. "I want you to clean these sheets completely and so well that I can use any one of them as a mirror by this afternoon," the chief engineer said, and handed them to the neophyte engineer. "I don't want to see one mark or smudge on any of them."

That afternoon, the five engineers met with the chief engineer again to present their completed projects to him. The new hire with the aluminum sheets proudly handed them to the chief engineer. They were bright and spotless. Anyone could have used one as a mirror. The new engineer had scrubbed each with steel wool before polishing it to a bright shine. Unfortunately, there was a problem. The ink smudges and grime were gone, but so were the etchings. The engineer had scrubbed them off to make the aluminum sheets spotless, just as he was instructed. John said that the chief engineer had instantly fired the new graduate.

John told me that he had never forgotten this experience, and he always remembered it when giving instructions to subordinates. "It wasn't the new hire's fault," he said. "It was the chief engineer's. The new hire had done exactly as he was told. The new engineer was too inexperienced to understand that the etchings were important and were to have been protected and not scrubbed off. I would have probably done exactly the same thing; any of us would have, given the chief engineer's instructions."

Peter agreed that this was exactly the sort of thing he was talking about. But he went further. "There is," he said, "something that can prevent just this sort of occurrence, and I recommend it to all of you whenever you change employment, or receive a new job assignment. It is in your interests, as well as those of your boss, to have a signed charter or performance contract."

Drucker Recommends Writing a Charter

"There are numerous opportunities for miscommunications," Drucker said. "Moreover, many executives forget what they have instructed their subordinates to do, especially over time. As a result, unless it is written down, and preferably signed by both the boss and his employee, the employee may well assume he is doing a satisfactory, or even an exceptional job in whatever he is doing. Yet, it may not be what his boss wanted done at all. Frequently the plan changes and not all subordinates are told. A charter describing what is expected over the coming period can ensure that both you and your boss are working towards the same goals.

"If you are a new employee," he added, "it is even more important that you get such a charter. Most bosses will not suggest this. So, as a new company manager, I would suggest that you develop a draft of such a charter yourself. Sit down and write out what you think your boss wants you to do over the coming year. Show it to him and get his input. Make corrections or changes as required. Date it and sign it, and ask him to sign it, too. Ask him if you can review it with him periodically to determine if you are reaching the goals he has set for you.

"Few will object, and such a charter will save you, your boss, and your organization a lot of trouble."

Much later I learned that it was Peter who had first articulated the concept of management by objectives in one of his early books, *The Practice of Management,* (New York: Harper & Row, 1954). What was Peter's "charter" but a version of management by objectives?

Peter also told us that if we were "the boss," we would do well to initiate such a process with our subordinates. Alas, I had already stumbled as a manager due to the lack of such a technique. I had, unfairly, not given an increase to a subordinate because I did not make my priorities clear, and no charter existed. Fortunately, I was able to correct my error and I never repeated this mistake in the future.

Peter gave us one additional important piece of advice that night. "Communication works two ways," he said, "and information moving in both directions is equally important. As a boss is accountable for information from the top down, those who report to him are responsible for information from the bottom up. Some bosses are readers, others listeners. However, every boss prefers one of these two methods. What is important is that there will be a significant improvement in comprehension when the method preferred by your boss is used. If you have a boss, it is your responsibility, and you are accountable for discovering and using whichever of these two means of communication your boss prefers."

Drucker Lesson Summary

Everyone in a corporation, both management and labor, is responsible and accountable for various aspects of the success of any of the organization's endeavors. Executives cannot avoid this accountability when they have the ability to take action which avoids a threat, solves a problem, or takes advantage of an opportunity. Mid-level managers cannot avoid accountability even when it springs from an action that might have been taken, but was not, by a boss. And workers, too, are part of the team. They and their union are also accountable for actions which help or hinder the organization that employs them. Accountability is enhanced by means of a written charter and attention to communications both by boss and by employee.

CHAPTER THIRTEEN

You Must Know Your People to Lead Them

*D*rucker knew that knowing his students was a major responsibility of a classroom leader, and he knew that this was an important function for any leader and manager in any environment. Leadership is complex. To lead successfully, you must see every single person you would have follow you as a separate individual. For a start, you can learn the names of those you lead. It doesn't really matter how large an organization you lead.

Peter was a real leader who led by example. He himself had almost been a dean at Bennington College in Vermont early in his career. Because of this leadership wasn't theoretical; he knew how to lead from personal experience. Drucker's demonstrated leadership in the classroom led me to the conclusion that to be a classroom instructor of the first order, one had to be a good leader. As evidence, I noted an important lesson from him. A good leader knows his or her followers.

Drucker Really Knew Those He Led

I was surprised as to the extent that Drucker knew and was able to master the names of his students and how much he knew about each one. I have seen Peter ask about a student's son or daughter. But, by the very way he inquired, you knew that he already knew quite a bit. He didn't just ask, "How is your daughter doing?" It was, "How is your daughter doing in law school?" Or if he heard something from the parent more recently, "How is your daughter doing in law school with that exam she was concerned about?"

After I left Claremont, Drucker would sometimes ask me about something that I had been working on or was concerned about the last time we had spoken, something that I may have actually forgotten about myself. Peter, however, did not forget. He strived to learn about his students at every opportunity, and he remembered who he met and what they said to him. I learned this from an experience at the beginning of my second year as his student.

At the start of every academic year, Claremont's business school hosted a party for all the graduate students. My wife Nurit met Peter at one such party at the beginning of my first year as a new doctoral student. He probably met a hundred or more wives of his students at the party that evening. Peter was his usual gracious self as he conversed with Nurit. He talked with her for a couple of minutes, and that was it.

I should add that Nurit was very favorably impressed with him. This is not always how she feels on meeting well-known people. Too many, she says, are "full of themselves." (She is quick to point out that I also sometimes get into such a mode, and when I do, she let's me know it.) However, being "full of himself" was never Peter's way. So when I asked her about her impressions of him, she told me he was, "sincere, a good conversationalist, and self-confident without being arrogant." Then she added (and Nurit was already headed toward becoming a clinical psychologist): "He knows who he is and what he has accomplished without feeling the need to prove anything to anyone. I liked him."

A year later we attended the annual beginning-of-the-year party again. In the interim, Nurit had not seen or talked with Drucker at all. We became separated at the event and she ran into Peter without my being present. She greeted him and began to say, "You probably won't remember me but I'm . . . " Before she could complete her sentence he interrupted. "Of course, I know you. You're Nurit Cohen, Bill Cohen's wife." This was all the more amazing because my wife is an Israeli and her Hebrew name, Nurit, is not exactly a common name with which Drucker would have been familiar.

A General Does Even Better

I told this story about Peter's phenomenal memory of his students to a group of senior military people once, and someone topped it. He told me that when he attended National War College in Washington D.C., the commandant, the War College's equivalent of a campus president, was a major general in the Marines.

Like Claremont, the school year began with a party for the new class and their spouses. There was no second party as the course was only a year long. He said that when each officer and his spouse entered they were greeted by a receiving line consisting only of the commandant and his wife. In the military, that itself was unusual. The modus operandi is for a receiving line in which an aide is the first to greet the guests. The aide takes the names of the military member and his spouse and introduces them to the senior officer. The senior officer then introduces the couple to his or her own spouse. In this case, there was no aide to first hear the names of each couple.

The commandant had met few of the hundred or so officers from all branches of the armed forces in the new class previously, and probably none of their spouses. Yet he amazed each couple by addressing them by their correct first and last names and introducing them correctly to his wife. Moreover, according to the senior officer telling me the story, the general seemed to know about their children and their off-duty activities and interests. His new students were dumbfounded. When occasionally asked by someone how he knew so much about them, he would only smile and say, "A good commander makes it his business to know those for whose well-being he is responsible."

Now I have heard of professional memory experts being able to do things like this, but never anyone else, much less a military commander. The general's students thought he was beyond having a photographic memory—that he had to be some kind of a psychic. The social talk that night at the party was about the commandant and his remarkable performance.

The next day the general addressed the entire class as a group for the first time. He explained the mystery of how he was able to know not only the names, but so much else about his new students and their families. Months before their arrival, all students were asked to submit a family picture and facts about their career and interests. This information would be circulated to the entire class so that they would more quickly get acquainted for this intensive year of top-level learning.

The commandant had assembled these responses and taken the time to study these photographs and learn all of his students' names and a few facts about them. He told his assembled students that he had done this for an important reason: all leaders must know everything they can about their subordinates. Only in this way can a leader lead in such a way as to maximize success of the organization to reach its objectives.

"Moreover," he said, "I wanted to demonstrate that it could be done. No one is obligated to learn so much about so many subordinates and their families in such a short amount of time. But it can be done."

Then the commandant told them that from his study of the material they had sent in months earlier, he knew that they had a great class. As this commandant had shown beyond any doubt that he really knew their backgrounds, he wasn't just speaking "out of his hat." He was sincere, and his sincerity was based on fact.

A College Dean Goes Even One Better

Barry Richardson is an editor at AMACOM, the publisher of this book. Barry told me the following story: "When I was a freshman at Trinity College (Hartford, CT) our dean memorized all the incoming students' names and hometowns by studying the freshman handbook. Trinity had about 2,000 students altogether at that time, so I guess he was memorizing approximately 500 faces, names, and hometowns. When I ran into the dean on the campus quad and he said, "Hi, Barry. How are things in Rockville Centre?" I was floored. The dean's remarkable 'feat' was mentioned time and again in any conversation with fellow freshmen that first week."

Now you may consider the actions of this general and dean a bit overboard. Maybe we don't need to go as far as they did to learn about the people we work and interact with. Nevertheless, it is a fact that without those people we cannot succeed, no matter who we are, or what heights we have reached in our professions. Knowing and understanding people we work with is an important secret of success for any leader.

Timeless Advice

How To Win Friends and Influence People (New York: Simon and Schuster, 1937) by Dale Carnegie is one of the most popular books ever written. It has sold over 100 million copies in many editions since it was written seventy years ago. It is still selling today. In his book Carnegie wrote: "Remember that a man's name is to him the sweetest and most important sound in the English language."[1]

Carnegie devoted an entire chapter to how to remember someone's name and the importance of doing so. He pointed out that another Carnegie, Andrew Carnegie, the poor Scot immigrant who became one of the wealthiest men in America as a steel manufacturer, knew next to nothing about the manufacture of steel. Andrew Carnegie's strength was his leadership, and it was based on knowledge of his employees. Andrew Carnegie was proud of the fact that he knew many of his workers by their first names. He bragged that there was never a strike when he personally was in charge.[2]

I don't know whether Peter, the Marine general, or Barry Richardson's dean, read *How To Win Friends and Influence People* or not, but they certainly followed many of the key concepts taught in it.

As a professor, I tried to follow Drucker's example. I must have succeeded to some extent, because many students asked me how I knew their names and facts about them. Fortunately, I never had to duplicate the performance of the Marine general or dean. However, I did have a procedure which worked very well for me.

I would study the roll I was given before the first class. At the universities at which I taught, I was required to take the roll at the first two classes. Both times that I took roll, I watched who responded. I also had each student introduce him or herself the first day of class. I didn't ask them to describe what they hoped to get from the course. Let's face it, 99.9 percent just wanted to get through the course with a passing grade. However, I did ask them to tell the class something about themselves. While they were doing this, I took notes. Whenever I could, I tried to use their names and I asked them to correct me if I mispronounced a name, or had it wrong.

I don't mean to say that I was celebrated by all as a "psychic" teacher and never made a mistake in identifying who was who in dealing with my students. However, I do believe that I was a much better instructor because I learned my students' names and remembered important things about their interests and backgrounds. I believe that they were able to learn more due to my efforts, because they realized that they were important to me as individuals, not just students.

I have since discovered that there are many techniques and books on how to memorize people's names and learn them with minimum effort. Of course, just knowing someone's name doesn't mean that you really know them. There is a lot more that you must do. However, learning the names of those that report to you, even if the number is large, is a good start. It is certainly something that Drucker did. Following Drucker's example helped me both as a leader in the classroom and in the "real world." However, there is more that managers should do in knowing his or her workers and employees. Let's follow Drucker's way and look at some of these other aspects of knowing your people.

Get Out and Talk with Those You Would Lead

If Peter confined interaction with his students to the classroom, I doubt that he would have known his students as well or had the same impact on them. To the best of my knowledge, Drucker never passed up the opportunity to interact with his students outside of the classroom. He not only attended such university events as the beginning-of-school-year party, but every school event to which he was invited—and he was invited to many.

I have seen professors of far less stature than Peter who have declined invitations from their own universities to participate in activities, apparently because they considered themselves too important or too busy for the event. Peter was never too busy. Consequently, his students interacted with him frequently, even when no longer taking courses from him. This continued with alumni and other events after graduation. Consequently Peter was able to stay abreast of his students' activities after graduation much better than most professors.

This translates in other organizations to getting out of the office, meeting people face-to-face, and actually talking with people who you lead. It doesn't seem to make much difference who you are leading. You certainly can't lead from behind a desk, and what you can learn and know about your people is greatly expanded when you see them face-to-face.

Then McKinsey consultants Tom Peters and Robert Waterman found a technique in use by executives in a number of successful companies, including Hewlett-Packard, GE, PepsiCo, Lucasfilm, Corning Glass, 3M,

Disney, and Wal-Mart. They popularized this technique in their best-selling book *In Search of Excellence* (HarperCollins, 1982) and called it MBWA, which stands for "management by wandering around."

The technique is hardly new. Two thousand years ago, Julius Caesar was popular with his soldiers because he wandered around seeing for himself what was going on and learning the names of even the most junior subordinates.

You've got to see those that you lead and let them see you. Robert W. Galvin, was chief executive officer and later chairman of the board of Motorola, Inc. Under his leadership, Motorola sales grew from $216.6 million to $6.7 billion. As a practicing top manager, Galvin knew the value of going around to really get to know his people. He told his managers: "I believe we in top management must circulate."[3]

Douglas D. Danforth, then chairman of the board at the Westinghouse Corporation, echoed this sentiment: "The better the CEO knows his key people personally, the better he will be able to correctly estimate their strengths."[4]

Of course, you can't manage only by wandering around and talking with people. And while you wander around making decisions, you need to be careful that you don't take authority away from middle management leaders functioning between you and the people you are visiting. Still, when you go out and see and are seen by those you lead, you greatly increase the effectiveness of communications up and down the chain of command. You find out what's right and what's wrong in your organization. And you can correct things instantly. You can dramatize your ideas to your followers. That way the word gets around . . . fast.

Perhaps even more importantly, when you go out to see and be seen, you not only learn what's going on, you learn who your people really are. A subordinate isn't just a peg in a round or square hole with certain skills, who is paid a certain amount of money and has a certain position in your organization. A subordinate is much more. He or she is a person of flesh and blood. This person has a wife or husband, girlfriend or boyfriend, children, hopes, dreams, problems, victories, defeats, and opportunities. Each individual has unique qualities, abilities, capabilities, and limitations. Faced with a certain situation, each person will usually react differently. Each person has the potential of contributing much to your organization, or of committing errors which can drag it down and cause it to fail.

Management consultant Harry K. Jones developed the following ten suggestions regarding how you implement MBWA:

1. Appear relaxed as you make your rounds. Employees will reflect your feelings and actions.

2. Remain open and responsive to questions and concerns.

3. Observe and listen, and let everyone see you doing it.

4. Make certain your visits are spontaneous and unplanned.

5. Talk with employees about their passions—whether family, hobbies, vacations, or sports.

6. Ask for suggestions to improve operations, products, service, sales, etc.

7. Try to spend an equal amount of time in all areas of your organization.

8. Catch your employees doing something right and recognize them publicly.

9. Convey the image of a coach—not an inspector.

10. Encourage your employees to show you how the real work of the company gets done.[5]

Another Advantage to Knowing Your People

When it comes to making staffing decisions, knowing the people you lead is a big advantage. Peter told us once that General George C. Marshall, Chief of Staff of the U.S. Army during World War II, and later Secretary of State under President Truman, probably knew more about his senior leaders than any other Chief of Staff in the history of the United States. Marshall kept a diary in which he listed all those he met and important facts about each person, including strengths and weaknesses and where each person could fit in time of need or crisis. When World War II came and the army expanded from a couple of hundred thousand soldiers to more than five million within a year, he knew just who to put where for maximum effectiveness.

Dwight Eisenhower was one of the officers he rapidly promoted. Eisenhower was an unknown lieutenant colonel commanding a few hundred men in 1940. Marshall quickly made him a general; and four years later, he commanded the D-day landing, the largest invasion in history, with more than a million men from many nations under his command.

Other Means of Getting to Know Your People

There are other ways of getting to know your people. Many of these are activities in which you can initiate yourself and can assign people to different roles if you are the head of the organization. These include:

- internal social activities;

- internal job-related activities;

- internal societal-benefit activities;

- external professional activities; and

- external societal-benefit activities.

All of these are important for you in observing and getting to know your people in a wide variety of situations. Many of these activities require a number of management and leadership roles. That's good, too, because it gives you an opportunity to observe your people in action and see how they themselves perform as leaders in different roles. I once worked for an executive who used these outside-of-the-normal-workday opportunities to test the leadership potential of those managers reporting to him. I call these "uncrowned" leadership roles because the leaders have limited and only temporary authority over others in these situations.

INTERNAL SOCIAL ACTIVITIES

Parties, such as those I spoke of that Drucker attended, are examples of internal social activities. However, these kinds of parties are just one example. There are also company picnics, sporting events, management clubs, retirements, award ceremonies, and more. All of these activities require someone to organize and run them. If your subordinates know that you use these activities to help you decide about future promotions, you'll probably have many who will volunteer for the jobs. Of course, this is true about all five categories of activities we will look at.

INTERNAL JOB-RELATED ACTIVITIES

There are many job-related activities that cut across organizational lines and for which you do not need a permanent organization. I was not a fan of the Total Quality Management (TQM) movement, which was very popular several years ago, because of the way it was practiced in many organizations. I certainly agreed that quality was central and that ownership was important and that continuous improvement was an eminently worthy goal. The problem, as I saw it, was in the way TQM was applied, or rather misapplied, which actually caused more problems than it solved in some organizations.

Still, there were various concepts promoted as integral parts of "TQM" which were quite good. One was the process action team, sometimes referred to as a PAT team. The idea of the PAT team was that the team, made up of members from a number of relevant organizations, would study a problem or opportunity and then present a solution that would be implemented. This is where the concept, as practiced, sometimes ran into trouble.

The team was "empowered," and its solution wasn't merely a recommendation. Management was supposed to commit to implementation of whatever the team came up with, like it or not. That was the problem. Not only did the team operate without the benefit of an overall management perspective, but the situation might have changed by the time they completed their analysis. However, this doesn't mean that the idea of cross-discipline problem-solving teams wasn't a good idea. Emphasis on teamwork is here to stay, and problem-solving teams of this type present an excellent opportunity to see the leadership of participants at all levels of experience, profession, and management within an organization.

INTERNAL SOCIETAL-BENEFIT ACTIVITIES

Many companies take on tasks which are primarily for the benefit of organizations outside of the company, but are done on the company's premises and usually on company time. Community fund drives and savings-bond drives are a couple of examples. Some companies simply give these tasks to a secretary or to the most junior member of the organization. To me, that is a waste of an excellent opportunity to get to know and give leadership experience to some of your younger managers.

I once met a young man who had advanced very rapidly in his company as an engineer. I learned that his "breakthrough" assignment came shortly after his hiring, but had little to do with his regularly assigned duties in his company. Once a year the company and every organization in it conducted a savings-bond drive. No one wanted the additional work of persuading the organization's employees to sign up for additional bond deductions from their paychecks and keeping the records this effort required. Since no one wanted the job, they assigned these duties to the most junior engineer, or sometimes to a secretary. Most people assigned this project did the minimum work possible and made no serious attempt at convincing people to make additional investments. Predictably, results were generally very poor.

However, this young man was different. Given the unwanted assignment, he really took charge. He convinced every engineer and manager in his department that was working on location to buy more bonds. But he didn't stop there. He called all over the country to talk to company engineers who were traveling. He motivated them by telling them that they could be the top organization in competing with other departments in the company for bond purchases.

At first, many of the veteran engineers bought bonds because his enthusiasm and sincerity amused them. Then, almost in spite of themselves, they got caught up in the competition. No one had ever appealed to them in this way before. Of course, this organization finished first in bond purchases in the company by a large margin. That wasn't the end of it. The department head noticed that although savings bonds had very little to do with engineering, the bond drive had helped to increase productivity. People just seemed to feel better about themselves as members of the organization and wanted to perform better. When they actually won this competition, which no one had ever taken seriously before, they really felt good!

The president of the company noticed the unusual bond drive results and was impressed. He asked the engineering department manager about them. Shortly thereafter, an opening for a junior manager of a small project appeared. The department head remembered the young engineer's success at organizing the bond campaign and selling bonds. He knew that if this engineer could accomplish so much with a bond drive, he probably could do the same with a project in his own profession.

The young man was promoted over twenty other engineers who had more seniority in the company for this small engineering project. He did so well in this job that when the next opportunity came up, he was promoted again. All of this was years ago. The young engineer went on to even greater success, eventually including a company presidency. I've often thought about management's success in discovering this young engineer's leadership abilities so early. Perhaps they should have considered using the bond drive and other similar opportunities to help them better get to know their people and their potential for early promotion.

EXTERNAL PROFESSIONAL ACTIVITIES

There are leadership positions in all sorts of professional organizations outside of a company's activities, as well as opportunities to demonstrate professional leadership by writing articles for publication in professional journals.

Make certain that external professional activities like these are promoted in your organization. When someone is active as an accountant, engineer, salesperson, marketer, or human resources worker in a professional organization, take note of it. Write a letter of congratulations, publicize and encourage these activities. Your paying attention to what people are doing demonstrates that you are taking the time to know them. It rewards their extra work and contribution, and it also helps give your organization a good name.

EXTERNAL SOCIETAL-BENEFIT ACTIVITIES

An example of external societal-benefit activities might be a fund-raiser done outside the company for a good cause, cleaning up a park, or anything else that needs to be done and benefits society. Again, there are many opportunities to develop leadership here.

These activities provide powerful opportunities for you to learn more about your workers. The only cautionary note is to be careful about stressing these activities to the extent that it takes away from the organization's main mission. Done correctly, however, these activities can support the mission of your organization, as well as help you to really know and understand your people and to develop and make the best use of their talents.

Drucker Lesson Summary

There is little question that the leader of any organization of any size has an amazing impact on that organization and the outcome of whatever activity in which it is engaged. All of us have seen organizations that were previous failures, flourish when a new leader is put in charge. The new leader may have the same resources as the previous leader, or he or she may have more or less resources. It doesn't seem to matter. What does matter is the leader himself. If it is the right person for the right job, frequently the turnaround is almost instantaneous.

For leaders at all levels, what this means is that it is critical that you know your people, their capabilities and limitations, and how they are likely to react in any situation. The more you can do this, the better you are able to lead them. Drucker knew this, and he taught and practiced it. By getting to know the people, without whom you will accomplish nothing, you can:

- Know what's going on in your organization every day.

- Help those who need help.

- Get help from those who can supply help.

- Discover the real problems.

- Uncover opportunities you didn't know existed.

- Praise and recognize those that deserve it.

- Correct or discipline those that need it.

- Get your word out fast.

- Communicate your vision for the organization.

- Insure everyone understands your goals and objectives.

CHAPTER FOURTEEN

People Have No Limits, Even After Failure

O ccasionally I have been asked whether the Peter Principle was one of Peter Drucker's concepts. It was not. The Peter Principle came from a best-selling book of the same name, written by an academic named Laurence J. Peter. Moreover, Peter (Drucker, that is) thought the "Principle" was badly mistaken, easily disproved, and likely to lead to serious problems at many levels of management if the "Principle" were actually applied as presented. But I'm getting ahead of myself.

In Peter's class, we had been discussing staffing and the selection of senior executives. Peter gave us a case which we were to write up and later to discuss regarding a failed promotion. Basically, the case concerned a senior appointment as a deputy to the CEO of a corporation. The appointee, a man by the name of "Novak," had a fine record of increasing responsibility over many years with the company. The CEO, who Drucker called "McQuinn," felt that there was no question that this was the right man for the job, and he made the appointment without stopping to think twice. However, for the first time in his career, Novak failed miserably.

McQuinn felt that Novak had no excuse. He decided that the appropriate solution was to fire Novak for his demonstrated incompetence at this higher level of management. However, the chairman had a policy that all senior firings had to be discussed first with him. So, McQuinn met with the chairman.

The chairman asked McQuinn for his analysis of Novak's failure. McQuinn told him that Novak made serious errors in judgment which had cost the company a great deal of money. When pressed further, McQuinn could not offer much, other than that clearly the job was too much for Novak to handle and that he had gone about as far up the corporate ladder as he could.

Much to McQuinn's surprise, the chairman blamed him for Novak's failure. He told McQuinn that, "The one thing we know for certain is that you made a mistake, since Novak was your appointment." Moreover, the chairman told him that to fire Novak was not only unfair, it was stupid. "Why should we lose a proven manager as valuable as Novak, just because you made a mistake?"

Drucker asked us what we thought of the chairman's argument. Almost immediately someone brought up the Peter Principle.

The Peter Principle

Dr. Laurence J. Peter was at the time an Associate Professor of Education at the University of Southern California. His well-known book based on what he called the "Peter Principle" was published in 1968. It was followed by several other books by him on the same general topic. His central concept was: "In a hierarchy every employee tends to rise to his level of incompetence." Being incompetent, they would be promoted no further, yet must be removed from his responsible position. If not, the organization could collapse when the number of incompetents among its ranks reached a critical number, resulting in the inability of the organization to perform its functions efficiently, effectively, or competitively.

The Peter Principle is based on the observation that organizations have hierarchies. New employees typically start in the lower ranks. As they do well and prove to be competent in their duties, they get promoted to the next higher rank. The process is then repeated. According to the principle, this process of promotion, followed by demonstrated competent performance, can go on indefinitely, or at least until the employee reaches a position where he or she is no longer competent. Then the process stops and the employee remains in the position without external intervention.

Returning the employee to his previous job at which he performed well is very difficult if not impossible. However, if some action to remove someone who had risen to his level of incompetence was not taken, the company would eventually suffer. The net result, according to Laurence J. Peter, was that most of the higher levels of any organization gradually would be filled by people who attained their positions because they were good at their previous job assignments, but were incompetent in their current positions. This concept resonated with many people who were delighted to consider their bosses as having risen to positions in which they were now demonstrating their incompetence.

While the Peter Principle paid some attention to cautioning that an employee promoted to a new job should be qualified for it, the general solution was that since the corporation could not demote these incompetents who had arrived at their final and incompetent level, it had to get rid of them, or suffer the consequence of inevitable failure due to a preponderance of incompetents in critical high-level positions. This made the Peter Principle a possible argument in McQuinn's defense in wanting to fire Novak.

Peter Drucker strongly disagreed.

Do People Really Rise to Their Levels of Incompetence?

Peter objected to the Peter Principle for several reasons. First, he suggested that the concept was overly simplistic. He stated that those who worked more with their minds, what Peter called "knowledge workers," were becoming more important in the workforce due to developing technology. Therefore, increasing numbers of managers were likely to be placed into positions in which they failed to perform in certain situations. Everything possible should be done to avoid this situation happening.

Peter said, "We have no right to ask people to take on jobs that will defeat them, no right to break good people. We don't have enough good young people to practice human sacrifice." The selection of the right person for the right job was the manager's responsibility. But even more importantly, the notion that people rise to their levels of incompetence was dangerous to the organization.

The Dangers of the Peter Principle

According to the Peter Principle, if an individual has arrived at his or her level of incompetence, logically the organization has little choice but to get rid of the incompetent employee before the entire organization becomes overloaded with incompetent managers who make more and more bad decisions. Yet, the concept and the recommended action has many down-sides. The only antidote to "incompetence" under the Peter Principle is dismissal. However, before one should even consider dismissal, the basic question concerns the assumption that failure is due to incompetence.

There is a story that Thomas Watson, founder of IBM, once asked to see a newly promoted vice president who failed on his first assignment and cost the company a million dollars. The young man reported to the IBM chief ready for the worst. "I guess you called me in to fire me," he said on entering Watson's office.

"Fire you!" exclaimed Watson, "We just spent one million dollars as part of your education."

A company that believes and applies the Peter Principle puts significant additional pressure on its managers not to make a mistake, even though mistakes are an inevitable part of taking action and a reasonable balance of risk taking. This additional pressure is hardly conducive to the manager's willingness to take risks or even assume full responsibility, both of which are essential. Such a "zero failure" climate will inevitably create problems.

An organization which buys into and practices this solution to the assumed reality of the Peter Principle is hardly encouraging or a morale booster for employees at any level. It says that a long term, hard-working, talented, and loyal employee must eventually and inevitably meet his fate. He will be plummeted headlong out of the corporation, or, at best, be "kicked upstairs" or put out to pasture in a nonentity job. Accordingly, every manager at every level had better take actions to ensure no mis-takes, no failures.

This particular problem recalls the 1970's movie *Logan's Run*. The movie involved a society which required that its members be killed upon reaching the age of thirty, thus maintaining a societal membership that was forever young. The movie's hero, Logan, was a member of this murderous society who was told he had reached the maximum age limit of thirty. This wasn't true, but has nothing to do with the point of my telling you the story.

Even this brutal society at least gave the appearance of giving its victims a fair break. Those reaching the magic age of thirty were forced to pass through a gauntlet of lethal laser beams. Those avoiding the beams, and thus surviving an instantaneous death, were allowed to leave the society with their lives. Reportedly, they now lived somewhere else and were never heard from or seen again. In reality, no one survived the lethal laser gauntlet, but no one in the youthful society knew this, except those who ran the system. However, this idea at least left some hope to those when they reached the age of life termination.

The Peter Principle doesn't leave even hope. It is ruthless in its dictate that managers reaching their level of incompetence must be removed for the good of the corporation.

Implicit in the theory is the assumption that if a manager is incompetent for one particular job, he or she couldn't function well in any job at the same or, of course, a higher level. It assumes that if a manager demonstrates incompetence and fails in one job, he or she cannot rebound to become a success in another. Both assumptions are in error and therefore not only unfair, but incredibly wasteful in human potential, for history is rife with "incompetents" who were later proved to be great successes.

The Peter Principle Disproved

Rowland Hussey Macy was a Nantucket Quaker. He studied business and then started a retail store. It failed. He started another. It failed, too. This happened six times, and he failed each time. Were his stores divisions of a Fortune 500 company practicing the Peter Principle, he would have been discharged after his first attempt as he would have clearly demonstrated his incompetence at retailing, business, and entrepreneurship. However, Macy's seventh attempt succeeded and he died a wealthy man. A hundred and fifty years later, Macy's still exists and earns roughly $30 billion in annual sales in approximately 800 stores. Not too bad a legacy for someone who had clearly risen to his level of incompetence six times before his overwhelming success.

Winston Churchill reached his level of incompetence as First Lord of the Admiralty during World War I, during which he succeeded in convincing the British War Cabinet to undertake the biggest Allied disaster of the war, the Dardanelles Campaign, including an Allied landing at Gallipoli. This resulted in the worst Allied defeat, with over 200,000 casualties, and Churchill's forced resignation from that particular job. Yet the same man, with much higher responsibilities as Prime Minister during World War II, saved England and possibly the world during almost a year, when the British stood alone against Hitler and his minions. Moreover, this "incompetent" is now considered the greatest British political figure of the 20th century.

Politicians are often great examples disproving the Peter Principle. While U.S. President Abraham Lincoln had his share of successes, he had more of his share of failures. He failed in business, ran for the Illinois State Legislature and at first was defeated, went into business again and went bankrupt, ran for Speaker of the Illinois State Legislature and was defeated, was defeated in his efforts to secure nomination to the U.S. Congress, was rejected for an appointment for the U.S. Land Office, was defeated in a U.S. Senate race, and two years later was defeated again in a nomination for vice president. Then, in 1860, he became our 16th president and saved the Union. To the best of my knowledge, not even his present-day detractors call him incompetent.

Drucker's Three Key Rules on Staffing

Peter's basic thought in the area of staffing was that you must first lower the failure rate. To do this, the appointing executive must staff for strength. Consequently, Drucker recommended three prime rules for staffing:

1. Think through the requirements of the job.

2. Choose three or four candidates for the job, rather than immediately settling on just one.

3. Don't make the selection without discussing the choice with a number of knowledgeable colleagues.

Let's look at each of these rules in turn.

(1) Think Through the Job Requirements

A poorly designed job, one in which the requirements have not been clearly thought through, may be an impossible job that no one can do. An impossible job means that work intended to be accomplished is accomplished poorly or not at all. In addition, this risks the destruction, or, at best, the misallocation of scarce and valuable human resources. To design a job properly, the objectives and requirements of the job must be thoroughly considered to decide those few requirements that are really crucial to the job's performance. That way, the executive seeking to fill the position can avoid filling it with a candidate who minimally meets all requirements rather than staffing for strength, based on the few critical areas of the job that are essential.

During the Civil War, President Lincoln wanted to promote Ulysses S. Grant to be general-in-chief of Union forces. One of Lincoln's cabinet officers offered the opinion that Lincoln should not think too highly or expect too much of Grant, because he drank hard liquor to excess. Lincoln retorted: "Please find out his brand, that I may send a case to all my generals." Grant was Lincoln's only general who consistently won victories, and he eventually defeated Robert E. Lee which finally ended the war. Grant, by the way, was another individual who while successful in the Mexican War, had failed miserably at various previous appointments in the peacetime Army and even as a clerk in a retail store before the Civil War.

Drucker also felt that by thinking through the job with an emphasis on the few essential requirements, a manager would avoid the danger of structuring a job around a specific individual. He was very much against this. In his opinion, this could lead to conformity, favoritism, or both, and accordingly he opposed this practice. Moreover, a restructuring of a job around an individual would create a chain reaction, with everybody changing their work and responsibilities to fit in with the new person's personality and way of doing business, causing immense disruptions to the organization. New bosses may cause disruptions anyway, but nothing compared with a complete redesign for the incoming personality.

I Disputed Drucker on This Rule

The only time that I challenged Peter was on this point, because of his emphasis on avoiding, or at least minimizing, these disruptions. I didn't argue that a chain reaction of disruptions would not occur due to restructuring a job. My argument was that such disruptions might be necessary in certain instances and could have an overall positive result, despite the drawbacks which Peter mentioned. In thinking through the requirements of the job, I made the point that a manager needed to anticipate potential disruptions and weigh them against the potential benefits that might ensue.

To support my position, I gave the example of General Pershing's assumption of command of the American Expeditionary Force during World War I. Despite considerable pressure from America's French and British allies, Pershing insisted that U.S. forces be employed as a separate entity under him, rather than integrated piecemeal into established allied units.

In effect, Pershing structured the job around himself. Indeed, one of the arguments against his doing this was the disruption of the established ways of "doing business" within the Allied command. Moreover, the Allies argued that they had the experienced commanders and units, the necessary artillery, aviation, and tank support, and that they lacked only the men. Pershing's force had none of these, only men. However, keeping his men as a separate organization meant that the fresh American forces were employed as a single fighting force, rather than used to provide additional manpower filler for the war-weary English and French units.

Pershing stuck to his demands and, when they tried to go around him, the French and English found that he was supported by President Woodrow Wilson. The organization built around Pershing is credited with a significant contribution toward the Allied victory, despite the disruption it created. After I made my argument, Peter did not dispute my theory that sometimes a disruption was justified. This made me feel pretty good.

This, too, was part of Drucker's character. If your argument made sense, he would listen. Admittedly, it was a rare instance that he would agree with your argument. In most cases, Peter's own positions were so well thought through that mere practitioners, or even academic researchers, could not successfully challenge them. Quite simply, he was almost always right!

Back to the Basics

Now let's get back to Drucker's main point. Thinking through the basic requirements of the job means determining those qualifications for the job which a successful executive must have to accomplish it successfully. If this were done in every case, it would minimize the chance that a selection would be made on less relevant factors.

Years ago, during a brief period when I worked as an executive recruiter, I learned that the modus operandi was for a recruiter to submit three to five candidates for any position, all of whom met the basic requirements, which the headhunter had helped the hiring executive to develop. The reason, as explained to me by a more experienced executive recruiter, was that this was to ensure that "the chemistry is right." "Sometimes a candidate won't like his potential boss," I was told. "Sometimes, a potential boss won't like the candidate. And yes, there are times when neither one will like each other. However, with three to five candidates, chances are that in at least one case the candidate will like the potential boss, and vice versa. But in all cases, the candidate must meet all the main requirements for the job."

This proved to be good advice. In one case, I spent considerable time with a hiring executive in developing the "job specifications" for the position. One very important qualification in this instance was geographical experience in the area where the executive would be operating. This was necessary because of local customs and other technical requirements peculiar to the locality. I then went about my business finding the three to five candidates to present to the hiring executive.

Some clients preferred to have candidates submitted and interviewed "piecemeal," that is, as soon as each was recruited. However, some clients didn't want to start interviewing until all the candidates had been recruited and were ready to go. I preferred the latter approach, as I thought it would give the client a better feel for the range of what was available before making a decision as to which candidate to extend an offer. However, just before I was ready to submit the candidates that I had recruited for this assignment, the client called off the search. "Just luck," he said, "but some guy happened to hear that we were looking and I interviewed and hired him."

I asked to go over the job specifications against the individual's qualifications with the client, to which he agreed. Everything looked good until we got to the requirement having to do with geographical experience. My client became evasive. Finally, he admitted that the candidate had no experience in the geographical area whatsoever. "But it's okay," he said. "We'll help him. He is so strong in other areas that he'll do a great job."

This was a perfect example of what Drucker was talking about. Here the client himself had stated that prior geographical experience was an essential requirement for any candidate. Yet he had disregarded this requirement because the candidate was strong in some other, less essential areas. Did the new hire succeed in this instance? I really don't know. However, there is no question that his chances of succeeding were significantly reduced, because the candidate lacked what the hiring executive himself had thought through and determined as a major qualification.

This sort of occurrence is far from uncommon. In the executive recruiting business, there is a saying, "Once a candidate meets face-to-face with a client, all bets are off." What this means is that personality and "chemistry" prevail in most cases over experience and accomplishments documented in resumes. There is nothing particularly wrong with these aspects of a candidate being considered. Personality and the ability to fit into different organizations are extremely important. However, this doesn't change Drucker's main point. Meeting basic, well-thought-through job requirements cannot be ignored. You need to think through the requirements of a job and staff for the strengths that are needed. If a candidate doesn't meet an essential requirement, don't promote or hire him or her for the job.

(2) Choose Multiple Candidates for a Job Before Selection

This sounds obvious, but it is not. The fact is that many promotions are made with only one or two candidates being considered. According to Drucker, the correct way is to consider three or four candidates, all of whom met the minimum qualifications of staffing for strength.

The reason that this wisdom is frequently ignored is that the hiring executive makes assumptions about other candidates' suitability before considering any one candidate's qualifications against the prime job requirements.

A Cautionary Tale

In one organization, the staffing executive, who had been with the company for a year, wanted to appoint a particular manager from within the company to a senior position. He sent forward the recommendation, which had to be approved by his boss. His boss asked to see the resumes of at least two additional internal candidates for the job. His boss was also curious about a particular aspect of the staffing executive's choice for this promotion.

The staffing executive used the old ploy of choosing straw candidates. He picked three, rather than two, additional candidates for the position. He thought this would give the impression that he had considered many subordinates for the promotion and would show how superior the candidate really was. He did not think the three additional candidates were anything special. One could say that he selected them for that very reason.

He sent all four resumes to his boss. In addition to demonstrating questionable integrity in his ploy, he made two major errors. First, he did not think through all the job requirements. His boss had. In addition, he relied on his personal knowledge and opinion of the candidates without investigating other aspects of their work at the company. That would have been bad enough. However, he even failed to read the resumes he sent forward. He merely attached a strong letter of recommendation for his candidate.

What the staffing executive did not know is that one of the three additional candidates had been with the organization for many years and had a reputation as an up-and-coming manager with superior capabilities. However, for the past year he had been on special assignment away from corporate headquarters, so the staffing executive did not know him very well. As it happened, this candidate's background and proven experience were particularly suited to the obvious requirements of the position to be filled. He was so well-suited in fact, that he, of all people, should have been the prime candidate.

This was one reason that the staffing executive's boss had asked to see the resumes of additional candidates. If this manager was not even included in consideration, he wanted to find out why. If he was included, but was not the candidate selected, he wanted to see if he was missing some important information before he approved the promotion. At least the staffing executive included this candidate's resume along with the others. Otherwise, he probably would really have been in real trouble. However, had he looked closely at the resumes, he would have immediately grasped the fact that he was not recommending the best candidate for the position. Of course, he may have known something about this candidate not known to others, but he did not.

What his boss saw was that the executive was clearly not recommending the best candidate for the job. In a face-to-face interview with the staffing executive, the boss soon determined that he did not know who should have been the obvious candidate, or his background as well as he should have. He could perhaps be forgiven since this manager in question had been absent during most of the staffing executive's time with the organization. However, it still did not reflect well on his ability as a high-level manager. Had he promoted the wrong manager, it might have caused a number of problems in the organization, not to mention the fact that the organization would not get the manager most suitable for the job.

After a discussion of the requirements and the qualifications of the candidates, both the boss and the staffing executive agreed that this ignored candidate, and not the candidate who the staffing executive had earlier recommended, should be promoted to the job.

(3) Discuss Your Choice with Colleagues First

Had the executive in the example above discussed the appointment with his staff or colleagues, he wouldn't have embarrassed himself in front of his boss. I want to state emphatically that Peter was not saying that such a promotion should be a group decision. It is not, and you must take responsibility for the outcome, regardless if those you consult give you erroneous information or possibly a poor recommendation. You are still responsible. However, it makes sense to share your plans and get others' opinions and ideas whenever it is possible to do so. Even if you decide to promote someone who others don't recommend, at least you'll know the pitfalls of your appointment. You'll learn more about what others think and know regarding the various candidates you are considering.

After the Promotion

Once you have made a promotion, your work is not done. You are responsible for what happens next. There is always "care and feeding" that is involved. New appointments do not automatically hit the ground running. It would be well to prepare the way as much as possible, including with specific job-related training. Sure, you can leave it to the new promotee to work it out by his or herself. If it's the right selection, the individual will know in what areas he or she needs help or additional training. But why wait? There is much that you know already that the new appointee probably does not. Unless letting the individual struggle is part of his or her development, why do it? You want your new promotee to be successful and make you look good, don't you?

Without doing everything for the promotee, you want to do everything possible to ensure his or her success. As a retired CEO once told a group of recently promoted vice presidents about leading their subordinates, "Don't you let them fail!"

Drucker's Six-Year Principle

We can't leave this discussion of Drucker's obvious dislike for the Peter Principle and its implications without one final thought. There was one element of top management departures that Peter felt should be encouraged.

He felt that top executives, or at least most top executives, should remain in their jobs no more than six years. However, this had nothing to do with incompetence.

Peter just felt that top management had to change periodically to allow for upward mobility and new ideas and new corporate directions. Moreover, this succession and its success was the responsibility of the top executive himself and had to be planned for well ahead to ensure a smooth transition. He may have got this notion from the organization we're going to look at in the next chapter.

Drucker Lesson Summary

The idea that managers rise to their level of incompetence is a dangerous myth. If a manager isn't performing, of course he needs to be relieved of his or her duties. But to automatically fire a manager due to failure with no further thought is, as Peter said, "human sacrifice" pure and simple. There may be an equally challenging job available at which the manager will be successful. Find something or put him in a holding position until you do. Don't waste individuals who have previously done well over long periods of time due to one job failure. In any case, you can minimize these problems by performing due diligence in the ways recommended, that is:

- Think through the requirements of the position and plan on staffing for strength.

- Have multiple qualified candidates before settling on one.

- Share your intentions with colleagues before promoting.

Do this and you should have an excellent "batting average" of promoting the right person into the right job. Once the right person is in the job, it is still your responsibility to get the person off to the right start. Take these actions and your organization is on the way to being top heavy with the best and most qualified managers. In any case, if it's your organization, these are your responsibilities.

CHAPTER FIFTEEN

A Model Organization That Drucker Greatly Admired

*P*eter had an extraordinary, in-depth knowledge of so many topics. Yet there were a few areas of business which he seemed to exclude as a distinct element to study and I never thought to ask him why. For example, I was surprised that he did not emphasize leadership more in his writings or in his classroom presentations. After all, almost every management writer you can name has also written one or more books on leadership, and some of them focus on leadership to the exclusion of other aspects of management.

I always thought this was because he thought leadership was so basic to every aspect and functional area of management. I still believe this was the reason. In fact, he did not minimize the importance of leadership; it ran through most of his lectures and many of his writings, especially over the last ten years. However, one day one of my classmates asked him about the fact that he had not written a book on leadership. Peter replied, "The first systematic book on leadership was written by Xenophon more than 2,000 years ago, and it is still the best."

Who Was Xenophon?

Some of us were immediately motivated to research Xenophon, the ancient Greek author. I am ashamed to say that I was not in this group. I felt that I had more important things to read, and anyway, translations into English from the ancient Greek always struck me as stilted and boring. When I finally decided that after all, this work was cited as the best book on leadership, a field of prime interest to me, and was recommended by Peter Drucker, I reversed myself. I learned that Xenophon was a general and the leadership he wrote about was leadership in battle. Here was the greatest management thinker of our time claiming that the best book on leadership (at least as of 1978) was not written by Warren Bennis, Tom Peters, or Kenneth Blanchard, but by a somewhat obscure Greek general who died two millennia ago! The importance of Drucker's statement had finally sunk in.

Drucker's Interest in the Military

Drucker spoke with such confidence and expertise in so many areas that I did not notice anything special about his use of military examples while I was his student. I rarely felt compelled to get into a discussion with him on military matters. However, after my graduation from Claremont, and as I advanced in my Air Force career, Peter and I had a number of conversations about the military, war, and its political involvements and relationships. The extent of his knowledge was surprising. Peter wrote for *Foreign Affairs* as well as *The Harvard Business Review*, but his understanding of military strategy, especially about the American Civil War, was considerable. However, he did not share the knowledge that he had this particular interest with many.

His knowledge of the organizational structure and culture of the German and Austrian-Hungarian military of the World War I era was also impressive. I learned much from our discussions, including that it was the use of the railroad during the American Civil War on which the German Army based its system of mobilization and which enabled them to bring together such large numbers of troops so rapidly at the beginning of World War I.

In class, Peter had told us the basis of modern business structure came from the military and from the Catholic Church. That is, both had hierarchies and forms of organization that were copied almost exactly by business. In addition to his occasional use of examples from the military, he stated that the U.S. military had the fairest system of promotion of any large organization. According to Drucker, this was because the system minimized favoritism, nepotism, and other elements which discouraged promoting the best. To many of my younger classmates who had not been in the military, this was a startling statement. Most of them had matured during the Vietnam era. They had been brought up with the notion that the military was inflexible, unfair, operated on the brutish of principles, and was peopled with individuals of lower intelligence at all levels. Only in recent years and since the first Gulf War has this feeling somewhat abated.

Much later on Drucker's beliefs regarding military management got more publicity. This occurred mainly from Frances Hesselbein's book, *Hesselbein on Leadership* (San Francisco: Jossey-Bass, 2002), and in *Be, Know, Do* (San Francisco: Jossey-Bass, 2004), a book Frances adapted from the official Army Leadership Manual and which was developed by the Leader-to-Leader Institute (formerly the Drucker Foundation), of which Frances is the chairman. Frances Hesselbein became a close friend of Peter's. In fact, Peter said that she could be a successful CEO of any company in the country, although her background is mostly nonprofit. She is one of the few management experts to notice the similarity between ethical leadership in what Peter taught and leadership as taught by our military services.

For the first time, the extent to which Drucker both understood and approved of the military's unique mastery of management was publicized and documented. For example, in recommending the Leader-to-Leader Institute's adaptation of the Army Leadership Manual, Drucker was quoted as saying: "The Army trains and develops more leaders than do all other institutions together—and with a lower casualty rate." Note that Drucker said "the Army." The book he was recommending was from an Army manual on leadership. He did not mean by his statement to disparage or put down any of our other armed services. From our conversations, I knew that he could have easily substituted any of the others, since all operate very similarly in training, leadership, and other aspects of management.

Three Areas of Military Management Drucker Recommended

In revisiting Drucker's lectures and our conversations, it was clear to me that Drucker thought military management should be studied by business and other civilian leaders mainly in these three areas:

- Training

- Promotional Systems

- Leadership

That's not to say that there weren't other major aspects of military management that Drucker thought would be good for businesses and other groups to look at. Only that these areas were the top three. Also, that it was not that other organizations should copy what the military was doing in all respects. Drucker was no fan of the concept that "business is war." He simply thought that other organizations should examine what was being done by the military and adapt them to what made sense to their own organizations. Finally, Drucker did not mean to give the idea that military management was perfect and without blemish. He knew there were always challenges that any organization must constantly work on to overcome, and he knew the military had shortcomings, despite what he saw as exemplary.

Military Training

Peter greatly admired the training and the philosophy behind it in our armed forces. All military training rests on two basic assumptions. These assumptions go back through the millennia of history to the much admired Spartans who began training at age seven and continued for twelve years. Thereafter they required military service of all and trained year around, as opposed to their adversaries, who began to train only when threatened or before a campaign.

The first of the two assumptions is that the harder you train, the easier the actual military actions would be and the better your performance. Famed World War II General George S. Patton put it this way: "A pint of sweat in training is worth a gallon of blood in combat."

The other basic assumption is that even the lowest ranking private has the capability of reaching the highest levels of responsibility and command. The old saying is that "in every private's knapsack, there is a marshal's baton." In the military, this practice is an absolute necessity because on the battlefield, officers and non-commissioned officers must sometimes be replaced immediately, without warning or additional training. This means that everyone has to be prepared at all times to assume higher responsibilities.

This practice places a significant emphasis on merit. Napoleon drew many of his top generals and marshals not from the wealthiest classes of French society, for most of these had fled France or been executed during the French revolution, but rather from battle-proved soldiers elevated through the ranks. Even the British, notorious for the Crown selling officer commissions to the upper classes of English society during this period, commissioned a percentage of their officers from the ranks during the Napoleonic Wars, without their having to buy their commissions. The only requirement was that those commissioned in this way be capable of reading and writing.

One of the most famous and successful Confederate generals during the American Civil War was Lieutenant General Nathan Bedford Forrest. He enlisted in the Confederate Army as a private in 1861. Within two years he had been promoted to the rank of brigadier general and given the command of a brigade. Many historians consider him the war's most capable cavalry general. Although I am aware of young men without degrees being hired by major corporations and rising over the years to positions high in management, I am unaware of any that accomplished this within two years.

Peter liked all aspects of military training: that it was continuous, that the training was hard and serious, and that the training assumed that anyone could reach higher levels of responsibilities.

This practice goes on even today. Most officers in the U.S. armed forces are graduates of college ROTC, the service academies (West Point, Annapolis, and Colorado Springs), or else they are given direct commissions due to their specialties (e.g., they are doctors, dentists, lawyers, or chaplains). But a significant number are graduates of officer training programs designed to commission qualified soldiers, airmen, sailors, and marines from the ranks, and some still receive battlefield commissions on the spot in combat when the need is pressing and immediate.

The concept of every soldier having a marshal's baton in his knapsack means that from the first day, the most junior soldier must be trained for increasingly higher levels of leadership. In contrast, it is rare that even new hires that are college graduates are prepared for higher responsibilities in industry. Many college graduates remain in the functional jobs and at the same level for which they were hired—specialist engineers, lawyers, scientists, accountants, or salesmen—throughout their careers. A few people in corporations or nonprofits do rise higher, but there is no expectation that they will do so. In the military, there is.

Every officer can aspire to be a general (or admiral in the navy) and is given the training to enable this promotion to happen, even though it is recognized that only a very small percentage will actually reach these highest of ranks. Similarly, every enlisted rank is given the necessary training to reach the highest non-commissioned officer ranks, even though only a small percentage can achieve this goal. And, as noted, the mechanism is in place to permit significant numbers of soldiers or sailors to seek commissions and become officers. Why not? If they have the ability, they have been given the necessary training since the day they donned a uniform.

In the military, all are exposed to re-occurring training, upgrading training, advanced training, and professional military education. These types of training vary dependent on the service, military specialty, career path, and other factors. However, the training is ongoing, required, and merges into a system of higher military education. While no career is identical even in one service, including with respect to training, the first eleven years of my own U.S. Air Force career provides at least an example.

CASE IN POINT: MY MILITARY TRAINING

I graduated from West Point with a BS in engineering. This is nominally an Army school, but I was commissioned in the Air Force. A small number of graduates from any of the three commissioning academies are allowed to switch services, army to air force, air force to navy, etc. I was immediately sent to attend primary basic navigation training (11 months), advanced navigation radar navigator training (9 months), B-52 ground and flying training (5 months), and survival school (1 month). I then reported for duty at my first assignment, a heavy bombardment wing. Nowadays, all newly commissioned officers take a basic airpower course lasting several months before receiving specialized training in the Air Force.

During the next five and a half years of my first assignment, I was sent to two advanced courses for air to ground missiles, each course lasting several days. I was encouraged to begin graduate school at night and completed half a dozen courses toward a master's degree. I was required to complete

Squadron Officers School either in residence or by correspondence. If I went in residence, the course was 4 months. In my case, my unit could not afford to lose me for that long, so I took the course by correspondence. I also completed the next level of professional military training, Air Command and Staff School, by correspondence. Had I taken it in residence, the length of the course would have been 10 months.

During the same period I flew approximately 200 training missions lasting on the average about 10 hours each; and more than 20 airborne alert flights with nuclear weapons lasting 24–27 hours each—in total more than 2,500 hours flying time. I was also on ground alert with my airplane, ready to take off and go to war within minutes, on the average about once a month for a week. While on ground alert, I received additional ground school training of various types eight hours a day.

Then I was selected to go for my MBA at the University of Chicago. On completing my MBA, I was sent to A-26 (attack aircraft) school, completed several Special Ops/Air Commando courses, and attended jungle survival school in the Philippines. I was then sent to my second operational assignment, an air commando squadron in Thailand, flying night interdiction and close air support missions against targets in North Vietnam and Laos. During that year I flew 174 combat missions lasting up to four hours each. As I flew almost all night missions, I was free during the day. I took a correspondence course from the University of Wisconsin in a foreign language.

On completion of my combat tour, I was reassigned to research and development. I completed several short courses on research and development and acquisition and worked as a program manager, developing new Air Force life support equipment for two years. That encompassed eleven years of service.

The above is typical of training and a career in all the military services. It is intensive, and it never ends, for both officers and enlisted ranks. I have omitted various short seminars and workshops which are more or less identical to what is offered in corporations.

At the top level for professional military education for officers are the war colleges. These are the Army War College, Air War College, Navy War College, Marine Corps War College, National War College, and the Industrial College of the Armed Forces (ICAF). You only attend one. I was fortunate enough to be selected for ICAF. Non-commissioned officers have non-commissioned Officer Academies. And by the way, in today's military, officers aren't the only ones whose education is encouraged. I have known non-commissioned officers with both doctorates and master's degrees.

It is expected that to make full colonel or Navy captain you must have completed a war college either by correspondence or in residence. The in residence course lasts 10 months. However, it is highly competitive to attend in residence, and only a very small percentage of eligible officers are selected to attend. Most general officers or admirals are graduates of the in resident courses of the war colleges.

From this description, I think you get a general flavor for training in the military, and maybe why Drucker thought it important for these standards of training to be examined by organizations outside of the military. There are certainly elements of this type of training in all organizations. However, there are underlying differences which go back to the two basic assumptions that I mentioned earlier.

THE HARDER YOU TRAIN, THE BETTER YOU'LL PERFORM

In the military, the thinking is that the harder you train, the more effective, efficient, and successful you'll be. While there are exceptions, much of the training in business is done on a one-time basis to achieve a minimal acceptable standard. It is generally assumed that thereafter, proficiency in performance will be gained and maintained through experience on the job, not through expending resources in perfecting or improving something already taught.

Some corporations have developed good leadership programs which are the equal of those in the military. Most, however, do not have such programs, and many are restricted to the upper levels of management, not for all employees. For some companies, the only thing done training-wise is the occasional workshop or seminar. Seminars and workshops are good, but in the military, this type of training represents a small part of total training time. For many in the corporate world, they represent the major allocation of training resources.

Many corporations view training mainly as an expenditure of time and money. The military views training as one of their most important investments. The more resources invested in training, the greater the payoff in performance. Drucker would have liked to see the same serious emphasis that the military placed on training in all organizations. He felt that the training concepts in use by the military would mean fewer failures by managers as they advanced up the corporate ladder.

Promotion Systems

You can sense much of Drucker's dissatisfaction with some of the standard means of selection for promotion in the corporate world (see the last chapter), but there is more. Drucker thought that the systems in use for promotion selection in the U.S. military, while not perfect, were the fairest in use by any large organization. While there are some differences among the services, these are minor. So what I will describe next is the general system of promotion in use in all services.

At most levels in the U.S. military, promotion is based strictly on merit. This is absolutely a Drucker concept. Beginning at the junior non-commissioned officer ranks through the rank of major general, there are promotion boards which meet and decide on who will be promoted. In most cases, the boards are very competitive and promote on a "best qualified" basis. For example, there usually are several thousand colonels vying for a handful of promotions to brigadier general, so the promotion rate may be something like 1 or 2 percent. At the junior non-commissioned officer and junior officer levels, promotion may be on a "fully qualified basis." This means that all who have performed satisfactorily are considered qualified and promoted. Usually, failure to win a promotion at these lower levels with officers eventually ends in discharge from the military.

For the top two ranks, lieutenant general and general, and for the naval services, vice admiral and admiral (those whose insignias of rank are three and four stars, respectively), there are no promotion boards. Candidates are nominated for specific jobs, and, if selected, promoted to one of these two highest ranks.

EVALUATION REPORTS

The main tool for promotion selection is always the evaluation report, which usually is accomplished annually, but is also done at any change of assignment. While these reports vary somewhat among the services, and also for officers verses enlisted ranks, they typically involve the rater evaluating on a number of specific criteria. For example, the current U.S. Army form for officers involves a written description evaluation in communicating, decision-making, motivating, planning, executing, assessing, developing, team-building, and learning. Many service evaluations I have seen ask for an overall evaluation potential for promotion and frequently some sort of ranking of where the individual rated stands compared with others of the same military rank being evaluated.

Usually, the rater's supervisor must add his or her endorsement and comments, especially as to whether he or she agrees or disagrees with the evaluation and why. If the evaluation is especially good or especially bad, the rater's supervisor must also get into the act and add an endorsement as well. The evaluation is discussed with the individual rated before forwarding in a counseling session. Currently, at least one of the services requires quarterly counseling regarding progress made after the annual evaluation.

At various times different variations have been tried. For example, in order to control evaluation inflation, that is, a rater giving all of his subordinates a high rating, the Air Force at one point required raters to assign those rated a "1," "2," or "3" score, with 1 being the highest score. However, raters were severely restricted in the number of "1's" they could assign depending on the number of subordinates which they rated. This procedure was discontinued because it was found to be unfair for many and counterproductive for the Air Force as a whole. For example, a selective all-volunteer unit might have all top people, all actually performing at a "1" level. Yet, if the group were small enough, few, if any, "1's" could be awarded. So a "2" or a "3" evaluation awarded in such an organization might in reality be describing performance that would be awarded a "1" elsewhere.

Another variation used is at the general officer level. A so-called "closed" form is used, and with some services there is no formal evaluation counseling session. The rating is limited to a few short sentences, or even a single sentence, regarding the general's performance, and the ratee may not see the report. The idea here is that at that level you are working for the next higher ranking general anyway, and it is too late, and maybe unnecessary, to change or improve any personal quirks. The rated general's boss either likes the way his subordinate general is operating or he does not. It is also thought that after passing all the screens and being promoted to general officer, formal written feedback probably won't help all that much.

What if a subordinate is performing poorly, but has done nothing illegal or immoral and has not violated the Uniform Code of Military Justice (military law) in any way? If the position or the situation is critical, the rater can take action to have the individual immediately removed from his position, in combat or in a critical non-combat position. Normally, someone relieved of his duties in this way will automatically receive a bad evaluation and these are difficult, but not impossible to recover from. As a brigadier general, Colin Powell describes in his book *My American Journey* (Random House, 1995) how he made some mistakes and received a poor rating. Nevertheless, he went on to become a four-star general and the highest-ranking officer in the U.S. military.

Finally, the facts of evaluation can be disputed by the individual rated. He or she may have a particular evaluation removed from the records if cause can be shown that the evaluation was seriously flawed or unfair.

Peter was a proponent of fair and continuous evaluation and feedback of knowledge workers. The whole system of management by objectives (MBO), which he developed, was based on formal feedback regarding objectives jointly agreed upon and progress made toward achieving them. While the military doesn't use MBO, per se, the individual goals set and the reviews are very similar.

GETTING PROMOTED

Not everyone is eligible for promotion to the next higher rank at every year's promotion. This, generally, has to do with time in grade at the rank held and/or total years of service, and this may change, depending on the needs of the service at that time. For example, during the years between World Wars One and Two, Dwight Eisenhower held the rank of major for sixteen years from 1920 to 1936. This was not because he was performing poorly, but rather due to the fact that the U.S. Army had shrunk after its rapid growth during the First World War, and Eisenhower didn't have enough years of total service to be considered for promotion to the next higher grade of lieutenant colonel.

While required time in grade still varies by service, today a major (the U.S. navy rank equivalent of lieutenant commander) is normally considered for promotion to lieutenant colonel (the navy rank of commander) at his or her 16th year of commissioned service, although a few individuals may be selected for what is called a "below the zone" promotion a year or two earlier. Since Eisenhower was commissioned in 1915, under the U.S. Army's current needs, he would have been eligible for early promotion to lieutenant colonel as early as 1929 instead of 1936—seven years earlier.

The first step in getting promoted in the military services is meeting a promotion board. However, meeting the promotion board is only the first step. Even though all are trained and qualified for promotion, not all can be promoted. The number holding each rank is limited by law. At the officer ranks, which begin with second lieutenant in the Air Force, Army, and Marines, and ensign in the Navy and Coast Guard, those failing to be promoted usually are given several attempts. However, should they not succeed, they are usually required to leave the service. This policy is known as "up or out." It helps to ensure a young force and the highest quality personnel at every level.

The number that can be promoted in any one year depends on the need and the rules. According to recent figures, in the Army, and this may vary by service, the promotion rate to lieutenant colonel is about 70 percent of those eligible and meeting the promotion board. Again, this practice may vary by both time and service. I have seen promotion rates to the rank of major much lower than 40 percent. It probably was even lower than that when Eisenhower was promoted.

Promotion to colonel is much more difficult, and as I mentioned earlier to general is much tougher, say, 1 or 2 percent (or less) of those eligible. Yet, all are qualified and could actually hold the rank. As I once heard a retired Air Force four-star, (that is, full general) tell forty newly promoted brigadier generals, lest they be too "full of themselves" at their recent selection for promotions: "The Air Force could have reached into our pot of several thousand eligible colonels and pulled out forty other names at random, not yours. Can you imagine the effect on our ability to perform our mission over the next five years? Most likely none at all!"

That says a lot about how well the system works. Imagine that you are in a large organization and promote a number of vice presidents simultaneously. Could the same be said if entirely different vice presidents were selected?

THE PROMOTION BOARD

The promotion board meets annually and is made up of more senior people from various units throughout the particular service. The same individuals usually do not sit on successive boards.

Promotion boards consider everything: previous performance as demonstrated by written evaluation reports based mainly on demonstrated performance, types of experience, education (both degrees and professional military), awards and decorations, anything else positive and negative, and anything that the promotion board is instructed to give special weight to. For example, a promotion board could be instructed to give special weight to multiple tours of combat in Iraq or Afghanistan.

However, no one, no matter how senior, and not even the Chief of Staff of the service involved, can get a particular favorite officer promoted. In fact, if he tries, this is considered "undue influence" and can get everyone involved, including himself, in serious trouble. I remember the Commander of Strategic Air Command, a four-star general, bemoaning the fact that he knew some particular captain personally, and though he felt that this individual should be promoted to major, there was absolutely nothing he could do to get this officer promoted.

The promotion board reviews the records of every one eligible and considers them for promotion. They may do this in a committee of threes, with there being three committees or a total of nine on the board. Each committee scores each candidate's performance and record, say, on a 1–7 basis, with 7 being the highest score. The board compares scores on each candidate. If the score of a candidate by one committee differs by more than two points from another committee, that candidate is discussed by the entire board until consensus is reached and a score is developed on which all three committees agree. From my experience this difference of more than two points occurs rarely and on only a very small percentage of those candidates reviewed.

The board then ranks all candidates according to their numerical scores and further ranks them within the point scores achieved. Once this is done, the final decision mostly depends on the number of promotions that can be made.

Officer selections might be screened further, especially at the general officer level, which in accordance with the law, must be confirmed by the U.S. Senate. And by the way, the Senate is not a rubber stamp and has blocked promotions for various reasons, as has the Secretary of Defense. For example, the Senate refused to confirm the promotion of a naval officer from commander to captain because he was seen at a "strip show" performed during the Tailhook scandal in Las Vegas some years ago. The Secretary of Defense refused to promote an Air Force brigadier general to major general who he deemed to have failed to have taken sufficient actions to protect U.S. personnel when terrorists blew up the Khobar Towers in Saudi Arabia in 1996.

Of course, the system is not perfect, and mistakes are sometimes made, both in promotion and non-promotion, but you can see that everything possible is done to try and ensure fairness, and it is easy to see why Drucker liked it.

Drucker on Leadership

I began this chapter with Drucker's response as to why he did not write a book on leadership. However, leadership can be found on almost every page of Drucker's writings, and long after I left his classroom, Drucker did write about the leader of the future. He believed strongly in what leadership could accomplish in any organization, but he also believed that the purpose of leadership was for the benefit of the organization and of society, and not for the benefit of the leader.

Some writers have suggested that the reason that Drucker largely abandoned his emphasis on corporate management in the latter years of his life to focus on the world of nonprofits and nonprofit management is that he had lost faith in corporate management. I cannot confirm this assessment, but I do know that he was vastly disappointed in the prevalent attitude among many managers, even well known and well-regarded successful managers, that they practiced leadership first and foremost for their own benefit. He was appalled at the huge salaries taken by senior management of many organizations, not a few while their organizations stumbled and their workers were laid off.

Drucker was dumbfounded by the lifestyles promoted by many executives and the concept of the "trophy wife," as if all of this was a reward to themselves for their success in having fought their way to the top. Despite his immense success, Peter himself lived in a modest house on a middle-class street with Doris, his wife of more than sixty years. She has written that he never failed on wakening to greet her with "Good morning, my dearest darling." It was almost as if Peter was trying to set the example for managers worldwide that to be a leader was a calling and that one should live modestly, morally, and for the benefit of others.

In the late 1990's I did extensive research on battle leaders of all ranks and services who had gone on to extraordinary success leading other organizations once they had left the military. I wondered if they had learned principles during their military careers which had helped them to success as civilians. Surprisingly, most of their responses could be boiled down to only eight categories. I called these "The Eight Universal Laws of Leadership." The idea was that leaders in all types of organizations could use this information to help them.

In the fall of 1997, I shared this information with Peter. He was very enthusiastic about the idea and encouraged me in my desire to publish my research in an applied book for managers. The resulting book was

The Stuff of Heroes: The Eight Universal Laws of Leadership (Longstreet Press, 1998). It was on *The Los Angeles Times* best-seller list for two weeks. The book is now out of print, though I hope eventually to bring it up to date and have it published again.

The Eight Universal Laws of Leadership

To get some idea of Drucker's feelings about leadership, I would like to share his responses to each "law" at the time that I showed them to him.

1. *Integrity First.* "You are entirely right and absolutely correct in listing this as your first law. A leader can be well-liked and popular and even competent, and that's all well and good, but if he lacks integrity of character he is not fit to be a leader."

2. *Know Your Stuff.* "This seems obvious, but some managers do try to cut corners rather than mastering the knowledge that they must have and that is essential to the quality of their performance."

3. *Declare Your Expectations.* "I'm uncertain what you mean by this. If you mean that a leader should declare his objectives and his mission—by all means, yes."

4. *Show Uncommon Commitment.* "The failure of many is because they show no commitment, or commitment to the wrong goals. This gets back to your third law. Commitment comes from a worthy mission and then strong commitment."

5. *Expect Positive Results.* "There is a cautionary tale here: one must not be a 'Pollyanna'. Still, the central thought is correct: one cannot be negative and succeed in anything."

6. *Take Care of Your People.* "Many managers are failing to do this, and it will catch up with them."

7. *Put Duty Before Self.* "This should be the basis of all leadership. The leader cannot act in his own interests. It must be in the interests of the customer and the worker. This is the great weakness of American management today."

8. *Get Out in Front.* "Very true. As junior leader or CEO, the leader must be where the work is the most challenging. During World

War I, the losses among higher ranking officers was rare compared with the losses they caused by their incompetence. Too few generals were killed."

Drucker concluded by commenting that there were other useful principles of leadership, and that a manager must first decide to be a leader. While all of the principles I had uncovered from battle leadership would help, Drucker said that the prime principle was what I called "duty before self."

"A leader, any leader," he continued, "must act for the benefit of others and not for oneself."

Drucker Lesson Summary

Drucker believed that corporations should look closely at and analyze the practices of the U.S. military. He did not believe that "business is war." He was very much against any such notion. However, he felt that there were many ideas gained by experience under risk and uncertainty during several thousands of years of recorded history which pre-dated organized business. Many of these ideas could be usefully adapted to non-military organizations.

The Management Control Panel

*I*t was an early spring day in Southern California in May of 1977. Strangely, spring in Southern California is not what you might expect if you watch the Rose Parade on television on New Year's Day. Contrary to popular opinion, it is not sunny in Southern California all year around. While it does rain in the winter months, for some reason the Rose Parade is generally dry. However, beginning about April and extending through early June, additional rains are sometimes evident. This particular day in Southern California the sky was overcast and it was raining—heavily. You could see the results in Peter's classroom.

Raincoats were draped over the classroom chairs and umbrellas were laid out of the way in the hallway. A damp smell pervaded everything. Peter entered the classroom and immediately began discussion of a case study he had mentioned in a previous class.

The case concerned the president of a company who had recently learned about the capabilities of new computers and their application. After giving this some serious thought, he called for a meeting of the management hierarchy of the company. He wanted their input for a new management control system to help run the company and told them of his plans. He called it a "Management Control Panel."

Using Technology to Its Fullest

"Management is getting more and more complex in our industry," the company president told his top management staff. "Recently I've learned of the capabilities of the latest computers. I think we can be the first in our industry, maybe in the whole business world, to implement a new concept which can give us a significant competitive advantage."

"The idea," he continued, "is to list all of the primary factors which affect our business. We'll use computers to see how these factors work individually and together to create various quantified outputs. For example, if the economy changes, it may increase demands for certain of our products. No doubt our competitors will see the same changes and increases. The difference will be in response. Do we lower price? Do we raise it? Do we increase our research and development expenditures? Decrease them? Perhaps some combination of these options?

"Every change we make affects other important aspects of running our business," the company president said. "We'll be able to immediately see the changes in output caused by the external environmental or changes we cause ourselves. We can take advantage of these opportunities to best achieve our business objectives and to affect our overall performance positively. Most importantly, the computers will generate an array of correct actions for us, according to whatever objectives we set and the resources available. All we will need to do is to implement these actions. We'll have the edge over all of our competitors."

Then he outlined his ideas for implementation. "First, we need to decide which factors primarily affect what we do," he said. "I know there are many, and they affect all of the functional areas, including finance, marketing, manufacturing, and more. Of course, there are external factors as well, including our competition, the state of the economy, and the business in our industry. We'll need to list them as well. Then, we'll turn all of this data over to computer experts to develop the program. It may take us some time and cost us some money, but it will be well worth it.

"What I have in mind as a result is something like the instrumentation panel in an airplane's cockpit, coupled with the aircraft's control system as controlled by the pilot. On the panel, the pilot observes changes in heading, altitude, fuel consumption, progress toward the destination, and other inputs. Then he uses the aircraft's controls to make corrections based on these observations to continue to his objective. The only difference is that because of advances in technology, and the Management Control Panel, we'll know exactly what to do in every situation."

I knew that this was probably a fictitious case, or one that was heavily disguised. With my background in aviation, I could immediately appreciate the potential of what the company president in Drucker's case was suggesting. I had seen and even used many such systems. Some were electronic; others were based on log functions and used in handheld circular or linear slide rules. The big difference was that none that I had seen integrated all flying or mission functions. It was left to the human operator to make the final decisions based on his overall integration of this information. What was being suggested in this case study was to leave the analysis entirely to the computers. Company management's function would be to implement the results of the computer's analysis.

If a control panel for running a company like this were available, it would be of tremendous benefit. It would allow company management to do a better job in what needed to be done, and this could be accomplished faster than anyone not having such a system. It would be a quantum leap forward, and I wondered only why no one had thought of an idea like this sooner. I looked around the room and could see that the reactions of my classmates were similarly enthusiastic.

Drucker's Challenge

"This is a homework assignment," Peter continued. "Please consider two questions. First, I would like you to consider the input factors affecting performance, both from within a company, and in its external environment, that should be considered and how they would be measured. These are the things that the president of this company said will be turned over to those qualified to quantify this information and determine their relationship with performance output. You can use your own company as an example.

"Second, please think through and list the advantages and disadvantages of the president's proposal. We will discuss your analysis in class next week.

However," Drucker added, "even if you feel that you are able to identify all the relevant factors and would like to develop an actual Management Control Panel for your company, I caution you about beginning this project until we discuss the concept thoroughly in class."

Peter then went on to another topic. It was hard for me to follow his lecture that evening. I kept thinking of the incredible possibilities of the Management Control Panel.

I devoted more time that week to thinking about the Management Control Panel than I had many past assignments. I reviewed my textbooks from different classes covering other functional disciplines of management and eagerly noted potential internal and external inputs that should be included because they clearly affected the performance output.

I also talked with several managers within my own company, McDonnell Douglas Astronautics Company. Although computer systems were not my area of expertise, I knew that a large amount of data was collected and analyzed in the marketing department in which I worked. I got all the information I could. Remember, this was several years before the rise of the information systems or chief information officers. They just didn't exist at this time.

We were using a lot of this information in our decision making, but it was not integrated with other functional areas, as suggested by the president in Peter's case study. It certainly wasn't formatted in such a manner that it would automatically yield the required actions to be taken, based on the constraints of the situations and the resources inputted by the company.

Harvard Business School's Three Inputs

During that week, I also had an interesting discussion with an individual who was not a Claremont student but with whom I had become acquainted. He was out of work at the time and seeking a position as president of a firm. Because he had heard that I had worked as a headhunter previously, he asked my advice to help him with his job campaign.

This individual had an MBA from Harvard, then, as now, considered one of the leading business schools in the country. This man had an interesting problem. In those days, Harvard used the case-study method exclusively. According to my acquaintance, this method was followed because it was considered the best way of putting the student in the driver's seat as president of a company facing various challenges. Harvard's objective was the education of future company presidents, not lower-level managers.

There was much less emphasis at Harvard back then on turning out high-powered consultants or entrepreneurs than today. So for two years, students labored on case after case in a variety of industries in order to learn the secrets of running companies from the top.

This individual had met the expectations of his alma mater by becoming the president of a small company that manufactured furniture. It was his first job in business. He told me that he had never heard of the concept of a Management Control Panel previously. However, Harvard did consider something similar, which was the basis of their claim that their Harvard graduates could assume the presidency of any company in any industry, and manage it successfully, knowing just three aspects of the business: the product, the finances, and the firm's position in the marketplace.

More precisely, the theory was that given a mastery of how to apply basic management skills, if you understood the product, the finances, and the market position, you knew all that was necessary in order to succeed. Even West Point made no such claims regarding the education of their graduates as preparation for battle.

However, the young MBA had apparently confirmed Harvard's theory. With no prior business experience, he had taken control of a company and tripled sales and profits over an eight-year period. At the end of eight years, the owners sold the company. The new owners thanked him for his services and sent him on his way, putting their own man in charge. The former young company president now had an interesting problem: He had no job and no experience except in this one industry, and that only at the top level of management.

The furniture manufacturing industry, or at least this segment of the industry, was apparently too small to support many companies and, therefore, many company presidents. Outside of this industry, potential employers weren't convinced that his industry-specific experience as president translated into other industries at the same level, despite his success. With no experience except as a company president, they weren't particularly enthusiastic about taking him on for other positions. So he had quite a challenge in his job search, and this was the reason he was seeking my advice.

He felt, however, that as far as producing results based on certain inputs, Harvard was on the money. His conclusion regarding the Management Control Panel was that if computer technology had really advanced that much, he could see its value. Harvard's theory about being able to run any company given knowledge of the three basic inputs was some sort of fore-runner that confirmed the Management Control Panel concept.

Drucker's Second Question

I didn't spend too much time on the second part of Peter's homework assignment—the advantages and disadvantages of the concept. It seemed to me that the advantages were so self-evident that they far outweighed the cost of putting the whole system together, providing it could be done. The advantages I listed were that the company would be able to act proactively and react to external forces better and faster than any competitor. It could avoid threats, overcome problems, and exploit opportunities, and do so with great precision. I could not imagine why such a system hadn't been designed previously.

Quoting my job-hunting acquaintance, I noted Harvard's theory of having to know only of the product, finances, and position in the marketplace as an early harbinger supporting the concept. I felt ready and eagerly awaited the discussion in the classroom. I thought maybe my employer would be interested in implementing the Management Control Panel once I had fine-tuned my own inputs. I even thought that this might be worthy of my dissertation research.

My only nagging negative thought was, "Why hasn't someone thought of this previously? If it is such a great idea, why hasn't Drucker used it?" Or maybe he had, with a client, and the project was so far along that the client didn't care if anyone knew about it.

The Classroom Discussion

It was overcast, but not raining, at Claremont the following week, so rain-coats and umbrellas were not part of the regalia that had been discarded around the classroom. I arrived a few minutes early and found many of my classmates already present, a lot more than usual. Some were comparing their list of control panel inputs. One or two of them announced that they had already discussed the possibility of proceeding with the Management Control Panel within their companies. Peter strode in and one of my class-mates couldn't restrain his enthusiasm. His hand went up even before Peter made it evident that he was going to begin class.

"This Management Control Panel is a terrific concept!" the student blurted out. "Was this something that you developed for one of your clients?"

Peter didn't answer the question. "Let's defer questions of this kind until we discuss the case. Since you are all eager to get started, we'll begin immediately with the first question. Who would like to tell us his list of inputs?"

Many hands went up, including mine. Peter called on someone toward the back of the room. The student's list was quite long. I thought mine was lengthy, maybe too long. I had pruned my list to about fifteen items. I had purposely sought only what I thought to be the main inputs affecting performance output, recognizing that there would be a cost associated with each measurement. However, I noticed others writing down inputs they had omitted as the student holding the floor announced his items one by one.

For the most part, Drucker listened with no comment. When the student finished and sat down, Drucker asked only whether the student had used his own company as the source for his inputs. When he answered that he had, Peter asked the student to identify the industry. Then he asked for another volunteer from a different industry. Again, many hands were raised. Drucker, called on someone else. This student had a number of items which the first student had not used, even though the second student's list was considerably shorter. After asking this student's industry, Peter repeated the process several times.

It soon became evident that a complete list was almost infinite, depending on your tolerance for using more and more inputs. It was also obvious that different industries probably considered different inputs more important than others. After several students, Drucker stopped calling on volunteers.

"I think we can conclude that the number of inputs is limited only by our imaginations. Also, companies in different industries will consider different inputs from both the internal and external environments to be basic drivers to output that should be included," Peter said. "This is as we might expect. Basic requirements are different in different businesses; core competencies, strengths and weaknesses vary from company to company and are part of this picture. Let's leave this for a moment except to conclude that this information and the interaction of the various factors is extremely useful for a manager making decisions and taking actions to reach the goals he has set to accomplish. Such a system is not however a control panel, but rather very much like an instrumentation panel on an aircraft.

"Now, tell me please," he asked, "what are the advantages and disadvantages of the Management Control Panel which the president proposes?"

Again, many hands were raised. The Management Control Panel was clearly a concept of high interest, and many students were eager to participate in the give-and-take.

The answers to this question were essentially what I had come up with on my own. Of course, the more inputs that were included, the more complex the system and the more costly. But considering the benefits offered, the Management Control Panel had everything to recommend it. By class consensus, it was worth the price irrespective of cost.

One student added, however, that such a system, delineating the actions that management was to take and leaving only implementation, eliminated much of management's decision-making, responsibility, and present duties. Peter nodded his agreement, but did not respond further to this statement.

Drucker's Analysis of the Management Control Panel

Peter now paused before going on. "Earlier someone asked me whether the Management Control Panel was something that I developed for one of my consulting clients. I deferred from answering, but I will answer now. Not only was the Management Control Panel not something that I proposed or developed, it was an idea suggested by a client which I opposed until the idea was finally dropped."

Several sighs of amazement were heard from the class. Most of us were surprised, to say the least. We had thought the concept brilliant. "Why? What was wrong with it?" one of the students asked.

"The Management Control Panel is not a good concept because it is unworkable. No matter how many inputs, there are always additional factors which cannot be included and cannot be quantified in any given situation. These factors might be the personality of one or more of the prime executives, recent experience, either good or bad, or even the weather on a given day. A single factor, sometimes differing only slightly, can cause entirely different results from those intended. It doesn't take much, and most of these factors are random and unpredictable. Therefore, the results of such a system must be unreliable and misleading.

"This is what differentiates the instrument panel of an aircraft from that anticipated with the Management Control Panel," Drucker explained. "It is not that inputs may not be equally reliable in an aircraft, although they usually are. However, the number of relevant inputs for nature and machinery is always much less than for human beings combined with nature and machinery. The president in this case proposed to include many factors that depend entirely on human beings."

"But what about an airplane autopilot?" someone asked.

"An airplane autopilot works well within strict parameters," Peter answered. "However, even for the autopilot, it is a human manager who stands by the controls of the aircraft. The human manager is capable of analyzing the variables in any situation and can take actions or react to external inputs to achieve the intended objective, despite the variables and the unexpected. This human manager always has the capability of overriding the autopilot, which is engaged within strict limits. Even with current technology, one cannot expect a system to substitute for the abilities of a manager or team of managers. Consider the fact that there are so many human variables involved for a business operating in an environment which includes competition, the economy, and more, and is also largely driven by human beings.

"Now the idea of a Management *Information* Panel is very good," Peter said. "Being able to view the spectrum of the internal and external environments, and even understanding the relationships between them if one takes certain actions, is not only essential, but extremely valuable. However, analyzing these variables and thinking you will obtain consistently repeatable results through exact managerial actions to be taken will invariably lead to disaster."

Drucker concluded by saying, "The manager is the one who must take the information provided, including a computer's analysis, and make a judgment as to what decisions to take. It has been said that the human brain is the world's best computer. This is only partially true, since a computer can make accurate and precise calculations much faster. However, human beings have something else which, combined with the human brain, is superior to the use of a computer by itself. This is the manager's gut feel and instinct as to what is important and critical in any situation, what must be considered at all costs, and what can be safely ignored."

Practical Proof of Drucker's Insight

Later reflection on Drucker's comments caused me to recall one of the courses I had completed the previous winter. Computerized simulations were just becoming popular. The idea was to give students experience in making real business decisions based on a simulated business situation in competition with other student teams representing competing "companies." The environmental conditions changed every week, representing a fiscal quarter in real life, as did the performance of each "company" based on inputs provided by the students in reaction to the previous quarter's (i.e., last week's) situation and also the reactions of and inputs of other student teams.

For example, one could shift dollar resources from research and development to sales. That decision might help out in the short run, but it could hurt in other areas or in several quarters later. The simulation was supposed to teach the principles of business and how the various functions worked together under competition to produce various results. Claremont made it a little more interesting by assigning a psychologist along with the regular professor to observe the team meetings held during several hours of class time. Of course, teams spent much of their time meeting during the week out of class.

This was not a course Drucker taught, but the similarity to the lessons from the concept of the Management Control Panel was striking.

The course was required for our doctoral program. However, like many graduate courses at Claremont, it could be taken for either masters or doctoral level credit. Only a few courses were reserved just for doctoral students. In any case, this particular class had only four of my doctoral classmates out of a class of about thirty, both masters and doctoral students. Since a team consisted of four students, we decided to form a team of four "aces."

We anticipated that our team would easily win the competition between the companies. We definitely had advantages. Not only were we at a higher educational level, but at a higher managerial level as well. Of the four members of my team, I was the only one who was not at least a corporate vice president and accustomed to making decisions involving all business disciplines. And I had worked with all functional areas while running a department of research and development. Only a few of the masters level students were corporate officers, and no other team had more than one of these on their team. We had three!

Despite the educational advantage of being doctoral students, and the advantage of this top level managerial experience, we did not easily finish as the top team in this competition. In fact, we did not finish as top team at all. We finished somewhere in the middle of the pack. We couldn't figure it out. More than once, one of our members would say something like,

"I can't understand it. We had something like this in our industry just last year. We made exactly the same decision and allocated proportionally just about the same resources, but the results in this simulation came out entirely different." We concluded that something must be wrong with the computer program.

Something was "wrong" with it, and now I knew exactly what. Drucker had said that it didn't take much deviation to create different results, and it didn't. I realized that you couldn't run a business with a machine or a computer program making the decisions and management simply implementing what the computer said to do. The use of computers to collect information and cross-tabulate relationships that did not vary with other inputs was absolutely needed. But these were guidelines for taking actions which only the manager, interpreting the computer's results—and not the computer itself—must make.

Our team didn't necessarily make a mistake in our simulation game. However, assuming similar results with identical actions when there was a slight variance in environment is incorrect. This meant that past experience, too, is only a guide to present action. To me, this experience also confirmed that management was far more an art than a science.

Some years later, both Harvard and my own alma mater for my MBA degree, the University of Chicago, modified their MBA programs extensively. Harvard had been known for its reliance on case studies. The University of Chicago was known as a "high quant" school, emphasizing the quantitative end of business and making decisions based mainly on an analysis of numbers. Both schools wisely introduced courses to round out their curricula. These courses recognized the fact that every situation is different, and that managers had to manage with their heads and guts as much as they did by relying mostly on computers or past experience.

In combining these different approaches, I believe that due to Peter's significant input and his judgment about combining these different approaches, Claremont was ahead of business educational theory at that time.

Drucker Lesson Summary

The Management Control Panel that Drucker introduced us to in his classroom sounded almost too good to be true. And it was! Technology can do wonderful things—whether giving a pilot valuable information needed to help fly his plane or providing sales projections based on different variables. But technology needs a human hand to guide it, to put it to use, to interpret results, and to make decisions based on the information output.

Use of technology and automation to gain assistance in making decisions is important, but this cannot replace the manager in making the final analysis and determining the actions which any organization must follow to lead to success.

CHAPTER SEVENTEEN

Base Your Strategy on the Situation, Not on a Formula

*S*ometime in 1977, I took Peter's class in "Policy"—an academic mis-nomer which I still don't like. To me, policy is a rule an organization has as a guide for decision making. So a retailer has a policy of "no returns after thirty days," or a company has a policy of an annual salary review, or another that "the customer is job number one." What academics generally term "policy" is really "strategy." Strategy is what a company plans to do to reach a goal or objective. Drucker actually taught strategy, not policy, and I believe that most of the academic courses of this type would be bet-ter described as strategy, which is what they are really about.

In Drucker's classroom, during one of the first sessions in the course, Peter began to cite various historical examples of strategy that worked or did not work. None of them had to do with him. This was how Peter normally taught. He rarely talked about his own successes, even when we pressed him for personal examples. Occasionally, he would cite an example of success in a company he had consulted for. However, he never took credit. He would just say the XYZ company was faced with such and such situation, and here's what the executive in charge did. He was never trying to convince us of how brilliant or what a great consultant he was. Without being arrogant or intentionally modest, Peter was very comfortable with himself.

On this particular evening, Peter went through a number of companies and industries, giving us the situations they faced and how they responded to them. I don't recall whether he used the phrase "captains of industry," or whether one of my classmates used it in asking a question. However, I made the immediate connection to a course on "great captains" I had taken when I was a cadet at West Point, where of course, we had studied strategy. The phrase "great captains" meant the great military thinkers on strategy. It too, by the way, went under a misnomer. The course was called "Military Art." I suspect that someone reviewing our academic transcripts probably thought it was the military version of a course in the humanities having to do with paintings of battles. However, the fact was I had been studying strategy, albeit in a different form, for a long time.

Strategy is Strategy

The origin of the word "strategy" is the Greek word, "*strategos,*" which means the art of the general. Maybe so, but as I heard Peter's presentation, in a flash it came to me that strategy was strategy, whether in warfare or business. I listened more closely as Drucker told of a particularly well done strategic action where, with limited resources, a company had challenged a much larger competitor.

It was a small company called ICS, Inc., which in the early days of computers and with ninety-six employees, successfully outdid industry giant IBM. The strategy is one we call niching today. That is, ICS, Inc. did not try to be everything to everybody, but concentrated its resources in a small segment of the market, computers for education, and for that market it was the best—with the better product, better service, and better marketing. In that niche, IBM suffered a significant decline in sales due to ICS, Inc.'s efforts. After a couple of years IBM waved the white flag and pulled out of that market completely. It wasn't that IBM couldn't have chased the small company out of this niche had it wanted to do so. But IBM had other fish to fry and places to put its resources, and so it left this particular market to its tiny competitor.

Hearing the ICS story, my mind went to one of the "great captains" I had studied some years earlier at West Point: This was the Carthaginian general, Hannibal. With inferior forces and cut off from his homeland, he had come close to nipping the Roman Empire in the bud while it was still relatively small, before it had grown into the colossus it eventually became.

At the Battle of Cannae in 216 B.C., Hannibal faced a well-trained, well-equipped Roman opponent named Varro who had between two to four times Hannibal's men and resources. Moreover, Varro had "the home team advantage" as he was fighting on Roman soil. Rather than retreat or surrender, Hannibal fought, employing a strategy which not only created victory, but resulted in the most decisive battle in the history of warfare. He annihilated the Roman force of 72,000 and left 80 percent dead on the field of battle. It sounded like an ICS, Inc.-type action to me, although of course ICS didn't leave anyone lying dead in the marketplace. But to those from IBM that had directly opposed ICS in that niche, it probably felt like a crushing defeat on the scale of a Cannae.

Don't Develop Strategy by Formula

Like Hannibal, Peter Drucker did not believe in developing strategy by formula. At least I never saw him teach such a method. Other professors might teach strategy by what is now termed "portfolio management." This included Bruce Henderson and the Boston Consulting Group's well-known four-celled matrix with their division into "problem children," "stars," "cash cows" and "dogs," or the nine-celled matrix developed by the General Electric Company with the McKinsey Consulting Company. Both of these rote methods of strategy development and modifications based on quantitative analysis were taught in almost every class on strategy in every graduate school at the time. Even in marketing, a student spent time analyzing the product life cycle of products, with certain specific strategies recommended at each stage.

Though modified over the years, Bruce Henderson's methodology was a detailed numerical analysis of all businesses, with a resultant grouping of them into categories by a common factor or factors causing these businesses to perform similarly. A grouping based on customers might be one example. These groupings were called Strategic Business Units, or SBUs. The strategist then placed each SBU in the matrix.

The matrix was defined by two axes denoting quantitative measurements of business strength and market growth rate. Each axis was divided equally by a line either vertical or horizontal. So the matrix outlined by the two axes had one horizontal and one vertical line which divided it into four quadrants or cells. From then on, the strategist simply followed standard actions according to their place in the matrix. Those businesses in the dog quadrant you sold or closed down. You used those falling in the cash cow quadrant to fund your stars. You paid particular attention to the question marks, also called problem children, taking actions to turn them into stars, doing some watchful waiting, or withdrawing resources and considering them dogs to be dumped.

This system of strategy development by formula became extremely popular in the 1960's. Many companies found a quick way to dramatically change SBUs from problem children to stars, or even dogs into cash cows, without having to increase sales in individual businesses. All you had to do was to acquire a company in the same group as represented by the troubled SBU. The secret was acquisition, and the logical outcome was for a corporation to grow larger and larger.

Peter would have none of this formulaic nonsense, and, of course, he was proven right. Drucker was all for a logical approach to arriving at a strategy. His famous technique of asking questions which led respondents towards powerful strategic approaches was based on a system of applied logic. However, he avoided precise quantifying inputs to arrive at precise quantified outputs which were intended to direct the manager in exactly what to do and how it was to be done. Such was the four-celled matrix approach. According to the matrix, bigness was supposed to lead to profitability through economies of size. In fact, there were plenty of smaller companies making fortunes, while some giant corporations stumbled and choked on too much acquisition, their size and their loss of efficiency, and their inability to best satisfy the customer. Some failed in the marketplace before they could recover.

Peter was not against acquiring as much information as you could prior to making a strategic decision. He was certainly not against analyzing this information in whatever way brought clarity. He just didn't think that you could develop a successful business strategy by formula after doing this analysis, regardless of what method of categorization was used.

This was a theme that continued throughout Peter's teaching. The manager was supposed to think each different situation through, not to allow a formula or a system to make decisions for him.

It is interesting to compare the formula methodologies with one of Peter's best-known successes in strategy, which I noted in an earlier chapter. This success is known only because Jack Welch, the CEO of General Electric, went public with it. Peter had asked Welch only two questions. "If you weren't already in a business, would you enter it today?" and "If the answer is no, what are you going to do about it?"

This was Peter's way. He would ask questions. Some executives in companies he consulted with talked about being frustrated by his methods. He didn't tell them what to do. He analyzed a company's situation and then asked the questions which caused them to think through and articulate their own successful strategies. This made it a little more difficult for me to understand what he was telling us as his students. It was clear that he was definitely against some sort of formula for developing strategy. But how in the world does one analyze the situation and then begin asking the right questions?

The Search for Drucker's Methodology

Once I started teaching I used Hannibal and the Battle of Cannae as an example in teaching business strategy. Like ICS, Inc., it proved that with the right strategy, a smaller organization could overcome a much stronger competitor. I wanted my students to understand that managing a business was not simply reaction to environmental conditions, but formulation of unique strategies to reach the intended objectives.

Although Peter's injunction not to adopt a strategy based on formula was clear, and I understood that he had a certain way of looking at things, I did not understand his method. What was it, exactly? I know that the simplest thing would have been to ask him. However, many of us had done just that in the classroom. In reviewing his comments and explanations, he told us what to do, but not how to do it. I concluded that he himself might not recognize what he was doing to result in his successful advice based on his analysis. But I knew it was significant that he invariably posed questions which clients themselves had to think through. Why not simply provide the solution?

How Peter Analyzed Things

I went back over what Peter had taught in the classroom and also reread articles that he had written on the subject. It seemed to me that certain common characteristics emerged. He believed that general principles didn't change, but that they might need to be applied differently depending on the situation.

I believe that, as a consultant, Peter first looked at a company's overall objectives to see if they matched his basic injunction, which was to determine what business the company was in, who the customer was, what the customer wanted, and what the customer termed "successful" in fulfilling this want. Presumably if an organization had not first done this, he would have insisted that it be done before he would proceed to an analysis.

In his analysis, Peter would look at two classes of variables in any situation. One set of variables he considered "fixed" or "certain," or at least relatively fixed. Consider demographics. Demographics might change, and company executives could probably recognize a trend for the future. But for the period in which the strategy was to be implemented they could assume the demographics to be fixed, meaning, in this state, they were also certain. Such "certainties" had to be faced, whether or not they were unpleasant. For example, demographics might be a negative factor that must be considered by industry. Or they could be a very positive factor leading to an opportunity. In any case, the strategist had little control over them.

The other set of variables were those over which the strategist might exercise more control. These might include the product or service and its quality, pricing, and means of distribution, etc.

Increasing global competition was a real challenge. Here was an issue Peter was very much aware of, due to his consulting work, especially in Japan. He frequently cautioned us to consider the global competition factor. Even before the oil crises of the 1970's, he felt this "certain" variable had simply been ignored by most American industries. He pointed out that as early as the late 1950's, Detroit automobile manufacturers knew that overseas competitors were acquiring the capability of producing high-quality, low-cost cars. As quality increased, and with the right marketing, this development would invariably lead to their capturing a dominant share of the American market. They would do so unless a new strategy was implemented in what was then the present. Despite this, little or nothing was done.

The oil crises, and the fact that foreign cars, especially Japanese cars, were more fuel efficient than American cars, was simply the luck of the draw, which speeded an inevitable process. They would have still taken giant shares from the American companies without this unpredicted occurrence, although even the importance of fuel efficiency might have been predicted from an analysis of our dependency on foreign oil over which we had little control.

Drucker knew that risk could not be avoided. Risk was certain. There were unknowns in every situation, and the precise future was a mystery. He felt that these unknowns could best be dealt with and minimized by first deciding what a corporation wanted to do and then setting out to do it—that is, creating one's future (see Chapter 11). Therefore, one had to plan ahead and then take the actions necessary to achieve the desired goals. Of course, major threats should be identified, along with some alternative strategies should any of these threats occur. That might have been done by American companies in planning for stiffer competition from all foreign cars, those coming from Japan and elsewhere. Of course, it was not.

So, Peter's method must have started with an analysis of the situation in the marketplace and identifying what he called certainties, or factors that we could not control that would be faced.

In addition to analyzing the environment as one class of "certainty" variables, Peter also looked at the company and its resources on hand or those it could obtain at the particular time needed. Since this was only partly under control of the strategist, this would actually be considered a "certainty" and consideration would have been necessary as a reality check. Could the company reasonably attain its objectives given the resources it had at its disposal?

Strategic Solutions

How did Drucker come up with highly creative strategic solutions which were so simple, yet so powerful? By his own admission, he brought not his specific knowledge of a company or industry to bear, but his ignorance. So he must have had some means of quickly determining the strategy to employ to achieve the objectives desired.

Many observers noticed his ability to cut through an unbelievably complicated strategic situation to get right to the heart of the matter and drive listening executives, through questions, to what the organization should do to reach its objectives. I believe that he could only have been able to do this with basic principles which he employed in every strategic situation he encountered. Drucker never articulated strategic principles in the classroom, and he may not have been aware of exactly what he was doing himself, but there is no other explanation. As I indicated earlier, Peter felt that there were certain basic principles in all management that were unchanging.

I recall a successful executive who had a reputation of being extraordinarily successful in having a strong strategic sense under great pressure and limited time. When asked his secret, he stated something to the effect that he had immersed himself in studying his profession to such an extent that even under pressure, this knowledge and his experience was somehow integrated without his having to consciously weigh the various factors. As a result, he was able to make the correct decision; without suffering delay or introspection, he was able to articulate a successful strategy. I believe it was the same with Drucker. Through his study and work, he had unconsciously evolved certain principles of strategy such that he was able to look at a situation and immediately understand how to achieve the objective desired.

The question was, could I discover these principles without Peter's direct help? I believe that Peter showed me that they existed, but I had to uncover them on my own. This was a typical Drucker scenario which sometimes frustrated his clients. Almost like an oracle, he would give strong hints and point a student in the right direction. But it was up to the student to go the rest of the way. I succeeded, but this process took me much longer than I thought it would.

My Search for Drucker's Strategic Principles

To determine the essential principles of strategy that Drucker used, I researched not only his work, but strategists and strategic thinkers spanning more than 7,000 years of recorded history, from both east and west, and representing a wide variety of fields.

I studied the writings of ancient Chinese strategists like Sun Tzu, T'ai Kung Chiang Shang, and Sun Pin, as well as Epaminondas of Thebes, who at Leuctra in 371 B.C., defeated the "unbeatable" Spartans, although they outnumbered his forces, two to one. My research included the well-known German military writer Karl von Clausewitz, but also his contemporary and, some say, the superior strategist, the Swiss general Antoine-Henri Jomini.

Then there were more modern strategists such as the Englishman B. H. Liddell Hart and the Italian economist-strategist Vilfredo Paredo. In 1897, Paredo found he could statistically prove the value of economizing to concentrate resources. He developed the 80/20 principle: 80 percent of results are derived from only 20 percent of the effort—a crucial comment on the proper allocation of always-limited resources. I tried to relate what resulted in these successes to what might prove successful in modern business.

I wish I had been able to conduct my research on an ongoing basis, but other projects kept cropping up which forced me to drop this work temporarily and to do something else.

At first I identified several hundred principles of strategy. However, many were repetitive. I finally whittled this list to only fourteen principles of the original group which I thought were completely nonrepetitive. I extended the results of my research to other endeavors. I actually did some research including office politics, sports, and even romance. I was surprised, but the principles endured in many different areas of human endeavor.

I didn't share this research with Peter at the time. I thought that I'd better get it all together before approaching him. Also it looked like I had a way to go. Some of my fourteen principles were too specific to certain situations. Others needed to be reworked for clarity and emphasis. Eventually, I refined my original list again, this time to ten essential principles. I was pretty proud of myself. They were the distillation from the thinking of the greatest strategists who have ever lived in many areas of human activity, and in my opinion, they were applicable across the board to all areas on human endeavor, including, of course, business.

I saw Peter at Claremont after concluding this research at a conference held there in the spring of 2004. I had told him about my work sometime previously. I had hoped to speak with him at the conference as it was almost done, but I did not get the opportunity. He had stopped teaching, and his colleagues told me that he was clearing out his garage and getting his papers in order and turning them over to the university.

For various reasons, including both of our schedules and his declining health, I did not get an opportunity to share these strategy principles with him before publication of them as *The Art of the Strategist* (AMACOM, 2004). So I cannot say whether he would have agreed with them or whether he would have recognized them as those principles that had been drivers in his thinking. I did have a number of CEOs and others review them and comment. I believe they are the essential principles of strategy, but I cannot claim them to be Drucker's principles of strategy. Still, as was pointed out at his memorial service after his death, we, his former students, are all Peter's "apprentices." So, from one of many apprentices, here is what I came up with.

My Ten Principles of Strategy

1. *Commit fully to a definite objective.* You will probably note the similarity to Peter's requirement that you first have to decide what business you are in. My mantra has been that you can't get to where you are going until you know where that is. However, note the other components of this principle, too. The objective must be precisely defined, and you must commit fully to it.

2. *Seize the initiative and keep it.* The main reason for this is that not only business, but life, is competitive. How many stories have you heard about individuals who think that they have a great idea, but delay in developing it or bringing it to market? Maybe they never do and someone else does and is highly successful. Or maybe they do, but someone else gets in just a little bit sooner. So this principle says you must get the initiative and keep it until you achieve your goal. Although Drucker taught thinking, the thinking and planning were worthless if they didn't lead to taking action. If one didn't seize the initiative and retain it, a competitor would have.

3. *Economize to mass your resources.* You can't be strong everywhere. The idea is to economize or eliminate waste of time or resources on unimportant aspects of the situation, and concentrate them where they are important. The concept is to concentrate superior resources where they are important, at the decisive point. This is exactly what Drucker was saying when he asked Jack Welch his two famous questions: "If you weren't already in a business, would you enter it today?" and "If the answer is no, what are you going to do about it?" GE owned some businesses that were earning less money than others. The company was expending resources less than optimally. Welch made the decision that if a GE-owned business was not first or second in its industry it should be axed. This was the first of many strategies that led to his increasing GE's market capitalization by $400 billion during his twenty year tenure.

4. *Use strategic positioning.* To achieve any strategic objective, you will probably need to maneuver due to environmental or other unexpected changes. You may need to modify your approach and your positioning, even as you continue to work toward an objective. That's why if what you are doing isn't working you need to alter your strategy to something that will work. I have heard that continuing to take the same action but expecting different results is one definition of insanity. Although Peter told us that re-organization was the equivalent of major surgery, he added the cautionary note that sometimes major surgery was necessary.

5. *Do the unexpected.* When you have competition, it is most effective to surprise your competition and do the unexpected. Peter once pointed out that Sony did this with the transistor. Though the transistor was invented in the U.S., American companies were committed to the vacuum tube and estimated that the transistor could not be commercialized for many years. So they didn't try. Sony licensed the transistor patent and, in a couple of years, built a workable portable transistor radio which grew into a business which soon made vacuum tubes obsolete. This principle can also be profitably applied with customers, so long as the surprise is pleasant. It goes along with the concept of giving your customers more than they expect.

6. *Keep things simple.* Someone at NASA once calculated that if every single one of the parts in one of NASA rockets was 99.9 percent reliable, the rocket would fail 50 percent of the time. The more things that can go wrong, the more will go wrong. If you want less to go wrong, keep your strategy simple. Peter's concepts and the strategies they led to were never very complex. They were easy to implement.

7. *Prepare multiple simultaneous alternatives.* Since some actions inspired by your thinking are going to fail, you should always have "Plan B" in place and be ready to implement it. Peter felt that many strategies were not mutually exclusive. If one idea didn't work, don't abandon the objective, proceed with an alternative.

8. *Take the indirect route to your objective.* Moving directly against any human thought or endeavor arouses opposition. No one likes to be sold anything. However, most people are eager to take advantage of a bargain. The difference is subtle, but the results can be decisive. The same principle holds true in a situation where there is competition that must be faced. The strategy you use may make all the difference. Sony, for example, didn't set out directly to replace the vacuum tube with the transistor. Rather, Sony put the transistor in a product and proved its advantages. Sony didn't need to hit anyone on the head and sell the transistor's advantages. They were obvious.

9. *Practice timing and sequencing.* The Bible says that there is a time for every purpose under heaven. Implementing the "right" strategy at the wrong time or in the wrong sequence can be just as ineffective as if the strategy was all wrong.

Peter arrived in England as a refugee from Nazi Germany after having been previously accepted for a teaching position at a major German university. Yet although he wanted to teach, he didn't do so during the entire four years he spent in England. Instead, he worked in the insurance and banking industry as an analyst and spent much of his time devoted to writing a major book in English. Why didn't he teach at a major English university? My guess is either his verbal English was not yet fluent, or it was because of his Viennese accent, which he never lost. So he understood that the timing was not right and he proceeded to write a book, *The End of Economic Man,* which was considered so insightful and on target that it was favorably reviewed by none other than Winston Churchill.

10. *Exploit your success.* Don't stop or slow down when you are achieving your objectives. Not staying continually ahead of your competition is simply giving your competition another chance to stop you. Again, we can look at Drucker's career for an example of how this principle can be applied. Drucker didn't stop teaching, writing, and consulting until the very end of his life. While in his sixties, he would joke with us that he was thankful for the opportunity to teach us because the alternative was to go to a home for the aged. Drucker is an icon in management even after his death, with no serious competitor for the title of "The Father of Modern Management," because he never gave his potential competition a chance to catch up.

Presenting His Strategy

The fact that Peter Drucker always presented his strategic advice as questions has been mentioned previously, without much explanation. Most people simply thought this habit was a quirk of genius. The recipients of his questions may not have particularly enjoyed this method of receiving Peter's wisdom, but considering from whom it was emanating and its results, they were prepared to accept this guidance in whatever form it was presented. However, I think the reason for Peter's presentation in this fashion had to do with a number of real factors.

First, Peter was a one-man band. Unlike the major consulting groups, he did not arrive with droves of subordinates and someone to work his PowerPoint slides. He was Peter Drucker out there by himself. He didn't even bring along an assistant or a secretary. By this means of presenting his strategy, he didn't need a large team or elaborate equipment.

Also, Peter told people what to do, not how to do it. He did this in his books and articles, in his presentations to corporate management, and of course, in the classroom. Although there is probably a hierarchy of strategic actions which can be distinguished by an infinite number of divisions, traditionally there are but three.

Imagine a pyramid. At the apex and highest level is grand strategy. This is the strategy planned at the top level of a corporation or any entity. One level down, grand strategy is supported by what we could term operational strategy. Operational strategy would be performed to implement the strategy decided at the top. The final level is termed tactics. Tactics are the actions taken to implement the level above it, which again we called operational strategy.

Peter always dealt at the top level. When he advised Jack Welch or other CEOs, he wasn't giving advice on how to do anything. He didn't have the specialized knowledge. Remember, he came to any situation not with his knowledge and experience of the business, but with his ignorance (see Chapter 6). He was telling Welch and GE what to do, not how to do it. How to do it was the operational strategy. The grand strategy for GE was to wean out less profitable businesses. How this grand strategy was to be accomplished was decided by Welch: "If a business is not first or second in its market, get rid of it."

Drucker Lesson Summary

There were three key aspects of any situation that Drucker had to take into consideration. These were:

- what Drucker called the "certain" or fixed variables of the environment over which the strategist had little control, along with the resources already available or those that could be obtained.

- the variables over which the strategist could always exercise control, and which could support the strategy decided upon.

- the principles which he knew intuitively and applied unconsciously.

He then had to put all these variables together in such a way as to achieve the objectives desired.

Although Peter never explained it in detail, I believe his application of the strategy principles I described, or principles similar to them, were the basis of his ability to ask questions which led to highly effective strategies in implementation. At the same time, he had to consider the relevant "certainties" in each situation. We are not Peter Druckers. Perhaps we cannot see the best strategies in any situation so easily or as quickly as he was able to see them. However, knowing these principles and the model of what he did, we can apply them to any strategic situation for success—not by formula or computer simulation, but by thinking through each issue as it is presented.

How to Motivate the Knowledge Worker

*D*rucker was very sensitive to the role and work of the worker. As he saw it, companies were increasingly dependent on the "knowledge worker," a term he had created some years earlier to denote the new worker, who worked not primarily physically with his body doing physical labor, but with his mind. However, to Peter, all workers were of significant actual and potential value to the firm. He resented it when management talked of the *cost* of labor. And he didn't like to think of *managing* workers, either, although at times he used both of these terms. To Peter, labor was not an expense; labor was added value, a resource, potentially the greatest resource that an organization possessed. Managers didn't "manage" workers, they led them. Peter was the first person I had heard at the time to make the distinction between management and leadership. Moreover, Peter took on some of the leading researchers in motivation, whose theories are still discussed and followed: McGregor, Maslow, and Herzberg.

With his discussion of knowledge workers as a background from previous lectures, it was no surprise when Peter began his lecture one late afternoon by repeating that one did not manage workers; one had to lead them.

"Leadership demands ethical and effective motivation," he said. "This cannot be done by Theory X, the carrot-and-stick approach, which was the primary means used in the past. For one thing, the situation in the workplace is entirely different today. Workers have alternatives, and if they don't like the work situation, they can leave. This was never true a hundred years ago, or even fifty years ago. However, this isn't the only reason, and it is not because the carrot does not work. It does.

"The problem," Peter continued, "is that it works too well. The inevitable result is that both knowledge workers and managers motivated under Theory X want increasingly more and more carrot so that, eventually, the increase in productivity is outweighed by the increased cost."

At this point Peter paused. Then he continued, "However, the notion that Theory Y in the form promoted by most of its adherents is the solution, is nonsense."

Theory Y Is Not the Answer

Now this last statement was surprising. Theory X vs. Theory Y was the concept of the two alternative theories of motivation proposed by Douglas McGregor in his book, *The Human Side of Enterprise* (McGraw-Hill, 1960). Theory X was the old carrot-and-stick approach. The manager told the worker what to do. If the worker did what the manager wanted and did it well, he got the carrot. If he failed to do this, he got the stick. McGregor contrasted this with Theory Y.

Under Theory Y, the worker had a large say and participated in defining the work and how it was performed. According to many of Theory Y's adherents, the worker should have the final say, since it was the worker who was closest to the action. This was "new management," in which the manager was relegated to almost a figurehead, or maybe a cheerleader position, as opposed to the bad old authoritarian management style of times past.

This clearly was a precursor to the empowerment element of Total Quality Management (TQM), which fifteen years later led to the disappearance of a "man in charge" in favor of complete self-direction. The weakness in this notion was exposed by what Drucker said next. "It will always be necessary for an individual to be in charge," Peter said. "Without someone in charge you have a completely permissive organization without anyone at the helm. This will invariably lead to chaos."

When Peter made his statement rejecting Theory Y as most explained it, he was bucking a trend which was much in tune with the ideas of "real freedom" and "gentle treatment" advocated by the permissive culture of the previous decade. As with many of his predictions, he lived to see this one come true. Peter was not against TQM when it came on the scene a few years later. Total quality, empowerment, ownership, continuous improvement . . . who in his right mind would object to these objectives of a concept of motivational management? Still, the lengths that some organizations went in applying TQM concepts to reach unquestionably worthwhile ends could result in serious problems.

Shortly after the peak of TQM activities, *Fortune* magazine revealed the results from a two-part survey in which 750,000 middle managers from one thousand large companies were asked questions over two three-year periods which roughly corresponded to the introduction and implementation versus the continuance of TQM in their companies. These middle managers were asked to rank how their organizations were doing on several issues that a total quality program could be expected to improve.

Fortune was surprised to discover the overall results between the first survey and the second, that is, the time period that corresponded roughly to the introduction of TQM and to its firm establishment within an organization. The number of managers that said their companies' executives communicated well with employees, listened to employee problems, or treated managers with respect as individuals, all declined. In addition, fewer managers said that their companies were a good place to work.[1]

But there was even more evidence that TQM could be dangerous as many practiced it. Florida Power & Light, winner of Japan's Deming Prize for quality management, gutted its quality program because of universal complaints by an important segment of company employees. Not the managers or executives, but the very segment of the company that was supposed to benefit most within a company: the workers. Another corporation, The Wallace Company, a Houston oil supply company, won the prestigious United States Malcolm Baldrige National Quality Award, which was based completely on the implementation of TQM. Shortly after receiving the award, Wallace filed for protection under the Chapter 11 bankruptcy law.[2]

As Peter had foreseen, even a concept with the correct objectives could lead to chaos if empowerment of workers led to mostly disempowerment of managers. What, then, did Peter recommend?

Drucker's Recommendations

Peter again stated that Theory X was not the answer. Nor was Theory Y, if it was defined as a leaderless organization. He cited a number of successful companies that were successful in applying a type of non-permissive motivation, but not Theory X. This kind of motivation included the following elements:

- There is a responsible manager in authority.

- Workers are led, not managed.

- The workplace is participatory, but not "free-wheeling."

- Workers are not motivated through money alone.

- Each worker is motivated differently, according to the individual and the situation.

- Management recognizes that workers could leave the organization. Therefore, workers are treated as if they are volunteers, and, above all, treated with respect.

Secrets of Motivation

It was not until several years later that I dug out my notes from Peter's lectures and put them together in an organized fashion. On receiving my doctorate I had left industry to teach. I started teaching part-time at the University of Southern California and California State University, Los Angeles. A few months later I accepted a full-time professorship at the latter. A number of organizations began asking me to assist in training and giving workshops for their members. Motivation was a subject of prime interest.

I put together a program which I called "Secrets of Motivation." I went back to my notes and incorporated all of Peter's ideas. I have updated the basic presentation many times over the last twenty-five years. Still, Peter's basic concepts shine through.

One of the first questions that I asked my corporate students was: "Why are people motivated to do things for you or for your organization?" Then I answered my own question: "The truth is there is no one single factor which motivates all of your people all of the time. Also, different people are motivated by different things at any one point in time."

I did not have the following example when I first put my motivational program together. But it fit so well that I have included it ever since I discovered it.

Treat Your People Individually

While rummaging through old bookstores, Jim Toth, a professor at the Industrial College of the Armed Forces, found a little ninety-nine-page book written after World War I by Captain Adolf von Schell, a German officer who was attending a course in the United States as an exchange officer. Von Schell was highly experienced. He had served throughout World War I, first in command of an infantry platoon and later in command of a company. He wrote the book *Battle Leadership* while attending the Advanced Class of the U.S. Infantry School at Ft. Benning, Georgia from 1930 to 1931.

The book related von Schell's observations on leadership from the vantage point of a junior officer in the Imperial German Army. Toth realized the collection of lessons from von Schell was as valuable in the present as on the day von Schell first recorded it. Toth contacted the Marine Corps Association, which agreed to reprint the book. In a preface, Marine Corps Major General D. M. Twomey said that the book "should be required reading for all combat leaders."[3] Captain von Schell's lessons show the age-old importance of knowing and understanding your workers and managers and treating each individually, as he or she prefers to be treated. This is just as Drucker taught in the classroom.

In his book, von Schell cited a classic example of this art as practiced by a German brigade commander in the year 1917:

> This general said, "Each of our three regimental commanders must be handled differently. Colonel A does not want an order. He wants to do everything himself, and he always does well. Colonel B executes every order, but he has no initiative. Colonel C opposes everything he is told to do and wants to do the contrary."

A few days later the troops confronted a well-entrenched enemy whose position would have to be attacked. The general issued the following individual orders:

To Colonel A (who wants to do everything himself):

"My dear Colonel A, I think we will attack. Your regiment will have to carry the burden of the attack. I have, however, selected you for this reason. The boundaries of your regiment are so and so. Attack at X hour. I don't have to tell you anything more."

To Colonel C (who opposes everything):

"We have met a very strong enemy. I am afraid we will not be able to attack with the forces at our disposal."

"Oh, General, certainly we will attack. Just give my regiment the time of attack and you will see that we are successful," replied Colonel C.

"Go, then, we will try it," said the general, giving him the order for the attack, which he had prepared sometime previously.

To Colonel B (who must always have detailed orders), the attack order was merely sent with additional details.

All three regiments attacked splendidly.

The general knew his subordinates; he knew that each one was different and had to be handled differently in order to achieve results. He had estimated the psychological situation correctly. It is comparatively easy to make a correct estimate if one knows the person concerned; but even then it is often difficult, because the person doesn't always remain the same. He is no machine. He may react one way today, another way tomorrow.

Soldiers can be brave one day and afraid the next. Soldiers are not machines but human beings who must be led in war. Each one of them reacts differently at different times and must be handled each time according to his particular reaction. To sense this and to arrive at a correct psychological solution is part of the art of leadership.[4]

Von Schell's example shows us how important it is to treat your people individually. This is not only true in battle, but as Peter understood, in business, too. In fact, in all organizations.

But the biggest mistake that leaders make is not even understanding what motivates most of their followers most of the time. As Peter said more than once, motivation by material rewards is not the whole story.

What Do You Think Motivates Workers?

Social scientists have studied many industries to determine what factors workers consider most important in their jobs. Over the years, questionnaires have been given to hundreds of thousands of workers, to both knowledge workers and the ordinary garden-variety worker. While the results have been known for sometime, they aren't well-known. One of these studies was done by the Public Agenda Foundation and referred to by John Naisbitt and Patricia Aburdene in their book *Re-inventing the Corporation* (Warner Books, 1985).

Before I give you these results, maybe you would like to take the test yourself. I've given it to thousands of leaders in my seminars and courses. All you need to do is to rank the following factors in the order of importance you think your employees would put them. Take a couple of minutes to do this before going on. Rank each factor in its order of importance to those who work for you, with "1" being most important, "2" being second most important, etc. There are thirteen factors in all in this list to rank.

SURVEY: WHAT DO YOU THINK WORKERS WANT?

__ Work with people who treat me with respect

__ Interesting work

__ Recognition for good work

__ Chance to develop skills

__ Working for people who listen if you have ideas about how to do things better

__ A chance to think for myself, rather than just carry out instructions

__ Seeing the end results of my work

__ Working for efficient managers

__ A job that is not too easy

__ Feeling well informed about what is going on

__ Job security

___ High pay

___ Good benefits

Now, here are the results. . . . If you were looking for another chart show-ing you the rankings, you already have them! That's right, the factors in the Survey are ranked exactly in the order of importance to your employees.

I repeat, the factors are ranked exactly in their order as listed. You are probably surprised with these results. I was. These are the results after interviewing or using this survey for hundreds of thousands of workers. How many did you get right? Most managers put job security, high pay, or good benefits in the top five. Some managers put all three in the top five or even list them as the top three. The reality is that these three fac-tors are frequently far down on the workers' list, and in the overall results, these factors are last.

Now this doesn't mean that job security, high pay, and good benefits aren't important. They are. However, for most workers, the other factors are more important. Without a doubt, Drucker's contention that there is more to motivation than money alone is confirmed by this research.

Max DePree, is former chairman and CEO of Herman Miller, Inc., the furniture maker that *Fortune* magazine once named one of the ten "best managed" and "most innovative" companies. His company was also cho-sen as one of the hundred best companies to work for in America. In his best-selling book *Leadership Is an Art,* (Dell Publishing, 1989) DePree said, "The best people working for organizations are like volunteers. Since they could probably find good jobs in any number of groups, they choose to work somewhere for reasons less tangible than salary or posi-tion. Volunteers do not need contracts, they need covenants."[5] I've heard Peter say much the same thing: "If we want to motivate workers properly, we must think of them as volunteers."

Does This Organization Exist?

Can you think of an organization which has all of the following attributes?

- The workers work very hard physically, including weekends, with little complaint.

- The workers receive no money and little material compensation for their services.

- The work is dangerous and workers are frequently injured on the job.

- The work is strictly voluntary.

- The workers usually have very high morale.

- The organization always has more workers than can be fully employed.

- The workers are highly motivated to achieve the organization's goals.

Very few people are able to come up with the correct answer. How about a high school football team? "Ah," you say. "But that's not work—football is a game. That's play." Exactly right. And that's part of the secret of motivating your knowledge workers: we need to make work more like a volunteer game, more like play.

Work Needs to Be Interesting

Peter recognized that money by itself is not a good motivator. He referred to Frederick Herzberg, who had developed the concept of job enrichment in his book *The Motivation to Work* (New York: John Wiley & Sons, 1959). The idea was to improve and restructure work processes and their environments to make them more satisfying to workers. While workers could feel less than satisfied for many reasons, less than interesting work was an important element. This is probably the reason that it was ranked number two in the results cited in the survey in *Re-inventing the Corporation*.

Can you provide interesting work, or can you make the work that your workers must do interesting in some way? There are many opportunities to do this, if you think about it. This is why a competitive activity like football, even though dangerous and "hard work," can exhibit such positive motivational qualities.

Treating People with Respect Gains Respect

Isn't it within your power to treat people with respect and insure that others who work for you do the same? Certainly every human being deserves to be treated with respect. Many outstanding leaders maintain that you should treat those who work for you with even more than respect. Mary Kay Ash, the amazing woman who built a billion-dollar corporation, Mary

Kay Cosmetics, recommended that you should imagine everyone you see wearing a large sign saying, "MAKE ME FEEL IMPORTANT."

James MacGregor Burns, an American political scientist, wrote an outstanding, scholarly, book called simply, *Leadership* (Harper & Row publishers, 1978). In fact, the book won the Pulitzer Prize. Listen to his succinct advice, for Drucker himself could not have put it much better: "In real life, the most practical advice for leaders is not to treat pawns like pawns, nor princes like princes, but all persons like persons."[6]

Peter followed this advice. He treated virtually everyone with respect. I suspect that not only CEOs but heads of state were treated exactly the way he treated his students.

Recognition for Good Work Is Desired and Deserved

Peter taught that recognition for good work was required on two levels. First, human beings crave such recognition, and so it is desired and an important part of motivating achievement. Such recognition could be in many forms. He quoted Napoleon Bonaparte, who on speaking of the gaudy medals he awarded, is said to have exclaimed, "It's amazing what men will do for such baubles." Napoleon may have been correct, but Drucker was not so cynical. To Drucker, the fact that recognition is desired by all human beings, including workers, meant that it was in part compensation for the work performed. Therefore, it was deserved.

Everyone wants recognition when they do good work, including those who you may wish to motivate. There are so many ways to recognize your employees. Management expert Bob Nelson actually identified over a thousand! He published them in a book entitled, *1001 Ways to Reward Employees* (New York: Workman Press, 1994).

Workers Should Be Able to Develop Their Skills

Do you create the opportunity for those in your organization to develop their skills? Can you provide special courses in-house? How about a few hours off every week to complete a college degree? Maybe you can hire a physical fitness instructor to work with employees during lunch or after work. Sometimes an employee has the ability to do this, or has unique knowledge in a special area and may be willing to instruct other employees. All you need to do is ask. Don't forget that you and other managers or workers in your organization can act as teachers if any have expertise in special areas. Of course, those who teach also learn.

Listening Is a Sure Motivator

There is little question that listening motivates. It may be far more important in motivation than you ever realized, and as we will see in the next
chapter, Peter considered it an important part of self-development.

When Robert W. Galvin was chairman of the board and chief executive officer of Motorola, Inc., his company did $6.7 billion in annual
sales and employed 50,000 people around the globe. What did the head
of a billion-dollar company stress in his leadership practices? "I emphasize listening," said Chairman Galvin. "We strive to hear what other
people want us to hear, even though they don't always come out and say
it directly."[7]

Mary Kay Ash maintained that listening was an art. She said: "If I'm
talking to someone in a crowded room, I try to make that person feel as
though we're the only ones present. I shut out everything else. I look
directly at the person. Even if a gorilla were to walk into the room, I probably wouldn't notice it."[8]

Let Workers Think for Themselves

Are you open to letting your people think for themselves? Drucker said
that you could tell people what to do. However, he also taught us that
managers who motivate know that they must allow their workers to
decide how to do most parts of their jobs for themselves. Peter didn't
mean that you shouldn't give help if asked. What he did mean was that
we need to recognize that people have their own abilities, experiences,
and unique backgrounds. That's why they're such valuable commodities.
They have a lot to contribute. It's wasteful to do all of the thinking for
everyone in your organization. Try it and sooner or later you are certain
to run into difficulties.

Even if you could do all of the thinking for all of your workers, you
would be ill-advised to do so. If all of your people thought exactly like
you, your organization would have a pretty limited source of ideas. In
addition, researchers have discovered that there is a synergy created such
that the product of many separate brains working together is far greater
than the sum of each considered separately. If you try to do all the thinking in your organization yourself, you lose this important synergism. Let
your workers do their own thinking, and you'll be amazed and surprised
at what they come up with and how they use their expertise to solve
your problems.

What about Salary, Job Security, and Benefits?

Of course, salary, job security, and good benefits are important. But they are not of primary importance. You may think that it is different in your company. Let's analyze this and see if it is true.

If you've been in a company for any length of time, you've seen people leave voluntarily. When asked why they are leaving, they will usually respond that they have better offers elsewhere. They may even begin to detail all the advantages of their new positions: higher salaries, bigger jobs, more benefits, more opportunities for the future, etc.

If you listen carefully, however, you'll hear a message, even if it isn't precisely verbalized. The underlying message is this: "These people who just hired me really appreciate what I have to offer. They recognize my real importance to a much greater extent than those here. They are giving me all these benefits because I am especially important." In other words, although the higher salary and additional benefits were inducements to leave an organization, they may only provide the rationale for the real reason.

Remember, there are voluntary organizations for which pay, benefits, and job security are nonexistent. Yet those who work in these organizations perform to their maximum. There are those who for low pay work on dangerous archeological digs. There are also voluntary hospital workers and the Peace Corps, the "Big Brothers" programs, the Boy Scouts and Girl Scouts, and hundreds of other organizations. What part do salary, benefits, and job security play in motivation in these organizations?

Motivations Are Interrelated and Connected

In the 1950's, a social scientist by the name of Abraham Maslow developed a theory of how all motivations fit together. Maslow called his theory the hierarchy of needs. You may have heard of it before. Peter thought Maslow's work to be of importance, not only because of his including compensation at the bottom of the pyramid, but because of his insight that these needs were not fixed in magnitude, but that the more a need was satisfied, the less its satisfaction mattered.

According to Maslow, we are motivated by various human needs. These needs are at different levels. As one level of needs is satisfied, people are no longer motivated by them. People seek to satisfy the next higher level of needs.

Maslow's first level consists of physiological needs like eating or breathing. Once these basic physiological needs are satisfied, people seek the next highest level. These are security or safety needs. That's where salary, benefits, and job security come in. Note that they are also at the bottom of the pyramid.

On the next level are social or affiliation needs. After this comes the esteem level. Respect and recognition are motivational at this level. Maslow's highest level is self-actualization. That is, to be everything you are capable of, Maslow also identified two categories of needs not on his hierarchy. These were the desire to know and understand, and aesthetic needs.

Let's see how Maslow's theory might affect motivation from a practical standpoint. Once knowledge workers have achieved their needs at a certain level, they are no longer motivated by the levels below. Do you stop and worry about breathing? Not unless you have health problems affecting your ability to breathe. It is the same with salary, benefits, and job security. If an employee has a salary, benefits, and job security in amounts he finds acceptable, these may no longer motivate. Of course, if there is a threat of losing these three factors, they may become motivational once again.

Maslow's Hierarchy of Needs helps to explain why high salary, good benefits, and job security may not be as important as other motivational factors, except as symbols of these other factors.

Symbols are important. Some years ago, I worked at a company that gave a salary review every year. The amount of annual salary raise was keyed to performance. A top performer could get as much as a 10 percent increase. An average performer received a lower percentage increase for the year. Someone performing below par didn't receive an increase. One year the company had a very bad year. Company management felt that it could not afford the same percentage of increases as it had used in the past. It explained the situation to all employees and informed them of its decision. Everyone in the company, including top management, would be limited to a two percent increase for the top performers. Despite the fact that the actual amount of increase was much lower than in previous years, it was still a motivator because the increases were symbolic of high achievement and were not awarded to everyone.

Different Motivators Accomplish Different Things

According to Peter, considering Maslow's hierarchy by itself was insufficient. Frederick Herzberg, who I mentioned previously, built on Maslow's work. Peter felt that Herzberg's work was also a significant contribution because he recognized that as certain needs or wants become satisfied, they cease to be incentives for higher achievement.

Herzberg collected data on job attitudes among employees in hundreds of companies. From studying this data, he concluded that workers have two completely different categories of needs which affect satisfaction or dissatisfaction with a job.

The first category he called "hygiene" factors. He gave them this name because these needs serve the function of preventative medicine, at least in the workplace. They prevent job dissatisfaction. They are also distinguished by the fact that these needs are never completely satisfied. You have to keep maintaining them, or else you lose performance. You can't, however, increase performance with them. But if your organization is already performing well, you can help to maintain these high standards with the hygiene factors.

Hygiene factors include money, status, treatment of followers and security. This relates back to the example of compensation. Money is a good compensator in order to earn enough to survive, or to live at a certain level. Above that level, it ceases to be an incentive and becomes what Herzberg classified as a hygiene factor. This phenomenon is well-known in the management of sales teams, in which most of the salesperson's salary depends directly on the level of sales. Up to a certain point this increased compensation acts as a motivator for the salesperson to make higher sales. But above that point, salespeople have been known to actually quit trying to sell! They have achieved a satisfactory level of compensation, and are happy to go about their business until the next month.

The second category, according to Herzberg, includes motivating factors that relate to the job itself. They involve feelings of achievement, recognition for accomplishment, challenging work, increased responsibility, and growth and development. These are the factors that produce job satisfaction as contrasted with the hygiene needs that only prevent job dissatisfaction. And, as Peter taught, they are underutilized in many organizations, but are necessary due to the limitations of the hygiene factors.

Herzberg's work is important because it shows that if we reduce the hygiene factors, we're going to get job dissatisfaction. How would you feel if someone reduced your salary? To avoid job dissatisfaction, we maintain the hygiene factors at their present levels. Of course there are exceptions to this rule. Most workers will accept a reduction in salary or benefits if everyone gets them for the good of the organization, just as in the case of the percentage of salary raise mentioned above.

Can we increase job satisfaction by, say, increasing salary? Not according to Herzberg. Remember, salary is a hygiene factor. If we want those we lead to be more satisfied with their jobs, we must use the motivators. That is, we must look for ways that we can increase:

- feelings of achievement

- recognition

- challenge in the work

- responsibility

- growth and development

So we're back to Peter's original wisdom again: we cannot depend on financial rewards by themselves, or even as primary motivators. We must use the motivational factors as indicated both by Herzberg and the results of the worker surveys that I discussed previously.

Can You Give Workers What They Really Want?

Excluding the last three factors on the list of what workers want from their jobs (i.e., job security, high pay, good benefits), what do the other items on the motivational survey form have in common? For one thing, none of them will cost you very much to implement compared with paying high salaries, offering benefits, or providing perfect job security. For another, these are factors which you can improve regardless of restrictions or limitations on salary or benefits placed by your parent organization. This is good news if you have limited resources and want to motivate workers to higher performance.

Most of these motivators considered important by workers can probably be improved by you today, and they will probably cost very little in dollars.

Drucker Lesson Summary

Peter had many thoughts on motivation, some of which went against prevailing theory, but all of which were ahead of their time and have been proven right over the years. Here are his five key thoughts on motivation:

- Workers must be led, not managed.

- Don't use Theory X, but don't use a permissive form of Theory Y, either.

- Motivate each worker according to the individual and the situation.

- Work on the most important motivational factors first.

- Treat all workers as if they were volunteers, because they are.

CHAPTER NINETEEN

Drucker's Principles
of Self-Development

*P*eter had visibly aged since I had last seen him, so I slowed my pace to match his. We entered the restaurant at which he had already made reservations and were led to our table by the hostess. Peter sat with difficulty. He fiddled with the two large hearing aids he had begun using.

"These need to be adjusted for ambient noise," he explained. "Otherwise it comes through garbled and I can't understand a thing. Now, what are you working on these days?"

"Mostly an old project," I said. "I've been trying to write a strategy book for about twenty years or more, but I never seem to find the time to give it the attention it deserves."

"A common problem," he responded, as the waitress handed us menus. "Do you make a list of projects that you intend to work on?"

"Yes, I do."

"So do I," he said. "I, too, have a few books that have been on my list for years. Unfortunately, something more immediate always seems to come up and I write about this other subject instead. Strategy is certainly an important topic. I hope you get to complete the work this time."

"Actually, it's going well and nothing has interrupted me as yet," I told him. "Also, since I retired from the Air Force, I have much more time. I have high hopes that I'll be able to complete the work this year."[1]

Then I asked him, "What about you?"

"I always have a number of projects in progress," Peter replied. "It is surprising to me, though, how many people think this is easy. It is not. It requires a great deal of energy and discipline, as I am certain you know. But this is true with everything in life.

"I am sometimes both surprised and perturbed by managers who think that simply being infused with natural abilities will carry them through," Peter continued. "Or they see advancement in their careers as a matter of practicing the correct office politics. As they see it, managers get ahead, are promoted, or achieve whatever it is that they want with little effort. It's all due primarily to luck or influence.

"Where do they get these ideas?" Drucker asked. "It is true that everyone has abilities and liabilities to a different extent. However, it is up to every individual to develop his abilities in order to achieve his goals, but more importantly, to make a contribution. Of course, I assume that the manager we are speaking of is astute enough to establish goals. All of this involves self-development, which is necessary for everyone. One cannot plan success, but one can and must be prepared for it.

"For many years," Peter continued, "almost since the beginning of my work, I have followed a disciplined program of reading books on many different topics. Of course, I enjoy it, but it certainly requires effort and discipline. Such a program has many advantages. I have been successful in acquiring general knowledge in a number of different areas, which is useful in applying to supplement basic ignorance about any specific situation. There are, of course, those who have great depth of knowledge, but only in one narrow discipline. They know a great deal, but about very little. They are at a disadvantage."

"Yes," I responded. "I've heard it said that such individuals know more and more about less and less until finally they know absolutely everything about nothing at all."

Peter smiled. "That would be one logical outcome. However, the fact is there are serious consequences to overspecialization, not for society, but for the individual. Specialists and generalists are both needed by society as a whole, and they both make contributions. However, significant innovations frequently come from outside any particular discipline. For an individual, overspecialization can limit the available repertoire of ideas from which to draw. Yet, a new idea taken from one field and applied to another could result in what many erroneously term a 'breakthrough.' Many individuals have made what are considered major contributions because of this."

The Lesson of An Australian General

Then Peter shared a lesson. "Are you familiar with the name John Monash?

"As a matter of fact, I am," I replied. "He was an Australian general during the First World War. As I recall he was commander of all Australian troops on the Western Front in France. There is a university in Australia named after him. I have a friend who is a professor at that university."

"What you say is correct," said Drucker. "You may not know that Field Marshal Montgomery called Monash the best corps commander in that war. In fact, Monash was years ahead of his time. He achieved a success which could not be denied despite a singularly unique background for a senior British Empire officer.

"Monash was not from the upper classes of British or Australian society. He was a Jew whose family had immigrated to Australia from Prussia. If that weren't enough, he did not come from the regular army with the traditional military education and experience that this implied. He graduated from the University of Melbourne where he studied the arts, law, and engineering. On graduation, he obtained work as an engineer, but also became interested in the army and almost casually joined a reserve artillery unit associated with the university. Almost twenty years later, by 1913, he was a colonel. He wrote a book on junior officer leadership which was good enough to become an official army training manual.

"Soon after the war began, Monash was given command of an infantry brigade. In the bungled Gallipoli campaign against the Turks in 1915, his unit stood out due to his innovative ideas and his ability to implement them. Monash was promoted to major general and sent to France in command of a new division. Again, where others stumbled, Monash, with ideas borrowed from engineering, the arts, even law, won the day. From the law he brought the importance of preparation prior to action. The preparation he insisted on was so rigorous that some considered it ruthless. Nevertheless, these attacks were not only successful but resulted in much reduced casualties in attaining the victory, so he had the full support, respect, and loyalty of his troops. Monash's training of his corps in the combined employment of infantry, artillery, airpower and use of tanks together was unique at the time. This idea may have resulted from his engineering background and absence of bias toward one favored branch. He also pioneered various raiding techniques of the type which we today call special operations and a strategy which avoided the head-on attacks and the heavy casualties they required. His success in winning battle after battle was said to be a major factor in breaking the Hindenburg Line.

"Some members of the British High Command taunted him that he was only a 'Jewish colonel of the reserve.' Nevertheless King George V knighted him on the field of battle. Monash was not only a generalist; he had developed himself in the 'product' he became."

Self-Development Is Up to the Individual

Peter had a definite viewpoint on what self-development really means. As we continued talking over our meal that day, he shared more of his thoughts on the subject.

"Of course, acquiring general knowledge is just one aspect of what we term self-development. There are other aspects. In all, too many managers depend on others for development. That is clearly not self-development. This is a fault of our school system," he said. "Students are taught that their teachers and the system will help them learn everything they need to know, which is nonsense, of course. Growing up thinking this, they believe that the companies that employ them will just pick up where their schools left off. This rarely happens, and in any case never happens to a sufficient extent.

"Consequently, we have very bright and educated managers graduating from good schools whose development frequently progresses at a very slow pace, if at all. They are unprepared for unforeseen obstacles and sometimes retire years later knowing not much more than they did when they finished school.

"It is not up to others to develop us once we leave the comfort of the home or school, it is up to ourselves."

We then went on to other subjects. As I thought about this later, I realized that Peter probably considered his conversations with others, including myself, to be part of his personal self-development program. From the time he was a youth, Peter spent a good deal of time interacting intellectually with visitors in his parents' home; he said he considered this his real education. I knew that this aspect of his education and self-development continued throughout his life.

I spent some time thinking about Peter's comments. I had enjoyed some success since I had first met him almost thirty years earlier, and I had learned a great deal from him. Still, there is no doubt that it was my own responsibility to make use of the lessons he taught and the wisdom he imparted. I had applied many of his principles and benefited enormously from them. However, I realized that the potential was still not fully realized.

Peter did not promote his system of self-development. It may have been because he, himself, did not realize to what extent he was following one. Was a system of self-development yet another important gift that Peter had to contribute? I decided to look again at some of the things I had learned from him over the years, as well as what he had done, both purposefully and unconsciously, to develop himself.

Drucker's Basic Premise

Peter thought that all of us have strengths on which we could capitalize and use to develop ourselves. This was his first principle of self-development. Weaknesses in all individuals are inevitable; however, so are strengths. In building an organization, managers need to staff so as to capitalize on individual strengths, and to make weaknesses irrelevant. He believed the same about personal development. His beliefs were that you should concentrate on developing your strengths and, further, that you must accept responsibility for managing yourself. He did not exclude himself from this principle.

Once in the classroom someone had the audacity to ask Peter if he ever had any personal managerial experience. Where others might have considered this an affront to someone of his accomplishments and stature, he simply said, "Very little; I was, however, consultant to the president, almost a dean at Bennington College early in my career as an academic."

Now, that was something new. I had never thought of Drucker as a practicing manager. His achievements were too great as a management thinker, consultant, and philosopher. However, this announcement created an additional issue, which another one of my classmates instantly raised.

Just about every one in the class was a practicing manager. We were perfectly happy to learn from academics. We respected them for their knowledge and wanted to gain practical knowledge we could apply. To us, Drucker represented the very best. But most of us didn't understand anything about being a professor as work or a profession. There were two reasons for this. First, there was the old prejudice best expressed by the saying "those who can do; those who can't teach." Of course there have been many professors, in the past and in our time, who have moved in and out of academia and "the real world" and done well in both. However, there is one dictionary definition of the word "academic" that reinforces this prejudice: "Theoretical or speculative without a practical purpose or intention."

Secondly, as practicing managers, we all worked in hierarchies. A manager started at the first rung and worked up from there. We never gave it much thought that most professors stayed as professors and seemed content to remain at what we perceived to be an entry level of the academic hierarchy. Academia had a management hierarchy of department chairs, deans, provosts, college presidents, and chancellors. If we considered it at all, many of us would assume that professors should be seeking the same advancement as we did in corporations or other hierarchical organizations.

So the next question put to Peter by a classmate was not totally unexpected. It was, "What happened?" In other words, if Drucker had been performing as a dean some years earlier, why wasn't he now further up the hierarchical ladder, and not "only" a professor?

Again, Peter responded without being defensive. "I didn't like being dean or an administrator as a profession. It wasn't satisfying. I knew I would be better as a business teacher, writer, and researcher. I knew what a dean needed to do to manage properly, but I knew that to spend that effort was to take time away from what I really liked and was good at, and where I could make the maximum contribution."

The Basic Question for Managers

It was clear to me that this got back again to the basic question Peter felt all managers should ask. As individuals, we first need to decide, "What business are we in?" Only then could we continue to develop ourselves to support a particular goal or life profession. Once you answer this question, there is quite a bit you can do.

I do not know at what point Drucker decided to become the world's foremost management thinker, if he ever did. However, I believe his intent was to make the maximum contributions that he could, given his abilities. He decided on the general background that put him on this path and "his business" was decided fairly early in his career. As I mentioned in an earlier chapter, Peter decided not to go to the university immediately after completing the Austrian equivalent of high school. Moreover, he spent a full year at a business trade apprenticeship; which on completing that assignment, he left the trade. I suspect that it was even this early that he realized "what business he was in" and began work on developing himself and preparing for his goal in this general area.

I recall reading during the time I was his student that someone who knew Drucker before he came to the U.S. had written that Drucker always knew he wanted to become a professor, business writer, and corporate consultant. By the way, this individual had not meant this to be complimentary to Peter, but rather to imply that since he planned his career ahead of time, he had somehow done something devious. As we saw earlier, planning is an essential step to taking the right actions and making contributions in any profession. It escapes me how anyone could think this to be a negative. However, if true, it confirms my speculation that Peter decided fairly early on the course of his life's work.

This does not mean that if someone fails to find his life work early on, all is lost and one is forever limited. There are those that have identified "their business," fairly early, and equally as many who have not done so until mid-career, or even until late in life. Who would have thought that "spaghetti western" actor Clint Eastwood would develop into an Academy Award-winning film director, or that a retired restaurant worker living on social security, Harland Sanders, would found the worldwide Kentucky Fried Chicken (KFC) company. Still, that is exactly what happened in both cases.

Drucker's Four Vehicles of Self-Development

Peter employed four main vehicles for self-development. These were reading, writing, listening, and teaching. He read constantly throughout his career. He gave extensive reading as his source of his wide-ranging knowledge in an all-embracing variety of different fields of human interest and disciplines.

There is a saying that you don't have it until you write it down. Peter himself stated that writing was the foundation of his career. Again, he practiced writing from very early on in his career. Did he write for himself? Possibly. As a writer, I think maybe all writers write for themselves . . . for their own pleasure and to clarify their ideas. However, they wish to publish what they write for a variety of reasons, including to persuade others, to make a contribution, for a feeling of accomplishment, or perhaps for the income.

I think Drucker wanted to make his point with those he sought to convince or persuade. That it brought him fame and celebrity in the business world was probably only a by-product. In addition, he wrote in many different fields besides management, politics, and economics. He once said that on arriving in the U.S., he wrote articles on travel for a popular magazine. In any case, he definitely used writing as a vehicle for his self-development.

One doesn't normally include listening as a vehicle for self-development, although there is little doubt that Peter used listening in this way. He spoke about intellectual conversations he was allowed to participate in with visitors to his parent's home while he was still a teenager. He considered these and later conversations with others as important. However, he went further. He was one of the first people to understand the importance of what today is termed "self-talk." On one occasion in class, he was asked how he was able to make a certain statement which later proved to be accurate, although at the time he had made it "everyone knew" that he was in error and that the opposite was bound to occur. "I listened," he told us, "to myself."

This comment, of course, amused his students, but I suspect he was speaking accurately. To amplify on this vehicle, psychologists today tell us that everyone continually communicates by talking to oneself. Peter had discovered what we now know: it is important for us to listen to what we say!

Although Peter probably decided on university life for other reasons, he used his teaching as a self-development vehicle for himself. He told us that "the best way to learn is to teach," and that "I teach to find out what I think." The latter statement, of course, resulted in a good laugh. Like writing, teaching requires extensive preparation and organization of ideas. Moreover, because in the traditional classroom it is done in a public setting, teaching provides the additional motivation of having to get it right or suffering public embarrassment, even humiliation. All good teachers recognize this, and Peter was definitely a good teacher.

As I mentioned in an earlier chapter, some years ago I spoke to a number of audiences on self-development for becoming a strategic leader. I recommended several principles. They were all Peter's.

Further Principles of Self-Development

Peter never spoke of principles of self-development that a manager should follow. However, I have started with his basic premise that all managers have both strengths and weaknesses. One should develop and capitalize on one's strengths and contrive to make one's weaknesses irrelevant. Plus, he believed in always asking: "What business are you in?" Building off of these ideas, I have derived what I believe are the other principles he followed and that he would recommend to others. These are:

- Be prepared.

- Be true to your commitments.

- When change occurs, take immediate action.

- Be flexible.

- Establish fixed goals, but vary strategy as necessary.

- Don't be afraid to take risks.

Preparation and Risk

Peter thought that while you cannot guarantee success in anything, you can and must be prepared for it in order to achieve it. In the early stage of life, the manager prepares himself before entering any profession and begins to finalize what profession to enter.

Drucker's first preparation that we know about was his decision to do a merchant apprenticeship with a trading company. This was contrary to his father's wishes. His father wanted him to get a university education before seeking any job. This was Peter's conscious decision, and not that of his parents. This corresponds with the feelings and attitudes of many parents and recent high school graduates today. The parents want their son or daughter to go to college. For a variety of motivations, self-development included, the prodigy may have other ideas. Sometimes the parents know best. Other times, the son or daughter is correct. Clearly, Peter was in this latter category. He left home in Vienna for Hamburg, Germany. In Hamburg, he would not only get the practical experience of working, but also begin preparation for what was to follow.

This was also Peter's first big risk. He was risking a year of his life. If you consider this of minor importance, you have probably forgotten just how long a year is to a seventeen-year-old. Preparation and risk seem to go hand in hand. The more prepared and self-confident one is, the greater the propensity for risk. I think that Drucker had already begun his intentional preparation even while a teenager.

Be True to Your Commitments

Drucker stayed and finished his one-year apprenticeship in Hamburg, but then did not continue with the firm, or any other trading company. This decision would seem to confirm that this may have been some planned preparation on his part. He actually did follow his father's wishes to a certain extent, as he enrolled at the University of Hamburg Law School after his arrival to take up his merchant apprenticeship. He did both simultaneously. It is possible this enrollment was a parental compromise.

Peter either saw his apprenticeship as a necessary stepping-stone in his development, or it was a serious career move which did not go the way he thought it would. Either way, he remained a year and completed what he had started. He has stated that his apprenticeship was not demanding and left him lots of free time. So, he was able to study law on his own and without attending class, according to one account. However, he has also said that he began to read voraciously, not only non-fiction, mostly in the historical genre, but also novels.[2] His decision regarding the study of law at this time was also probably planned preparation for what was to follow next.

That he stayed in the apprenticeship and did not leave was also an indication of the strength of his commitment to any goal that he established. As we will soon see, once he decided that he wanted a full-time university position, this commitment did not waiver, though it was to require many sacrifices and took ten years to achieve.

More Preparation on Drucker's Part

Immediately after completing his one-year apprenticeship as a clerk, he enrolled at the University of Frankfurt, where he completed a doctorate in public and international law. At the same time, he began writing freelance articles on economics and soon afterwards became a freelance journalist, and then an editor in foreign affairs and economics for a widely read daily. Both jobs were part of his preparation. If Peter wanted to make his career in these areas as a journalist or professor, why didn't he pursue a doctorate in these disciplines, and not law? In class, he told us that he chose to pursue a doctorate in law because at the time it was one of the easiest and quickest doctorates to obtain.

The idea that his plans required an education which included a doctorate degree, but no intention to practice of law, seems confirmed by his subsequent actions. He never attempted to practice law, even though he did briefly do part-time teaching in this field. He began writing about political economics, which was clearly his main area of interest. This interest may have started with his father, who later immigrated from Austria to the U.S. and taught economics at a university in the United States.

According to some sources, Peter had already been accepted for a job as a journalist in Cologne, Germany. In any case, he visited the University of Cologne, where his uncle was a famous professor. This information may confirm his intention to use a professorship as a base for distributing the results of his research and thinking.

In summary, Drucker was no "Student Prince." Peter did double duty in attending both Hamburg and Frankfurt Universities, completing his apprenticeship while he attended one, and working as a journalist and writing while he attended the other, and beginning a lifelong habit of extensive reading.

When Change Occurs, Take Immediate Action

Frequently we encounter obstacles along the career path we've planned or in which we're already engaged due to change. It is important to assess the situation and, if necessary, immediately move on, rather than remain and wish that whatever changed had stayed the same. Spencer Johnson, co-author of the best seller, *The One Minute Manager,* wrote another best-selling book based on this single concept. It was entitled *Who Moved My Cheese?* (GP Putnam's Sons, 1998). The basic idea was not to waste time regretting change. Rather, accept the situation, move on and start again based on the new circumstances. In the early 1930's that is exactly what Drucker did.

Peter had early on recognized the danger presented by the Nazis. If his Jewish background weren't enough, he had written a pamphlet supporting the views of Friedrich Julius Stahl, an early-19th century political conservative, who was a college-age Jewish convert to Christianity. Unlike others, Peter did not fool himself into thinking that the Nazis would leave him alone, or that they would soon be ousted from the government. He did not waste time wishing that Hitler had not come to power, or hoping that his dominance wouldn't last. When Hitler was elected chancellor in Germany in 1933, Drucker immediately emigrated to England.

It is noteworthy that Drucker foresaw the likely course of events at a time when popular wisdom was that Hitler and the Nazis were a temporary aberration that would soon be reversed. Most likely, the two habits he had acquired, of extensive reading and engaging in an interchange of ideas with others, assisted him in coming to the conclusion that he should get out of Germany as soon as possible.

Every month that someone of Jewish ancestry remained in Germany made it more difficult to leave. Those who waited to see what was going to happen eventually lost all rights of citizenship, were not allowed to work in their professions, and were prohibited from taking any money out of the country if they emigrated. Soon after this period, Jews had their assets confiscated by the German government and were not allowed to leave the country at all. Eventually, most of them perished in the Holocaust.

However, Drucker's leaving Germany this early was again a risk. To give up what he had worked for—possibly even a full-time teaching position at a major university—must have been a difficult decision. It is sheer speculation on my part, but I am sure that many advised him against this move and to wait at least a little longer to see what was going to happen.

Be Flexible

When Peter arrived in England, he did not pick up his planned work as either a journalist or a professor of political economics. Perhaps a lack of fluency in spoken English or his heavy Viennese accent limited his ability to immediately continue in the career and the work he had previously planned to take up in Cologne. In any case, Peter remained in England for four years, working first as a security analyst with an insurance company, and then as an economist with a bank.

He did not teach at a university as he had planned. However, he continued to write, and not only articles. Most notably, he wrote a book, his first best seller, *The End of Economic Man: A Study of the New Totalitarianism.* An abbreviated version was also written in German and published in Vienna in 1936, two years before the Anschluss, which occurred in 1938.

However, it was the fully expanded English version of Drucker's book that brought him fame. It was published after he emigrated to the United States in 1937. This is the Drucker book that was favorably reviewed by Winston Churchill back in England. Without question, the success of this book encouraged Peter to continue his development. He was on the right track with his career aspirations.

Fixed Goals; Flexible Strategy

Four years after arriving in England, Peter left for the United States. At this point, he still probably defined his goals as making his contributions as a writer-journalist or writer-academic in political economics, not business or management, neither of which were the subjects of his first book.

Why did he not stay in England? Or conversely, why did he emigrate again, this time from England to the United States? He was asked this question once in class. His response was essentially that England was stuck in the past, while the United States was focused on the future.

In practical terms, this explanation may have meant that he could not secure the kind of teaching appointment he sought in England, but felt he could do so in the United States. This would be in line with his ideas of strategy; i.e., that one should change goals slowly, but be prepared and flexible to alter the strategy to reach these goals as required. Of course, Peter's strategy again involved risk, but he was able to secure a job as American representative of several English newspapers before he left.[3] This assignment made going to the U.S. more attractive.

Probably helped by the publication of *The End of Economic Man*, Peter landed an adjunct job teaching economics at Sarah Lawrence College, in Bronxville, New York, which is essentially in the New York City metropolitan area. Sarah Lawrence has a reputation for scholarship, it was back then a small girls' school, and it is still small, although it became co-educational in 1966. It was a strange academic starting place for the future Father of Modern Management and a huge step down from the world-famous University of Cologne, at which he may have originally hoped to teach five or six years earlier.

Meanwhile, Peter was not sitting on his hands. He continued to write, building not only on his past preparation, but now on war work he was doing for the U.S. government. He published another book in 1942, *The Future of Industrial Man.*

Drucker had begun working for U.S. intelligence, doing research and writing about German industry. In the cubicle next to him he befriended a man named Marvin Bower who was doing similar work. Marvin Bower founded the world-famous McKinsey Consulting Company. Then in 1943, Peter received a full-time offer from Bennington College in Vermont. There, at yet another small girls' school, he taught philosophy, government, and religion. Like Sarah Lawrence, Bennington too is now co-educational.

So it took Peter ten years to achieve a full-time university position at a school which, though it had a good academic reputation, was hardly in the same league as the University of Cologne. This speaks volumes for Drucker's self-development principles, including being prepared and flexible, but especially staying committed to a fixed goal, even though it might be necessary to vary one's strategy to achieve it.

The year 1943 was especially big for Peter. First off, he finally obtained a full-time faculty position after ten years. Also, General Motors contacted him about looking at its management practices, probably based partially on the book he had published the previous year. This was a major shift in activity for Drucker. He would not be analyzing macroeconomics, but microeconomics. Once he decided to do this work, he could not be dissuaded. Fellow academics advised against it as it would be out of his field and could affect his academic reputation negatively. Risk again.

Drucker completed the study. From all accounts, his study was not well received by Drucker's clients at General Motors. Nevertheless, it led to his ground-breaking book two years later in 1946, *Concept of the Corporation.*

Meanwhile, Peter had decided to try his hand at academic administration and performed many duties of a dean at Bennington for two years. Once again, he was taking a risk. As noted earlier, he decided this wasn't his thing. He returned to full-time teaching, research, and writing.

In 1949, Peter received another offer to teach full-time at New York University. This appointment allowed him to focus on where he defined his niche and where he could have the maximum impact with his contributions: executive education. He accepted the offer and remained at NYU for twenty-two years. By then, he was well established in his profession and doing exactly what he wanted: writing, speaking, and making major contributions based on his kind of research, along with his analyses, and thinking.

When he decided to come to California in 1972, it was by his choice and on his terms. Though many California universities competed for his services, he chose a small college which stayed small by intent, but developed into a world-famous university, which includes a school bearing his name, the Peter F. Drucker and Masatoshi Ito Graduate School of Management at Claremont Graduate University.

Drucker Lesson Summary

Peter's basic premise of self-development was that all managers have both strengths and weaknesses. You should develop and capitalize on your strengths, and strive to make your weaknesses irrelevant. He also recommended that all managers start their self-development by asking themselves: "What business am I in?"

Peter Drucker's career did not develop through luck or political favoritism. He encountered real obstacles which he had to overcome. However, through purposeful self-development based on the principles he practiced, hard work, and his own natural abilities, he not only made contributions which are unique and significant, he reached the pinnacle of the profession he chose.

A F T E R W O R D

*P*eter Drucker is gone, but his deeds, achievements, accomplishments, and contributions live after him, and they are significant. As Peter himself said when he first started writing about management, if you went into a bookstore and asked for books on the subject, you might find a few slim volumes if you were lucky. Today, you cannot go into even a medium-sized bookstore without finding an entire shelf filled with books on every aspect of management. This fact is largely due to Peter. He truly was the Father of Modern Management.

Drucker was the one who created management as a discipline considered worthy of study, not only in business, but by governments, universities, and organizations of every kind. Peter not only changed the discipline of management, he changed the world. The results of his research and study, his unique way of looking at things, his gift for cutting right to the heart of the matter, his insights, and his ability to

articulate truths that most of us did not readily see were all extraordinary and unprecedented.

Fortunately, the lessons he taught, both in and out of the classroom,
are still available to us. In many ways Peter was unique in this respect,
too. A Peter Drucker comes along perhaps only once in a century. Usually
the lessons of such an individual are restricted because the genius is so
successful that he is largely isolated from the rest of us. As a young boy,
Peter was introduced to a family friend, Sigmund Freud. Freud's genius in
psychology is acknowledged everywhere. Yet, not many of us know
exactly what he taught. We depend on others to interpret his teachings or
explain what he actually meant. Few are capable of doing this directly.
And even these experts fight and argue about what Freud said or did not
say, and whether his theories are true or false, or maybe were true once,
but are no longer true today.

Not so with Drucker. Peter left behind his lessons and insights through
many media. These included writings, speeches, recordings, and videos. To
me, it is his actual classroom lessons and personal teachings that offer such
a wealth of insight into his ideas on a wide range of topics, which were not
always restricted to management. Even more than that, he was accessible to
his students on a one-on-one basis, and to those he thought would value
and not waste what they would learn from him. I was extremely fortunate
enough to be one.

Because his productive life was more than three quarters of a century,
Drucker's lessons were many. Plus, he frequently taught in "shorthand."
That is, he gave us only guideposts which needed to be developed fully by
those who received them. Peter communicated his ideas to be understood.
It was sometimes frustrating that he told us what to do, and not exactly
how to do it. But, as attested to by his clients, readers, and students, this
method too was part of his genius. His general guidelines and hints invariably led the recipients of these lessons to unimagined rewards in application, which would not have happened had he simply told us how to
implement his ideas.

Just this morning, Dean Ira Jackson, Dean of the Peter F. Drucker and
Masatoshi Ito Graduate School of Management, announced that the
School's entire core faculty will soon be jointly teaching a new required
course for all entering MBA students, entitled "The Drucker Difference."
The course will share the best of Peter Drucker on topics ranging from
innovation to marketing, from purpose to the role of the civic sector. "The

Drucker Difference" will summarize Peter's original insights and update his teachings and writings to reflect Claremont Graduate University's own research and the contributions of others who have built upon the firm foundations that Peter left behind. This is a terrific idea.

I was privileged and blessed to be Peter Drucker's student. The impact that he had on me and on my life was profound. I was far from alone in this regard. In this book, I have tried to share some of these classroom lessons and what they meant.

As for myself, I can only say: Thank you, Peter, thank you for everything.

Bill Cohen
Pasadena, California
June, 2007

N O T E S

CHAPTER 2

1. Simon London, *Financial Times,* quoted in Christian Sarkar.com, January 2007, http://www.christiansarkar.com/2005/11/best_drucker_obituary_ft.htm (accessed January 17, 2007).

2. I have seen it published that the Nazis offered Peter a job if he would remain in Germany. I doubt this, or if so, it must have been a pretty ignorant Nazi. See "Trusting the Teacher in the Grey-Flannel Suit," *The Economist,* November 19, 2005, V. 377, N. 8453, pg. 84, no author listed. Also, I met Peter's cousin who had visited with the Druckers when her husband taught at Claremont as an adjunct professor who confirmed his Jewish background.

3. John A. Byrne, "The Man Who Invented Management," *Business Week,* (November 28, 2005), p. 96.

4. Author unknown, "Peter Ferdinand Drucker, A Celebration," December 10th, 2005, Claremont, California.

CHAPTER 3

1. Jerry Knight, "Tylenol's Maker Shows How to Respond to Crisis," *The Washington Post,* October 11, 1982.

CHAPTER 4

1. Richard Brem, "Peter F. Drucker: A Biography in Progress," http://www.peterdrucker.at/en/bio/bio_01.html (accessed August 15, 2006).

2. Richard Brem, "Peter F. Drucker: A Biography in Progress," http://www.peterdrucker.at/en/bio/bio_02.html (accessed August 15, 2006).

3. Author unknown. Claremont Graduate University Press Release, "Peter F. Drucker Passes Away at 95," (November 11, 2005), http://www.thedruckerinstitute.com/templates/cusdrucker06/details.asp?id=34682&PID=38488&style= (accessed May 25, 2007).

4. *AFM 35-15 Air Force Leadership* (Department of the Air Force, Washington, D.C., 1948), p. 30.

5. Arnold Schwarzenegger with Douglas Kent Hall, *Arnold: The Education of a Bodybuilder* (New York: Fireside, 1997), p. 24.

6. No author listed, "Mary Kay Ash," *infoplease®*, http://www.infoplease.com/ipa/A0880005.html (accessed August 12, 2006).

7. Charles Garfield, *Peak Performers* (Avon Books, New York, 1986), pp. 72–73.

8. Walter Anderson, *The Confidence Course* (HarperCollins Publishers, New York, 1997), p. 166.

9. Andrew Roberts, *Hitler and Churchill* (Weidenfeld & Nicolson, London, 2003), p. xviii–xix.

CHAPTER 5

1. No author listed. "History's Greatest Turnaround?" CNN.com, December 8, 2005, www.cnn.com/2005/BUSINESS/12/08/go.ibmgerstner/ (accessed April 17, 2007).

CHAPTER 6

1. James Flanigan and Thomas S. Mulligan, "Peter F. Drucker was the original management guru," *Los Angeles Times* (November 12, 2005).

The Seattle Times, Business and Technology, http://seattletimes.nwsource.com/html/businesstechnology/2002619549_druckerobit12.html (accessed February 10, 2006).

2. John H. Lienhard, "No. 1525: Liberty Ships," *Engines of Our Ingenuity.* http://www.uh.edu/engines/epi1525.htm (accessed February 21, 2007).

3. No author listed, "Silly Putty®," Inventor of the Week, at http://web.mit.edu/invent/iow/sillyputty.html (accessed August 9, 2006).

CHAPTER 8

1. Peter F. Drucker, *Management: Tasks, Responsibilities, Practices* (New York: Harper & Row, 1974), p. 285.

2. Richard Poe, "A Winning Spirit—It Takes Integrity To Lead Franchises To Victory," *Success* 37, No. 6 (August 1990), p. 60.

3. Leonard Roberts, telephone interview with the author, November 3, 1997.

CHAPTER 9

1. Thomas V. Bonoma, "Making Your Marketing Strategy Work," *Harvard Business Review.* Vol. 62 (March-April 1984).

CHAPTER 10

1. Author unknown, "Report: U.S. Ignores Bribes for Mideast Defense Contracts," *WorldTribune.com* (June 13, 2002), http://www.worldtribune.com/worldtribune/WTARC/2002/ss_military_06_13b.html (accessed October 12, 2006).

2. H. Norman Schwarzkopf, *It Doesn't Take a Hero,* (New York: Bantam Books, 1992), p.70.

3. William A. Cohen, *How to Make It Big as a Consultant,* 3rd ed. (New York: AMACOM, 2001), pp. 170–173. Questionnaire reprinted with the permission of Washington Researchers.

4. David A. Kaplan, "Intrigue in High Places," *Newsweek Business,* pg. 3, (September 5, 2006), Accessed at http://www.msnbc.msn.com/id/14687677 /site/newsweek/page/3/ (February 8, 2007).

CHAPTER 12

1. Jeanne Sahadi, "CEO Pay," CNN/Money, http://money.cnn.com/2005/08/26/ news/economy/ceo_pay/ (accessed December 3, 2006).

2. Ken Iverson, *Plain Talk,* (New York: John Wiley & Sons, Inc., 1998), p. 13.

3. Ken Iverson, telephone interview with the author, October 30, 1997.

4. Erick Laine, telephone interview with the author, December 22, 1997.

CHAPTER 13

1. Dale Carnegie, *How to Win Friends and Influence People,* (New York: Simon and Schuster, 1937), p. 108.

2. Ibid., p. 100.

3. Chester Burger, *The Chief Executive* (Boston: CBI Publishing Co., Inc., 1978), p. 48.

4. Jerome M. Rosow, "A View from the Top," *Success* (February, 1986), p. 69.

5. Harry K. Jones, "Does MBWA Still Work?" *The Achiever Newsletter* (Spring 2001). http://www.achievemax.com/newsletter/01issue/management-by-wandering-around.htm (accessed February 12, 2007).

CHAPTER 18

1 Anne B. Fisher, "Morale Crisis," *Fortune,* (November 18,1991), p. 70.

2. Jay Mathews and Peter Katel, "The Cost of Quality" *Newsweek,* (September 7, 1992), p. 48.

3. Adolf von Schell, *Battle Leadership,* (Quantico, VA: Marine Corps Association, 1982). Originally published Ft. Benning, Georgia: *The Benning Herald,* 1933, as the foreword.

4. Ibid., pp.11–12.

5. Max DePree, *Leadership is an Art,* (New York: Dell Publishing, 1989), p. 28.

6. James MacGregor Burns, quoted in William Safire and Leonard Safir, *Leadership* (New York: Simon & Schuster, 1990), p. 202.

7. Chester Burger, *The Chief Executive* (Boston: CBI Publishing Company, Inc., 1978), p. 48.

8. Mary Kay Ash, *Mary Kay on People Management* (New York: Warner Books, 1984), pp. 30–31.

CHAPTER 19

1. Unfortunately, many things did interfere. I was contacted by no fewer than three publishers about updating previous books, and it was not until the following year that I was able to do my planned work which eventually resulted in my book, *The Art of the Strategist* (AMACOM, 2004).

2. Richard Brem, *Peter F. Drucker: A Biography in Progress,* http://www. peterdrucker.at/ frmset_en_interview.html (accessed February 19, 2007).

3. John J. Tarrant, *Drucker: The Man Who Invented Corporate Society* (Cahner's Books, 1976), p.6.

BOOKS BY PETER DRUCKER

1. *The End of Economic Man*—1939
2. *The Future of Industrial Man*—1942
3. *Concept of the Corporation*—1946
4. *The New Society*—1950
5. *The Practice of Management*—1954
6. *America's Next Twenty Years*—1957
7. *Landmarks of Tomorrow*—1957
8. *Managing for Results*—1964
9. *The Effective Executive*—1966
10. *The Age of Discontinuity*—1968
11. *Preparing Tomorrow's Business Leaders Today*—1969
12. *Technology, Management, and Society*—1970
13. *Men, Ideas, and Politics*—1971
14. *Management: Tasks, Responsibilities, Practices*—1973
15. *The Unseen Revolution*—1976 (published in 1996 under the title *The Pension Fund Revolution*)
16. *People and Performance: The Best of Peter Drucker on Management*—1977
17. *An Introductory View of Management*—1977
18. *Adventures of a Bystander*—1978 (autobiography, reissued in 2001)
19. *Song of the Brush: Japanese Painting from the Sanso Collection*—1979
20. *Managing in Turbulent Times*—1980
21. *Toward the Next Economics and Other Essays*—1981
22. *The Changing World of the Executive*—1982
23. *The Last of All Possible Worlds*—1982 (fiction)
24. *The Temptation to Do Good*—1984 (fiction)
25. *Innovation and Entrepreneurship*—1985
26. *Frontiers of Management*—1986
27. *The New Realities: in Government and Politics, in Economics and Business, in Society and World View*—1989
28. *Managing the Nonprofit Organization: Principles and Practices*—1990
29. *Managing for the Future*—1992
30. *The Ecological Vision*—1993
31. *The Post-Capitalist Society*—1993
32. *Managing in a Time of Great Change*—1995
33. *Drucker on Asia: A Dialogue between Peter Drucker and Isao Nakauchi*—1997
34. *Peter Drucker on the Profession of Management*—1998
35. *Management Challenges for the 21st Century*—1999
36. *The Essential Drucker*—2001
37. *Managing in the Next Society*—2002
38. *A Functioning Society*—2002
39. *The Daily Drucker*—2004
40. *The Effective Executive In Action*—2006

BOOKS ABOUT PETER DRUCKER

1. *Drucker: The Man Who Invented The Corporate Society* by John J. Tarrant—1976
2. *The World According to Peter Drucker* by Jack Beatty—1998
3. *Business Masterminds: Peter Drucker* by Robert Heller—2000
4. *Peter Drucker: Shaping the Managerial Mind—How the World's Foremost Management Thinker Crafted the Essentials of Business Success* by John E. Flaherty—2001
5. *The Definitive Drucker* by Elizabeth Haas Edersheim—2006

I N D E X